Windows NT® 4.0 Visual Desk Reference

David C. Gardner, Ph.D.

Grace Joely Beatty, Ph.D.

David A. Sauer, M.S.

Windows NT® 4.0 Visual Desk Reference

Library of Congress Catalog Card Number: 96-72219

ISBN: 0-7897-1106-0

98 97   8   7   6   5   4   3   2   1

Interpretation of the printing code: the rightmost double-digit number is the year of the book's first printing; the rightmost single-digit number is the number of the book's printing. For example, a printing code of 96-1 shows that this copy of the book was printed during the first printing of the book in 1996.

Screen reproductions in this book were created by means of the program Collage Complete from Inner Media, Inc, Hollis, NH.

Printed in the United States of America.

Credits

Publisher
Roland Elgey

Publishing Director
David W. Solomon

Editorial Services Director
Elizabeth Keaffaber

Managing Editor
Michael Cunningham

Director of Marketing
Lynn E. Zingraf

Acquisitions Editor
Don Essig

Senior Product Director
Lisa D. Wagner

Product Development Specialist
Carolyn Kiefer

Editors
Lori A. Lyons
Linda Seifert

Product Marketing Manager
Kris Ankney

Technical Specialist
Nadeem Muhammed

Acquisitions Coordinator
Tracy C. Williams

Cover Designer
Jay Corpus

Production Team
Julie Geeting
Brian Grossman
Kay Hoskin
Steph Mineart
Kaylene Riemen
Lisa Stumpf

Indexer
Kevin Fulcher

Composed in *Stone Sans* and *Palatino* by Que Corporation

About the Authors

David C. Gardner, Ph.D., and **Grace Joely Beatty, Ph.D.**, are licensed psychologists who specialize in the human interface to computers. They are a husband-and-wife team and the co-authors of over 30 computer books with more than a million copies in print. Many of their titles have been best sellers. The Golden Gate Computer Society suggested that their books serve as a model of how to put together a book about a computer program. In their corporate consulting, they work with organizations going through major computer conversions.

You can reach them on the Internet at **writebks@aol.com**.

David A. Sauer, M.S., is currently Vice President of Information Services at CyberHelp, Inc. He has over 20 years experience in electronic information management, database design and administration, and online services. He designed and managed the online information management system at the Stone Science Library, Boston University, and is the co-author of 10 computer books.

Acknowledgments

Frank Straw and Dan Terhark of Computer Service and Maintenance provided the technical support for this book. Because they set up networks for their clients and provide ongoing troubleshooting and maintenance, they have special knowledge of the needs of small and growing businesses. They helped in the development of the outline for this book, tested each chapter, and maintained our network throughout the process. We could not have written the book without them. Thanks, guys!

Carolyn Holder helped us write chapters, organized several phases of the beta testing, and performed her usual stellar role as company social director. Carolyn, we don't know what we would do without you!

We are especially indebted to the people who took the time to test each step in our manuscript: Mark Allen, Heather Bowen, Ray Holder, and Tina Terhark. Each person added a perspective that improved the book.

A special thanks to Shawn Benson for consulting with us on Chapter 29, "Controlling Access to Workstations."

Chris Allen of ElectriCiti, our Internet Service Provider, gave us free accounts to test the online chapters of this book.

We are delighted to be working with the professionals at Que: David Solomon, Don Essig, Lisa Wagner, Lori Lyons, Tom Hayes, and Carolyn Kiefer. They contributed greatly to the book and made the process a pleasure.

We can't sign off without thanking Bill Gladstone and Matt Wagner of Waterside Productions. They've been good friends and terrific agents.

Trademarks

All terms mentioned in this book that are known to be trademarks or service marks have been appropriately capitalized. Que Corporation cannot attest to the accuracy of this information. Use of a term in this book should not be regarded as affecting the validity of any trademark or service mark.

Contents at a Glance

Table of Contents

Introduction

The visual format of *Windows NT 4.0 Visual Desk Reference* is based on research we did at Boston University on the best ways to teach technical information to nontechnical learners. In our consulting work with our corporate clients, we found that technical and nontechnical people appreciate the direct, results-oriented text. This book does not cover every possible permutation of hardware / software / network configuration issues. It does cover most of what the average employee of a corporation needs to know to use the workstation productively, as well as what the SOHO (small office / home office) executive needs to know about setting up individual workstations in a small network. It does not cover NT server issues.

How to Use This Book

Chances are you're migrating to Windows NT 4.0 from a Windows 3.1-type interface. This can be somewhat of a shock because NT 4.0 presents a totally different desktop. The first two parts of this book facilitate the adjustment to the new NT 4.0 environment. The information is presented step-by-step and tied to actual screen shots so that you can follow the directions with ease. The purpose is to get you up and running with a minimum investment of time but with maximum results. We tested every page of our manuscript with real people, and we know the steps work.

If you're new to the Windows NT 4.0 desktop, follow Parts I and II in sequence. These parts will help you adjust to the new interface. The most effective way to use this book is to sit at your computer, mouse in hand, and follow along with the steps.

After you're comfortable with the NT 4.0 desktop and file management system, you will be ready to take on more technical tasks. The rest of the book will help you keep your workstation operating at peak efficiency and take advantage of the many NT 4.0 features designed to enhance your personal productivity. Go to a section as you need the information it presents. Each part is independent of other parts, barring the occasional reference to other chapters.

How This Book Is Organized

Windows NT 4.0 Visual Desk Reference is divided into six parts and an appendix. The rest of this introduction includes an overview of each part.

Part I: Getting Acquainted with Windows NT 4.0

If you've been working on a computer set up with Windows 3.1, Windows for Workgroups 3.11, Windows NT 3.5, or a non-Windows operating system, you will find that the look and feel of Windows NT 4.0 is different from what you're used to. You may be more than a little frustrated trying to do things you could do easily in your old system. However, with a little help from the chapters in Part I, you'll find the transition easy to make.

Part II: Managing Your Files

The chapters in Part II will appeal not only to the person who has just upgraded from a Windows 3.x environment, but also to the person who is new to networking. Managing your files can be a chore on a single machine. When you have access to other machines, the task can be daunting. Windows NT 4.0 gives you several options for managing your files, including its unique Briefcase program.

Part III: Keeping Your Workstation Humming

In many ways, a computer is like a fine automobile. It can be great fun and can get you to where you want to go quickly. However, it does require periodic maintenance, fine-tuning, and sometimes the addition of accessories that did not come with the machine out of the show room. This part shows you how to maintain your workstation at peak performance.

Part IV: Communicating

Windows NT lets you communicate directly with the outside world. To do this you need to install Remote Access Services, Dial-Up Networking, and, most importantly, your modem. Part IV takes you through the steps of getting your equipment and NT set up for going online.

Part V: Setting Up Workstations in a Peer-to-Peer Network

Most small offices or home offices are set up as peer-to-peer networks where every machine has the capability to connect to all other machines and to share files, folders, drives, and printers. You also can restrict access to certain machines, folders, and files so that only authorized people can use them. Part V is designed to be used by SOHO (small office/home office) owners who want to set up workstations on an NT 4.0 network.

Part VI: Enhancing NT

The standard Windows NT 4.0 Workstation installation will probably give you everything you need for your day-to-day computer use. However, if you're like us, you have definite ideas about how to improve the way things work on your computer. This part explores numerous enhancements, many of which are available on the Web. Chapter 35 includes a comprehensive list of Web sites and newsgroups that will help keep you as knowledgeable about NT 4.0 as you care to be.

Part VII: Appendix

The appendix consists of a glossary that contains nontechnical definitions of some of the terms used in this book.

Getting Acquainted with Windows NT 4.0

Part I was written specifically for you if you've been working on a computer set up with Windows 3.1, Windows for Workgroups 3.11, Windows NT 3.5, or a non-Windows operating system. The look and feel of Windows NT 4.0 is different from what you're used to, but with a little help from the chapters in this part, you'll find the transition easy to make. Once you've adjusted to the new desktop, check out Chapters 9, 10, and 11 to learn ways to customize NT 4.0 to fit the way you work!

1   Booting Up Your Workstation

2   Starting a Program or Document

3   Shutting Down or Rebooting Your Computer

4   Changing Screen Colors

5   Selecting a Screen Saver and Other Display Options

6   Changing the Date, Time, and Time Zone

7   Customizing Your Mouse

8   Using Help

9   Working Smarter with Shortcut Icons and Desktop Folders

10   Customizing the Start Menu

11   Using the Automatic Startup Feature

PART

II

PART

III

PART

IV

PART

V

PART

VI

PART

VII

CHAPTER 1

Booting Up Your Workstation

If you're familiar with Windows 95, then you'll feel completely comfortable with NT 4.0. If you haven't worked with Windows 95, you'll find that the NT desktop looks very different from what you're used to. With a little help from this book, however, you'll find the transition easy to make. In this chapter, you will do the following:

- ✔ Boot up your NT workstation
- ✔ Enter your password
- ✔ Change your password if necessary

Advantages of Windows NT 4.0

As you have undoubtedly heard, Windows NT 4.0 uses a 32-bit operating system. This is an advantage over Windows 3.1's 16-bit system because a 32-bit operating system can talk to your applications and peripherals, such as modems and printers, in bigger chunks of information. Therefore, things work faster. Although your Windows 3.1 programs will still run, you'll have more speed in 32-bit applications. A 32-bit operating system also allows more colors to be displayed on your screen and more sophisticated multimedia and video conferencing. Perhaps the most obvious and most practical change is the ability to use long file names that actually tell you what the file is about. With the exception of the symbols \ ? : * " < > and x, you can use up to 255 characters, including spaces, in a file name. For example, a file name in Windows NT4 can be "Minutes of Feb 11 board meeting."

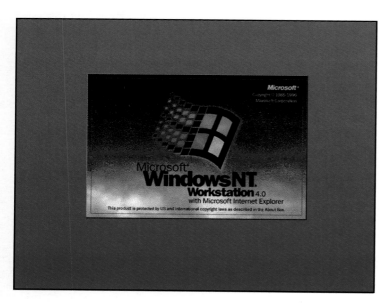

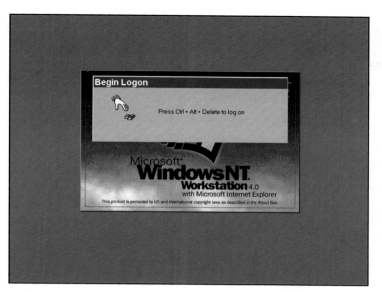

Logging on to Windows NT

When you first turn on your computer, Windows NT requires a password before you can proceed.

1. Follow the directions on your screen and **press Ctrl + Alt + Delete** to log on. The Logon Information dialog box will appear.

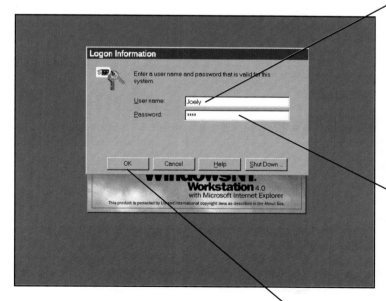

Your name will appear here. However, if you share this computer, the name of the person who last logged on will appear here. Simply do step 2.

2. Double-click in the User name box to highlight the name, and then **type** your own **name**. **Press Tab** to go to the Password box.

3. Type your **password**.

Note: If you see a Logon Message like the one at the top of the next page, it means that the network administrator set up your machine to give you the ability to change your password the very first time you boot up your workstation. If so, follow the steps on the next page.

4. Click on **OK**.

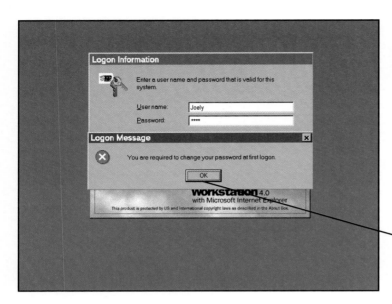

Changing Your Password the First Time You Boot Up

If the network administrator set your machine to allow you to enter a new password the very first time you boot up, you have the opportunity to enter a password that will be meaningful to you.

1. Click on **OK**. The Change Password dialog box will appear.

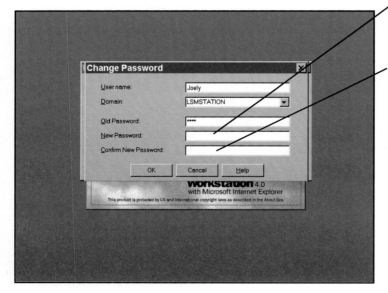

2. Type the **new password** you want to use, and then **press** the **Tab** key.

3. Type the **new password** again to verify it and check for typing mistakes.

4. Click on **OK**.

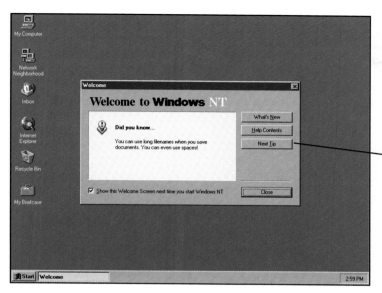

The Welcome Window

After you log on, you'll see the Welcome window with a Tip of the Day.

1. Click on **Next Tip** to see another tip. You can scroll through all the tips with this button.

The What's New button will show you an overview of some of the features of NT. You can check out the overview now or go through this book for step-by-step coverage of all of these features.

The Help Contents button will bring up the Help index. The Help feature has become more sophisticated in Windows NT. See Chapter 8, "Using Help," for details.

If you don't want to see this Welcome window each time you turn on your computer, it's easy enough to tell it to go away.

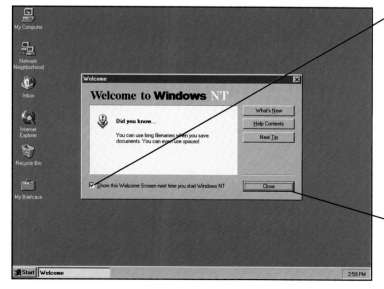

1. Click on **Show this Welcome Screen each time you start Windows NT** to *remove* the ✔.

Note: You can always get the Welcome screen back by typing "Welcome" in the Run dialog box. See "Opening a Program from the Run Dialog Box," in Chapter 2 for more information.

2. Click on **Close**.

The NT Desktop

This is the default Windows NT 4.0 desktop. If you are unfamiliar with Windows 95, you are probably thinking all sorts of things, the least violent of which may be, "What did they do to my desktop?! Where are my group windows?! Where are all my programs?!"

Not to worry. Everything you had on your 3.1 desktop is on the NT desktop. It's just arranged differently. This book will give you step-by-step directions for finding and using your files and programs. If you want, you can make this desktop function more like a 3.1 desktop. We'll show you how in Chapter 9, "Working Smarter with Shortcut Icons and Desktop Folders."

Starting a Program or Document

Given its name, it's not surprising that the Start menu is one of the ways to start the programs on your computer. It is, however, not the only way. In addition to the methods discussed in this chapter, be sure to see Chapter 9, "Working Smarter with Shortcut Icons and Desktop Folders," Chapter 10, "Customizing the Start Menu," Chapter 11, "Using the Automatic Startup Feature," and Chapter 13, "Using Windows NT Explorer." In this chapter, you'll do the following:

✔ Open programs with the Start menu and the Run dialog box
✔ Browse for a program
✔ Change the size of a window and switch between open programs
✔ Tile programs
✔ Open a recently used file
✔ Clear the Documents Menu

Using the Start Menu

The Start menu is "Command Central" in Windows NT. It takes a little getting used to if you're coming out of Windows 3.1 or NT 3.51 but once you adjust, it's very easy to use.

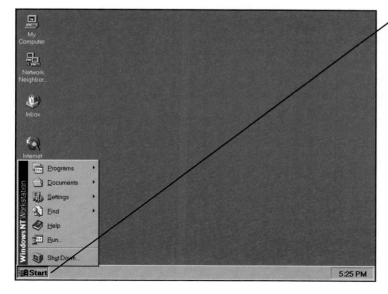

1. Click on the **Start** button. The Start menu will appear.

Yours may look like the standard menu you see here, or it may have been customized to have more or fewer items. You'll learn how to customize the Start menu in Chapter 10, "Customizing the Start Menu." Customized or plain vanilla, it works the same way.

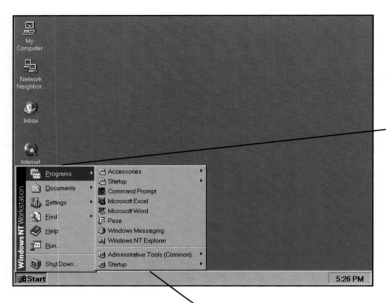

Notice that the top four choices on this menu have a ▶ to their right. This symbol means that a second menu, or submenu, will appear when you highlight the choice.

2. Move your pointer up the menu to highlight **Programs**. A second menu will appear. Depending on how slowly or quickly you move the pointer, menus may pop up as you highlight each choice with a ▶. Ignore the menus. As you move past them, they'll close.

Take a moment to look at the Programs menu. This menu, too, can be customized, so your menu may be different from the example shown here.

3. Move the pointer over to **Accessories**. Another menu will appear showing the programs on the Accessories menu. Notice, by the way, that you don't have to click to get the submenu to open. As soon as you highlight Accessories, the submenu opens.

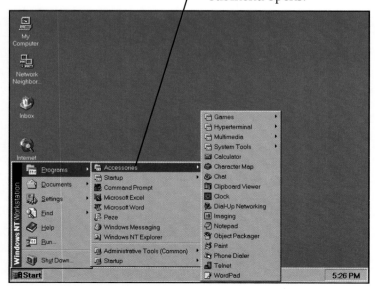

Note: The automatic opening can get annoying because the submenus tend to be hyperactive and pop up all over the place. If they get out of control, press the Esc key. This will take you back one pop-up menu. You can also press the left arrow key to go back one menu. If they simply will not behave, click anywhere on the desktop. All menus will close, and you can start over.

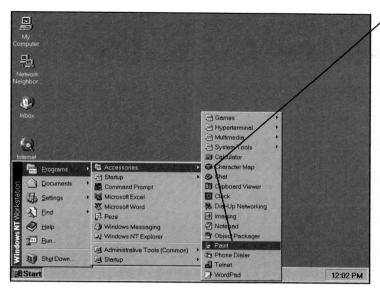

4. Move the mouse pointer over to the third menu and then down to **Paint**.

Note: If you try to get to Paint by sliding the mouse pointer down the middle menu and then over to Paint, the Accessories menu will close.

5. Click on **Paint**. The Paint program will open. Paint is a draw program that comes with NT 4.0. You're opening it here so you can see how to switch between programs. The process in NT 4.0 is different from what you're used to in Windows 3.x or NT 3.51.

Changing the Size of a Window

Windows NT 4.0 has new buttons for resizing windows.

1. Click on ▢, the Maximize button, to make the window fill your screen. Notice that after the window is maximized, the Restore button (▣) appears in place of the Maximize button. This new button will restore the screen to its original size. For the moment, however, leave the window maximized.

2. Click on ▬, the Minimize button.

The Paint program will disappear into the taskbar at the bottom of your screen. It is now running "in the background," which means it is still open and will immediately reappear when you click its button on the taskbar.

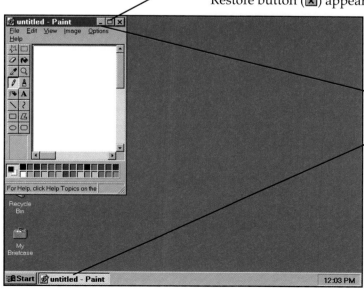

Opening a Program from the Run Dialog Box

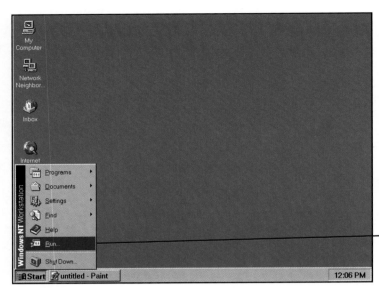

You can, of course, repeat the steps shown at the beginning of this chapter to open a second program, but in this section you'll use the Run command to open a program. If you used the File, Run command in Windows 3.x, you'll feel right at home with the Run dialog box.

1. Click on the **Start** button in the taskbar. The Start menu will appear.

2. Click on **Run**. The Run dialog box will appear.

3. Type the **path** for the program you want to run. In this example, we show Word 6. The typical path for Word 6 is c:\winword\winword.exe. If you don't know the exact path, click on the Browse button and see the next section, "Browsing for a Program."

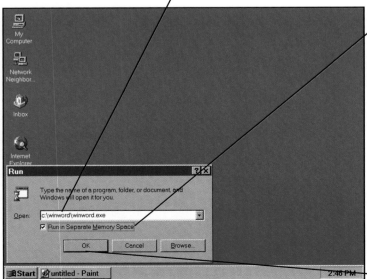

4. If this is a 16-bit program, **click** on **Run in Separate Memory Space** to put a ✔ in the box. The 16-bit programs in Windows 3.1 and NT 3.51 use memory differently than 32-bit programs. Not checking this option can cause problems with the application and/or memory. Don't start DOS programs through the Run dialog box. See the last page of Chapter 9, "Working Smarter with Shortcut Icons and Desktop Folders," for details.

5. Click on **OK**.

Browsing for a Program

You can either type the exact path of a program in the Run dialog box, or you can browse for it.

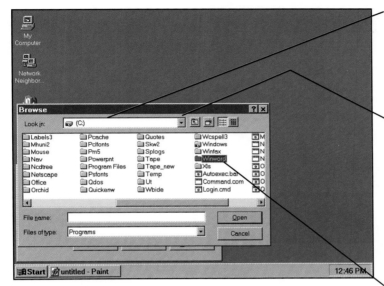

When you click on the Browse button in the Run dialog box (see the previous page), you will open a window showing the programs on the C: drive as you see here.

1. If the program is on a different drive, **click** on the ▼ to the right of the Look in box and select the appropriate drive.

2. **Drag** the **scroll bar** to the right until you see the folder (directory) for the program you wan to run.

3. **Double-click** on the appropriate **folder**. In this example, it's Winword. The Winword folder will open.

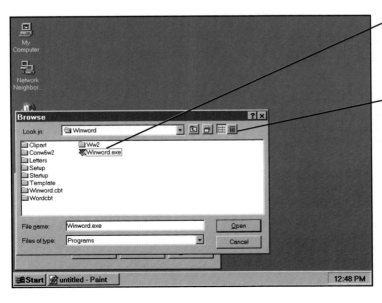

4. **Click** on the **icon** that will start, or execute, the program. Look for the .exe extension or see step 5.

5. If your file names do not show extensions, **click** on the **Details** button. The list will change to show the file type.

Note: If you want to set your computer to show the file extensions, see the section entitled "Showing File Extensions and the File Path" in Chapter 13.

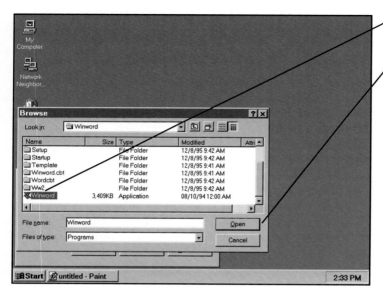

6. Click on the appropriate **Application** listing.

7. Click on **Open**. You'll go back to the Run dialog box.

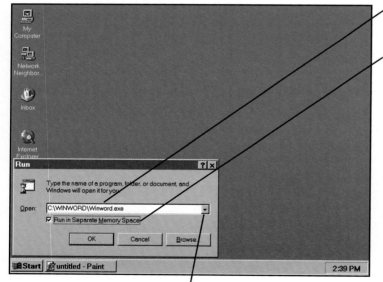

The correct path is now shown in the Open box.

8. If this is a 16-bit program, **click** on **Run in Separate Memory Space** to put a ✔ in the box. The 16-bit programs in Windows 3.1 use memory differently than 32-bit programs. Not checking this option can cause problems with the application and/or memory. Don't start DOS programs this way. See the last page of Chapter 9, "Working Smarter with Shortcut Icons and Desktop Folders," for details.

9. Click on **OK**. The program will start.

Note: The next time you open the Run dialog box, the path of the last program opened will be shown. However, the Run dialog box saves a list of all programs previously opened. Click on the ▼ to show the list. Select the program you want and you're off and running. Be sure to click on Run in Separate Memory Space if it's a 16-bit program.

Switching Between Open Programs

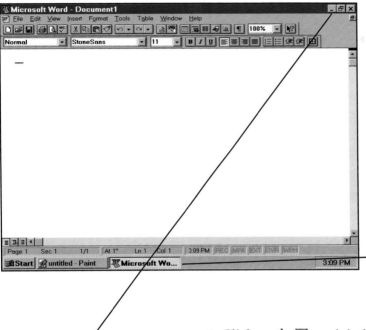

In Windows 3.x, you're probably used to using Ctrl + Esc to bring up the Task List or Alt + Tab to toggle through open programs. These don't work in Windows NT 4.0. However, you'll find the taskbar is a visual way of keeping track of open programs.

If you've been following along, you have two programs open and the second program is on your screen.

Both programs appear in the taskbar, with the button of the active program appearing to be pressed in.

1. Click on the ⬛ to minimize the active program. It will disappear into the taskbar.

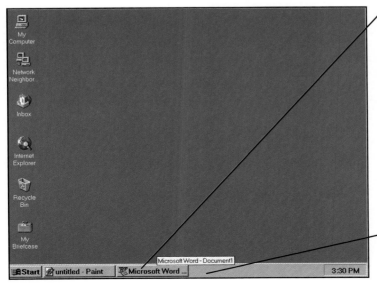

2. If the button on the taskbar is not wide enough to show the entire program or file name, **place** the mouse pointer on top of the **button** and a balloon, or label, will appear with the name spelled out in full. This is a handy feature because the buttons become narrower as you open multiple programs.

You don't have to minimize one program in order to open a second one.

3. Click on each **button**. The programs will layer over one another.

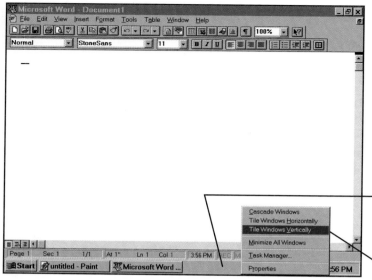

Tiling
Open Programs

You can make two programs fit side by side on your screen. If you don't have two programs open as in step 3 at the bottom of the previous page, follow the steps detailed earlier in this chapter.

1. Click the **right mouse button** on a clear space on the taskbar. A pop-up menu will appear.

2. Click on **Tile Windows Vertically**. The programs will appear next to each other. (If you click on Tile Windows Horizontally, the programs will appear one above the other.) If the options are grayed out, see the Note in the next paragraph.

Note: If this doesn't work, you didn't have both programs open on your screen. Repeat step 3 on the previous page and try again.

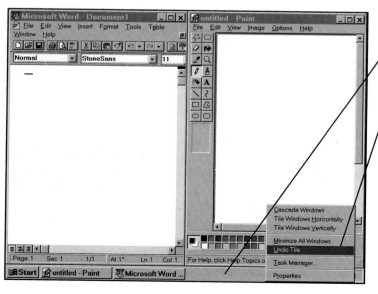

You can undo the tiling just as easily.

3. Click the **right mouse button** on a clear space on the taskbar. A pop-up menu will appear.

4. Click on **Undo Tile**.

5. Click on the ☒ (Close button) on the right of the title bar to close each program.

Opening a Recently Used File

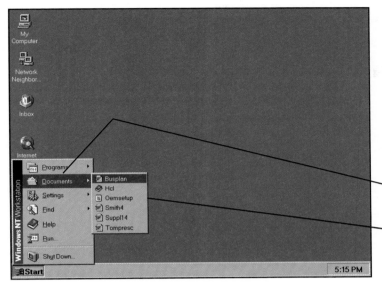

The Documents menu keeps track of the 15 most-recently opened files if you opened them in a new 32-bit program or in Windows NT Explorer (Chapter 13). Files opened directly in a Windows 3.1 program will not show on this list. They will show, however, if you open them in Explorer.

1. Click on the **Start** button. The Start menu will appear.

2. Move the mouse pointer to **Documents**. A list of recently used documents will open.

3. Click on the **file** you want to open.

Clearing the Documents Menu

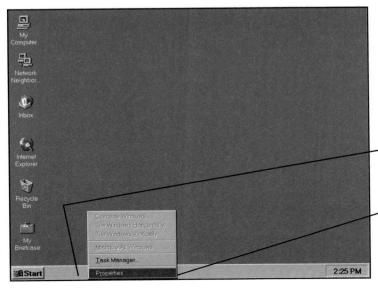

The Documents menu will not clear itself when you shut down for the day. You can manually clear the list if you want to keep it current or if you prefer that others not see the files on which you last worked.

1. Click the **right mouse button** on a clear spot on the **taskbar**. A pop-up menu will appear.

2. Click on **Properties**. The Taskbar Properties dialog box will appear.

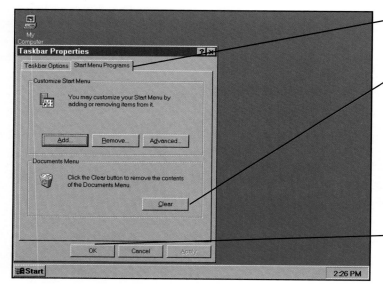

3. Click on the **Start menu Programs** tab to bring it to the front of the dialog box.

4. Click on the **Clear** button to remove the contents of the Documents Menu.

The list will begin again with the next file you open (provided, of course, that it meets the criteria described in the introduction to this section).

5. Click on **OK**.

CHAPTER 3

Shutting Down or Rebooting Your Computer

You and Toto are not in Windows 3.1 anymore. NT has a specific process you should follow when you shut down or reboot. This process guarantees that all of your data and the registry information is saved. In this chapter, you will do the following:

✔ Shut down your computer
✔ Reboot

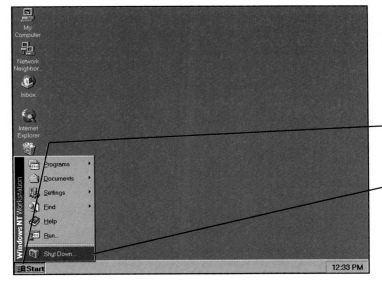

Starting to Shut Down

NT has a Shut Down command on the Start menu.

1. Click on the **Start** button in the taskbar. The Start menu will appear.

2. Click on **Shut Down**. The Shut Down Windows dialog box will appear.

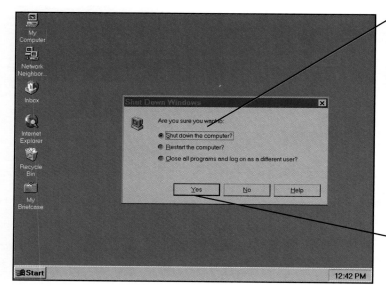

3. Click on the **appropriate choice**.

Notice that in addition to shutting down, the message box contains a Restart option if you change your mind about shutting down.

If you share the machine, you can choose the option to close all programs and log on as a different user.

4. Click on **Yes** (or press Enter).

If you're shutting down, wait for the message saying, "It is now safe to turn off your computer." At this point, you can turn off your machine.

Changing Screen Colors

Colors affect your mood, your ability to see items on your screen clearly, and can increase or diminish eye strain. You can change the colors on your screen to fit your personal preferences. In this chapter, you will do the following:

✔ Choose from a list of predesigned color schemes
✔ Customize a predesigned color scheme
✔ Save a customized color scheme
✔ Delete a color scheme

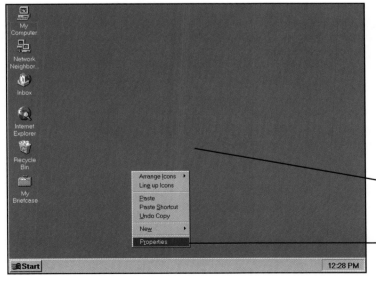

Changing the Colors on Your Screen

You change colors in the Display Properties dialog box. The quickest way to get to it is to use the following process:

1. Click the **right mouse button** on the desktop. The pop-up menu you see here will appear.

2. Click on **Properties**. The Display Properties dialog box will appear.

3. Click on the **Appearance** tab to bring it to the front of the dialog box.

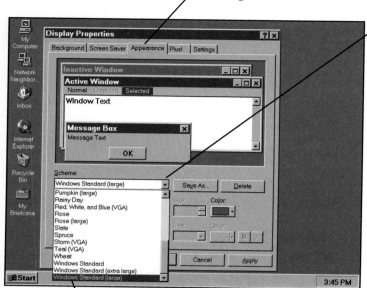

4. Click on the ▼ to open the list of predesigned color schemes.

Notice as you scroll through the list that some of the choices say large or extra large. These choices will enlarge the size of icons and the print on your toolbars and make things a little easier to see. Keep in mind that these settings only affect icons, menus, and other screen items. Settings within applications (such as the font size for a Word document) are still completely under your control. Some choices say VGA. These choices will display well on a VGA (video graphics array) monitor. All choices will look good on the much more popular SVGA (super VGA) monitor.

5. Click on a **scheme** on the list, and watch the sample screen change colors to reflect your choice.

6. Click on **Apply** to select the choice, or see the next section on customizing a color scheme.

Customizing a Predesigned Color Scheme

If you're not especially crazy about any of the color schemes, you can use one as a basis for creating your own. If, for example, you like one of the large schemes but don't like the colors, you can change them.

1. Click on the **color scheme** that comes closest to what you want.

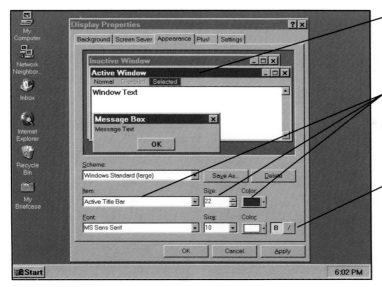

2. Click on any **item** in the sample window. In this example, click on the Active Title Bar.

Notice that the item you clicked (in this example, the active title bar) is shown in the Item box, and its size and color are shown to the right.

Details about the font in the active title bar are shown in the line below.

Try clicking on other items in the sample screen to see how the information in these two lines changes.

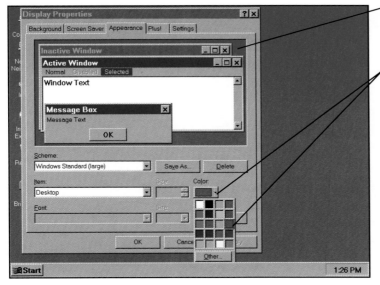

3. Click on the **item** you want to change. In this example, it is the desktop.

4. Click on the ▼ to the right of the Color box to open the color palette for that item. Notice that on the palette the current color is surrounded by a selection border.

5. Click on the **color** you want that item to be.

6. Repeat steps 3 through 5 to change other items on the screen.

When you've finished coloring your screen, see the next section on saving the scheme.

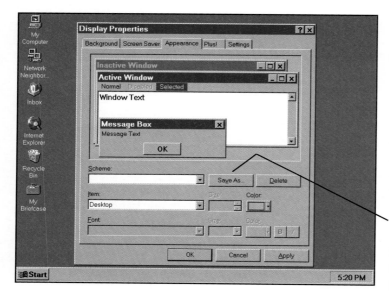

Saving a Customized Color Scheme

Don't save an existing color scheme with changes because you won't be able to restore the original settings without a lot of work. Save the changes under a new name.

1. Click on **Save As**.

2. When the Save As dialog box opens (not shown here), **type** a **name** for the new scheme and **click** on **OK**.

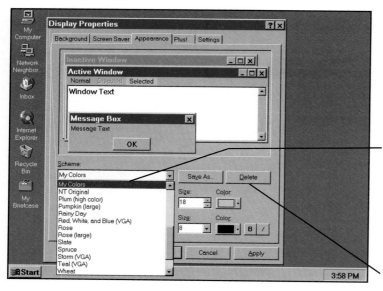

Deleting a Color Scheme

1. Follow steps 1 - 3 at the beginning of this chapter to go to the Appearance tab in the Display Properties dialog box.

2. Click on ▼ to open the list of color schemes if it is not already showing in the Scheme box.

3. Click on the **scheme** you want to delete.

4. Click on **Delete**. The color scheme will be deleted from the list.

Note: If the scheme you deleted was the one that was on your screen, you'll have to choose another color scheme before you close this dialog box.

Selecting a Screen Saver and Other Display Options

Seven or eight years ago, if you allowed an image to stay on your screen too long without any movement, it could burn itself into your monitor. Screen savers were developed to prevent this. With today's monitors, screen savers are no longer technically necessary, but they're still used for their entertainment value and the personalization they give to a humdrum computer screen. A screen saver can even provide some security for your computer. There are numerous ways you can affect what you see on your screen, from adding background patterns to changing the size of the icons and the number of colors you see. You can also hide or move the taskbar. In this chapter, you will do the following:

✔ Select and customize a screen saver
✔ Attach a password to a screen saver
✔ Create a customized marquee screen saver
✔ Explore additional display options
✔ Learn how to hide or move the taskbar

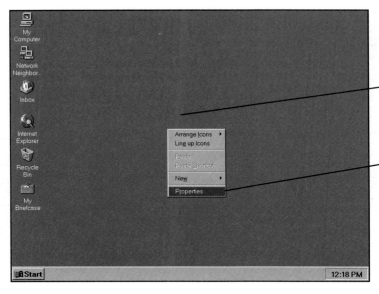

Selecting a Screen Saver

1. Click the **right mouse button** on a blank spot on the desktop to open the pop-up menu you see here.

2. Click on **Properties**. The Display Properties dialog box will appear.

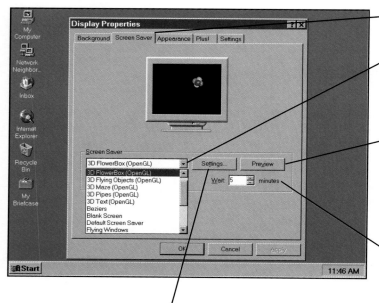

3. Click on the **Screen Saver** tab to bring it to the front.

4. Click on the ▼ to open the list of screen savers.

5. Click on a **screen saver**.

6. Click on **Preview**. After a pause, the screen saver you selected will appear on your screen. Move your mouse or press any key to end the preview.

7. Click on the ▲ or ▼ to increase or decrease the wait time before the screen saver comes on.

Customizing a Screen Saver

Most screen savers can be customized.

1. Click on **Settings** to open a Setup dialog box for the particular screen saver you selected in the steps above.

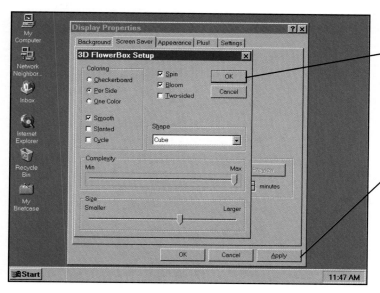

2. Make the appropriate **changes**.

3. Click on **OK** to accept the changes and close the Setup dialog box.

4. Click on the **Preview** button if you want to see the impact of your changes.

5. Click on **Apply** to put your choice into effect without closing the dialog box.

Attaching a Password to a Screen Saver

With this option, you (or anyone else) must enter your computer password to make the screen saver disappear once it has been activated. Although it would be a pain in the neck to have to do this as a regular routine, it could be useful if you expect to be away from your desk for a while.

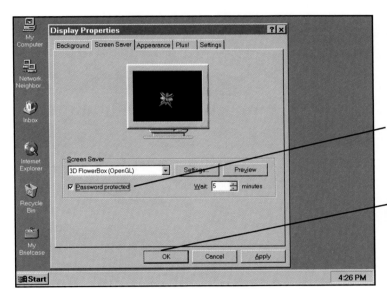

1. Follow steps 1 through 3 at the beginning of this chapter to open the Screen Saver portion of the Display Properties dialog box, if you aren't already there.

2. Click on **Password protected** to put a ✔ in the box. This will attach your logon password to this screen saver.

3. Click on **OK** to apply the password and close the dialog box.

The next time your screen saver comes up and you move your mouse, you'll see a message saying, "This workstation is in use and has been locked."

4. Press Ctrl + Alt + Delete to unlock it, and then enter your logon password in the screen that comes up.

Removing the Screen Saver

Sometimes a screen saver will interfere with the installation of new programs. You can remove it temporarily (or permanently) with the following steps.

1. Repeat steps 1-5 at the beginning of this chapter. In step 5, **click** on **None** and then **click** on **OK**.

Creating a Marquee Screen Saver

A marquee is a text message that scrolls across your screen. You can create any message you want from "It's a girl!" to "In a meeting until 3:30."

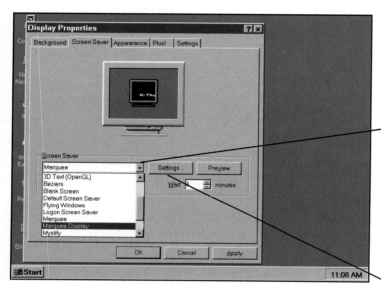

1. Open the **Screen Saver** portion of the Display Properties dialog box if you haven't already done so. See the steps at the beginning of this chapter if you need help.

2. Click on ▼ to open the list of screen savers, then click on **Marquee Display**. If NT was installed over Windows 3.1 or 3.11, you may have another "Marquee" listing as well as doubles of Mystify and Starfield Simulation. They all work the same.

3. Click on **Settings**.

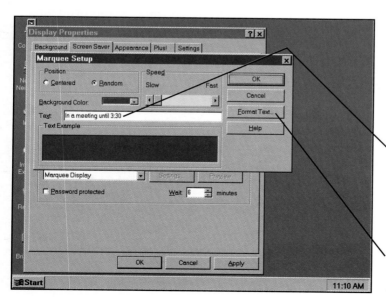

In addition to the actual text, you can select the color of the background—whether the text is centered or randomly placed as it scrolls across your screen—and the speed at which the text moves.

4. Click in the **Text** box and **type** the **message**.

5. Make the appropriate **changes** in **Position**, **Speed**, and **Background Color**.

6. Click on **Format Text** to select the font as well as the color, size, and style.

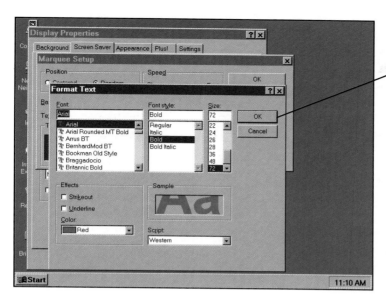

7. Select the **font, font style**, size, and **color** of the text.

8. Click on **OK** in this screen and in the Marquee Setup screen.

9. Click on **Preview** to check out the marquee.

Exploring Other Screen-Changing Options

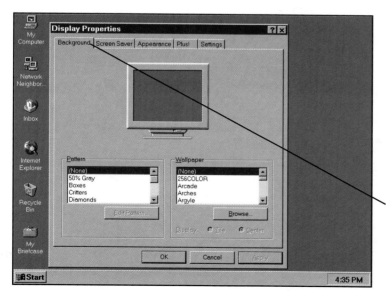

In addition to sections on Appearance (see Chapter 4, "Changing Screen Colors") and the Screen Saver, the Display Properties dialog box contains sections on Background, Plus!, and Settings.

Adding Patterns and Wallpapers

Background contains patterns and wallpapers that you can apply to your screen. Because they often take up a lot of memory and slow your computer's performance, we don't recommend them.

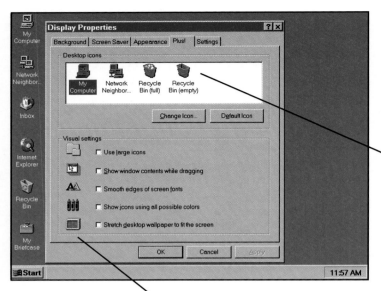

Using the Plus! Pack

The Plus! pack comes with NT 4.0 and it gives you even more opportunities to make your screen your own.

You can customize the four desktop icons shown here. Click on the icon you want to change, then click on Change Icon. Choose the one you want from the icons that appear (not shown in this example). If you decide you don't like the new icon after all, simply click on Default Icon to go back to the original.

The bottom portion of the Plus! page allows you to change several visual settings:

❖ **Use large icons** will make the icons on your desktop and in Explorer about twice as large as they are now.

❖ **Show window contents while dragging** means that when you drag a window, the entire window is dragged. With the default setting, only an "outline" is dragged and the window itself moves only when you release the mouse button.

❖ **Smooth edges of screen fonts** makes large fonts a little easier to read by smoothing their edges. It may bring up a message telling you that you must set your display's color palette to High Color or True Color with the Settings tab (see the next section). You may not have the system authorization (or the right equipment) to make this kind of change. See your systems administrator.

❖ **Show icons using all possible colors** may get a message similar to the one in the choice above.

❖ **Stretch desktop wallpaper to fit the screen** will, literally, do just that. See our comments in "Adding Patterns and Wallpaper" earlier in this chapter.

Changing Settings

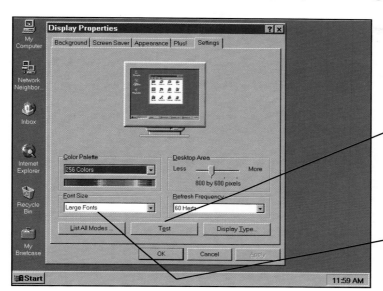

The settings on this page often require that you have system authorization to make changes because they depend on the kind of monitor you have and your video card.

If you have authorization, most changes ask you to test the changes by clicking on the Test button and then responding as to whether you can see the colors well.

You may need the installation disk to make a change in the Font Size box and to install large fonts.

Hiding the Taskbar

The taskbar is set to show at the bottom of your screen even when you have a program displayed in full-screen view.

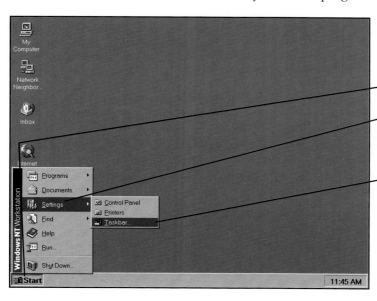

You can hide the taskbar from view and still have it immediately available on a simple mouse move.

1. Click on the **Start** button.

2. Move the mouse pointer to **Settings**. A second menu will appear.

3. Click on **Taskbar**. The Taskbar Properties dialog box will appear.

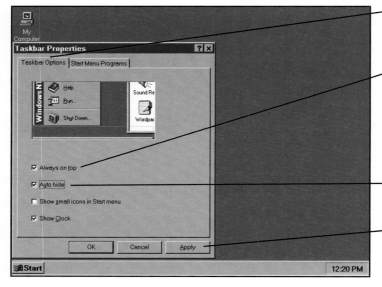

4. Click on the **Taskbar Options** tab if it is not already at the front of the dialog box.

Note: "Always on top" should have a check mark. Leave the check mark there. This option makes the taskbar available even when you have a program running in full-screen view.

5. Click on **Auto Hide** to put a ✔ in the box.

6. Click on **Apply** and watch the taskbar vanish from view.

7. Click on **OK** to accept the change and close the dialog box.

Using a Hidden Taskbar

Getting access to the hidden taskbar couldn't be easier.

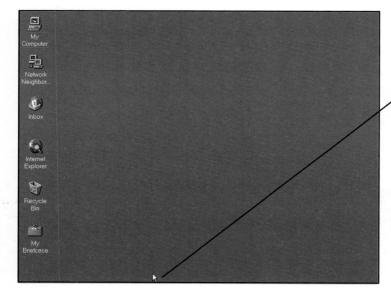

1. Move your **mouse pointer** into the **bottom of your screen** and the taskbar will come into view.

Unhiding the Taskbar

Repeat the steps you took to hide the taskbar but click on Auto Hide to *remove* the ✔.

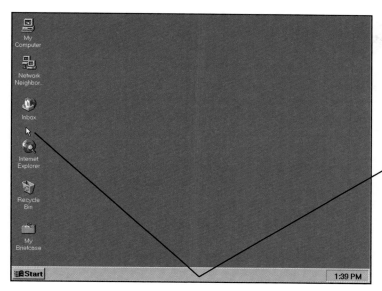

Moving the Taskbar

You can move the taskbar to any of the four sides of your screen. This is called "docking" the taskbar.

1. Place your **mouse pointer** on **top of the taskbar** and **drag** it to the left side of your screen. The taskbar will stay where it is and you'll see an outline being placed on the left side of the screen. When you release your mouse button, the taskbar will move.

Note: If you selected "Show window contents while dragging" back in "Using the Plus! Pack" section of this chapter, you won't see the outline. In fact, you won't see anything until you release the mouse button, at which point the taskbar will move.

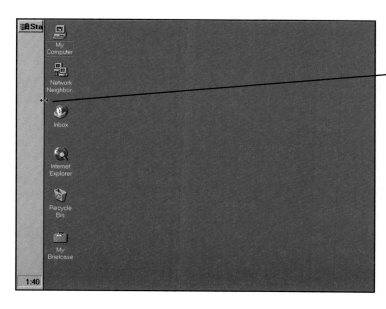

If the taskbar is moved to the side, it probably won't be wide enough to show all of the Start button.

2. Place your **mouse pointer** on the right edge of the taskbar. The pointer will change to a two-headed arrow.

3. Drag the **edge** of the taskbar to enlarge its area. When you start a program, it will run in the desktop space available.

You can, of course, put the taskbar back at the bottom of the screen with the same steps. Or the top, or the right...

CHAPTER 6

Changing the Date, Time, and Time Zone

If the date, time, and time zone were not set correctly during installation, it's easy to do. In this chapter, you will do the following:

✔ Change the date
✔ Change the time
✔ Change the time zone

Opening the Date/Time Properties Dialog Box

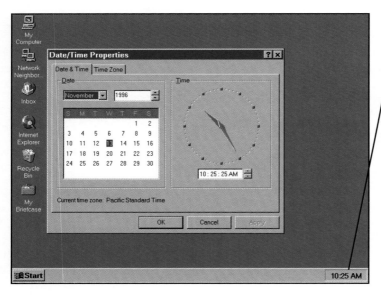

There is a Date/Time icon in the Control Panel. For even quicker access, use the Time button on the taskbar.

1. Double-click the **Time button**. The Date/Time Properties dialog box you see here will appear.

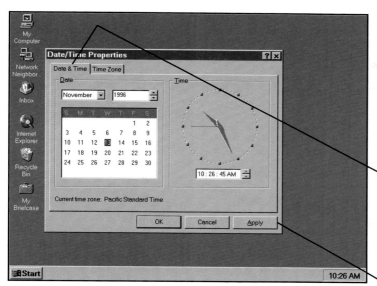

Changing the Date & Time

The date and time can, of course, be changed independently of the time zone; but if you have to change all three, do the time zone first.

1. Click on the **Date & Time** tab if it is not already in front.

2. Make the appropriate **changes** to the month, year, date or time.

3. Click on **Apply**.

Changing the Time Zone

Changing the time zone will automatically adjust the time and date as appropriate.

1. Click on the **Time Zone** tab to bring it to the front.

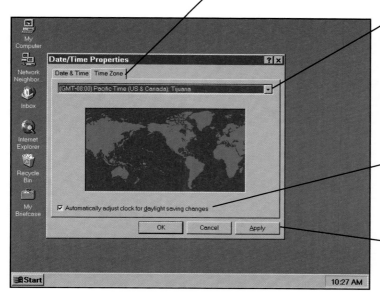

2. Click on the ▼ to open the time zone list.

3. Click on the appropriate **time zone** on the list (not shown here). The map will shift to bring the selected time zone into focus.

Notice that the daylight savings change is already selected. You can change this, of course, if you choose.

4. Click on **Apply**.

5. Click on **OK** to close the dialog box.

CHAPTER 7

Customizing Your Mouse

There are many ways to customize your mouse. In this chapter, you will do the following:

✔ Change to a left-handed mouse
✔ Change the speed with which you must double-click
✔ Choose from a selection of pointer sizes and shapes
✔ Change the motion or speed with which your mouse moves
✔ Make your mouse automatically go to the OK or Apply button in a dialog box

Opening the Mouse Properties Dialog Box

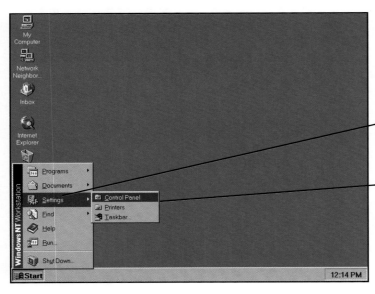

You go through the Control Panel to change the mouse.

1. Click on the **Start** button in the taskbar. The Start menu will appear.

2. Move the mouse arrow to **Settings**. A second menu will appear.

3. Click on **Control Panel**. The Control panel window will appear.

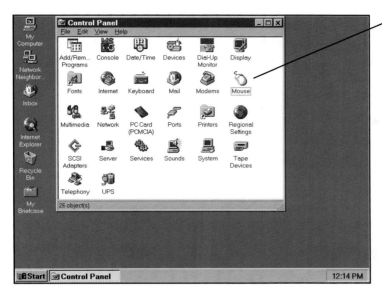

4. Double-click on the **Mouse** icon to open the Mouse Properties dialog box. Your mouse icon may be in a different spot in the window.

Switching to a Left-Handed Mouse

If you haven't already done so, follow steps 1 through 4 above to open the Mouse Properties dialog box.

1. Click on the **Buttons** tab if it is not already at the front of the dialog box.

2. Click on **Left-handed** to select this option.

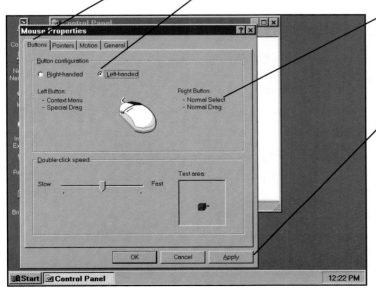

Notice that the functions associated with the Left and Right buttons have changed and that the highlighted area on the mouse moved from the left button to the right button.

3. Click on **Apply** to make the change take place *immediately*. You can now switch your mouse to your left hand and use the right button as your primary mouse button.

You can click on OK to close the dialog box or go on to the next section, "Changing the Double-Click Speed of the Mouse."

Changing the Double-Click Speed of the Mouse

There are certain functions in Windows that require a double click. If you make the double clicks too slowly, Windows does not connect the two clicks and, therefore, does not perform the appropriate function. You can easily adjust the time needed between clicks to fit your own style.

If you haven't already done so, follow steps 1 through 4 at the beginning of this chapter to open the Mouse Properties dialog box.

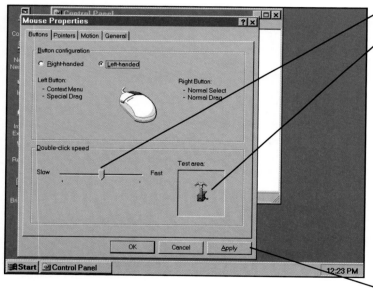

1. Drag the **arrow** toward Slow.

2. When the arrow is placed where you think best, **double-click** the jack-in-the-box in the Test area. Use the double-click speed most comfortable for you. If your double click is accepted, the jack-in-the-box will pop up. You can double-click again to put him back into the box.

3. If the jack-in-the-box doesn't appear, **repeat steps 1 and 2** until you find the speed that's right for you.

4. Click on **Apply** to make this change.

You can click on OK to close the dialog box or go on to the next section, "Expressing Yourself With Pointers," to see the new pointers included with Windows NT 4.0.

Expressing Yourself with Pointers

Windows NT 4.0 includes a variety of pointers of different sizes and shapes that will make your pointer easier to see or simply more interesting to look at.

If you haven't been following along with this chapter, repeat steps 1 through 4 at the beginning of the chapter to open the Mouse Properties dialog box you see here.

1. Click on the **Pointers** tab to bring it to the front of the dialog box.

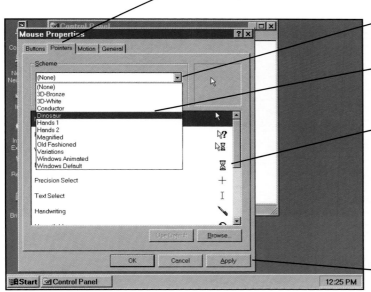

2. Click on the ▼ to open the Scheme list of pointer choices.

3. Click on the **scheme** you want. In this example, it's Dinosaur.

Notice that the pointers will change to reflect your choice. Experiment with choices until you find one you like. In terms of results, Windows Default, the last choice on the list, is the same as (None), the first choice on the list.

4. Click on **Apply** to accept this choice.

You can, of course, click on OK to accept the changes you made so far and close the dialog box, or you can continue on to the next section of this chapter.

Controlling Pointer Speed and Placement

You can make your mouse whiz around the screen or move more sedately. You can even make the pointer automatically appear at the OK or Apply button in a dialog box.

If the Mouse Properties dialog box is not already open, repeat steps 1 through 4 at the beginning of the chapter.

Changing Pointer Speed

1. Click on the **Motion** tab.

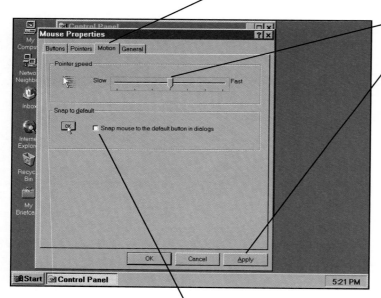

2. Drag the **arrow** toward the appropriate end of the scale.

3. Click on **Apply** and then move your mouse around. If you don't like its feel, repeat steps 1 and 2 until you do like the feel.

Changing the Default Position of the Mouse

When you open a dialog box, your mouse is in the spot where you last clicked. By choosing the "Snap to default" option, you can make your mouse automatically appear at the OK or Apply button.

1. Click on **Snap mouse to the default button in dialogs** to put a ✔ in the box.

2. Click on **Apply**. Nothing will happen with this option until you close this dialog box and open another.

3. Click on **OK** to accept the changes and close the dialog box.

Using Help

You'll find the NT 4.0 Help function much improved over the Windows 3.1 version. Each specific application, such as Word or Excel, has its own content-related Help, of course, but the NT desktop gives you immediate access to help on topics about NT. In this chapter, you will do the following:

✔ Check out the Troubleshooting Tips
✔ Print a Help topic
✔ Annotate a Help topic
✔ Find a specific Help topic

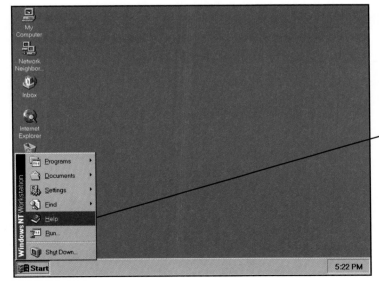

Using Help

Help is on the Start menu.

1. Click on the **Start** button. The Start menu will appear.

2. Click on **Help**. The first time you open Help, a small graphic will appear showing a pen writing in a book with the message, "Preparing Help file for..." Then the Help Topics window will appear.

Identifying Items

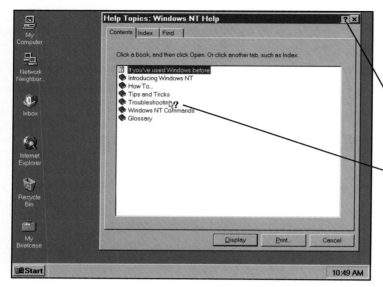

If you're not sure what a specific item in a window is for, Windows NT has added a help feature that will identify it.

1. Click on the **question mark** (**?**) in the title bar. The question mark will become attached to the mouse arrow.

2. Click on any **item** in the window. An explanation of the item will appear. In this example, we clicked on Troubleshooting.

The explanation can be a one-sentence definition or it can give you directions on use, as in this example.

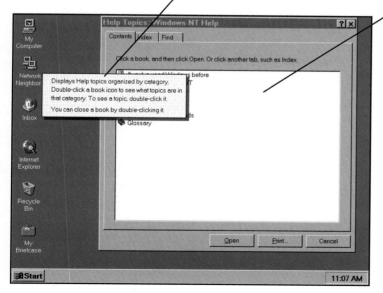

3. Click anywhere to remove the explanation.

You can use the question mark in any window or dialog box in which it appears. It's especially helpful when you don't understand the difference between specific options in a dialog box and need a little more information to make an informed choice.

Troubleshooting Help

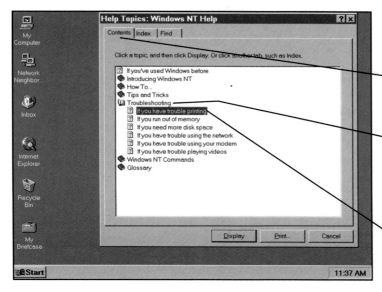

NT 4.0 Help contains trouble-shooting tips for a variety of topics.

1. Click on the **Contents** tab if it is not already at the front of the dialog box.

2. Double-click on **Trouble-shooting**. The book icon to the left will open and a list of items in the book will appear as shown here.

3. Double-click on **If you have trouble printing**. A Help window with the Print Trouble-shooter will appear.

Depending on the problem, NT 4.0 Help may ask you to define your problem more specifically.

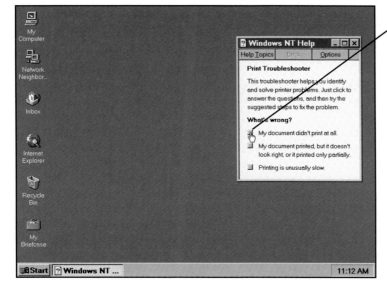

4. Click on the **appropriate description** of your problem. In this example it is "My document didn't print at all." Notice that the mouse arrow turns into a little hand. The hand tells you that this option is a link to another window.

We won't walk you through additional layers of this particular Help topic because the process doesn't change. However, in the next section, you'll learn some of the things you can do with information in Help topics and the Help window itself.

Choosing Options for a Help Window

There are a number of things you can do with the information in the Help window as well as the window itself. This example shows a Print Troubleshooter Help window. The exact topic doesn't matter – the Options button is in all Help topic windows.

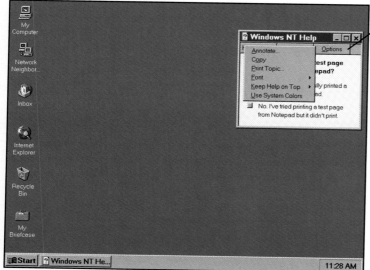

1. Click on **Options** in the Help window menu bar. The Options menu will appear. The items on the Options menu are as follows:

❖ **Annotate** allows you to make notes on this specific topic. See the next section for directions on using the Annotate feature.

❖ **Copy** copies the text in this window; then you can open a new document in Notepad or your word processor and paste the text into the document.

❖ **Print Topic** prints the text in the window.

❖ **Font** gives you the opportunity to make the font in the Help window larger or smaller than the normal size you see.

❖ **Keep Help on Top** gives you three options. The Default option has different settings for different types of Help windows. On Top means that the Help window will always stay on top of whatever comes on the screen. Not On Top means that if something else comes on the screen, it may open on top of the Help window, covering it.

❖ **Use System Colors** changes the color scheme of the Help windows to the color scheme you have chosen. (See Chapter 4, "Changing Screen Colors.") You'll have to close Help to put this change into effect.

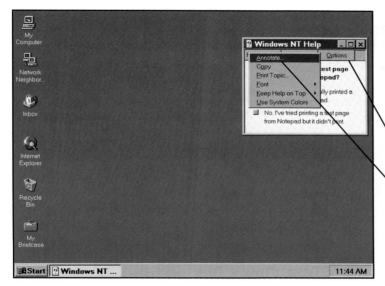

Annotating a Help Topic

You can make notes to yourself about a particular topic.

1. Click on **Options** in the Help menu bar.

2. Click on **Annotate**. The Annotate window will appear.

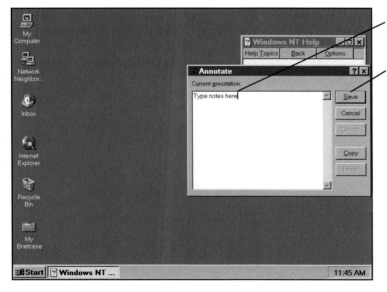

3. Type your **notes** in the window.

4. Click on **Save**.

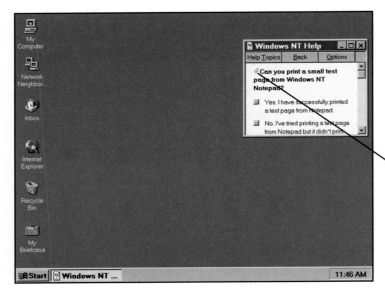

Opening and Removing an Annotation

Notice the paper clip next to the question. This indicates an attached note.

1. Click on the **paper clip** to open the note.

2. Click on **Delete** (not shown here) to remove the note.

Navigating Through Help Windows

A Help topic can have so many links and layers of windows that it's easy to get lost. No matter where you are, though, two of the choices on the menu bar will help you navigate through the maze.

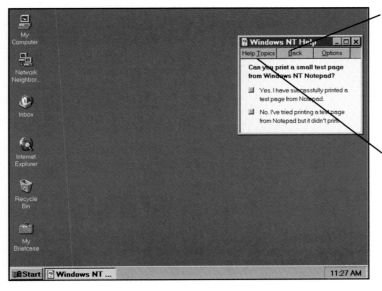

1. Click on **Back** to go back one window at a time. Clicking repeatedly will take you back to the very first topic window. However, this button will not take you back to the original search window or the Help Topics window.

2. Click on **Help Topics** to go back to the Help Topics window. Use this button when a particular Help topic is not particularly helpful and you want to start the search over again.

Finding a Specific Help Topic

Follow the directions at the beginning of the chapter to open the Help Topics window or, if you've already started to explore Help topics, click on the Help Topics button to return to the window you see here.

1. Click on the **Find** tab to bring it to the front of the window.

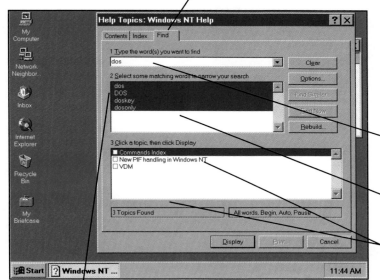

If this is the first time anyone has used Help on this machine, you may see the Find Setup Wizard that is shown later in this chapter. If it appears, click on Next and then Finish to build the Help database.

2. Type a **word or phrase** that describes your question. In this example, it is **dos**.

A list of possible matches will appear here.

This example shows that three topics were found that contain the term "dos."

Note: The search, or Find, function is case-sensitive in that if you had typed "DOS" fewer matches would have been identified. You can refine the search by clicking on one of the matches in the list. This will, in turn, shorten the list of topics in the bottom area.

3. Click on **DOS** in the middle box and watch as the list of topics is reduced to two.

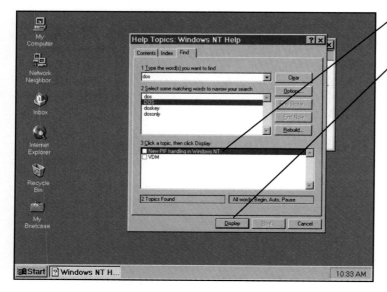

4. Click on **New PIF handling in Windows NT** to highlight it.

5. Click on **Display** to see the text.

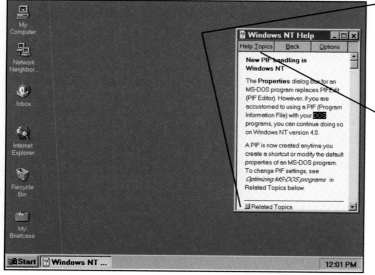

The Related Topics button at the bottom of the window is a handy way to expand your search. Another way to expand the search is described in the next section.

6. If you're following along with these steps, **click** on **Help Topics** to go back to that window.

Expanding Your Search to Similar Topics

If the initial list of matches is not exactly what you want or if you want to expand your search, the Find Similar command is a welcome addition to the search function.

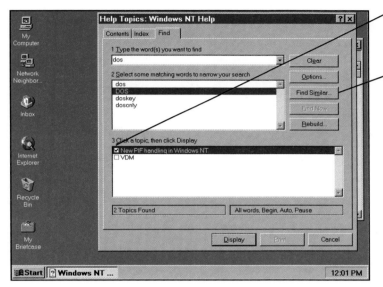

1. Click on the **box** to the left of **New PIF handling in Windows NT** to put a ✔ in it.

Notice that the Find Similar button is now active.

2. Click on **Find Similar**. A list of similar topics will appear.

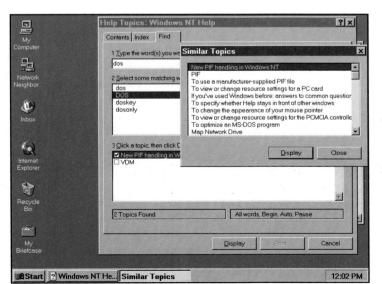

There are a multitude of paths you can take depending on your topic and your interests. The process of clicking on a choice, then clicking on Display to see the text is the same as previously described, so we won't repeat it here.

Go on to the next section to learn more about the Find function.

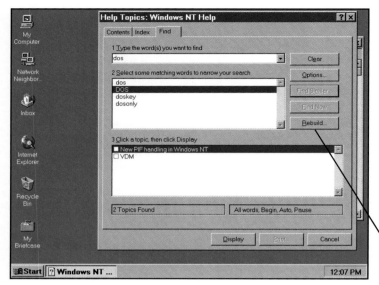

Rebuilding the Database

You can maximize your search capabilities by rebuilding the database to include all possible terms.

1. If you haven't been following along with this chapter, **open** the **Help Topics** window and **click** on the **Find** tab.

2. Click on **Rebuild**. The Find Setup Wizard will appear.

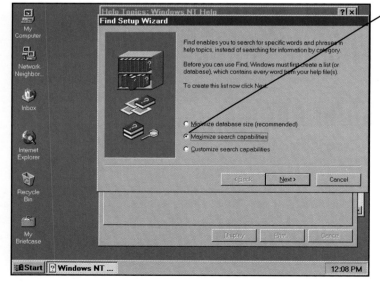

3. Click on **Maximize search capabilities**.

4. Click on **Next**.

5. Click on **Finish** (not shown here). The graphic of the pen writing in the book will appear again as NT compiles the expanded database.

Defining Find Options

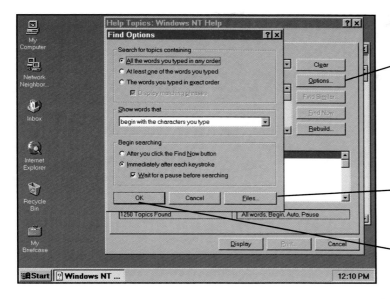

You can customize how your searches are done.

1. Click on **Options**. The Find Options dialog box will appear.

2. Select the **options** you prefer. Remember that you can use the ? if you're uncertain what these options do.

You can even confine the search to specific Help topics, such as Basic Tasks or the Glossary.

3. Click on **OK** if you make any changes.

Using the Index

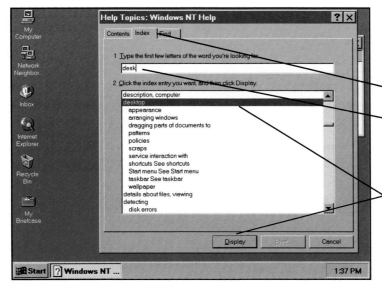

The Index is an alphabetical listing of Help topics.

1. Click on the **Index** tab.

2. Type a **word** or any portion of a word. For example, type **desk** to bring you to the first listing beginning with "desk."

3. Click on the **topic** you want to see, then **click** on **Display**.

Happy searching!

Working Smarter with Shortcut Icons and Desktop Folders

If you've just converted from Windows 3.x or NT 3.51, you may be a little frustrated because things don't work the same way anymore. Don't despair because in this chapter and the next two, we will show you how to customize Windows NT to work a little more like the way you used to work. In this chapter, you will:

✔ Install your favorite program icon on your desktop
✔ Fine-tune the icon if it is for a Windows 3.1 program
✔ Create a folder on your desktop in which to store programs
✔ Move an icon from the desktop to the folder
✔ Add a program icon directly to the folder
✔ Remove a program from the folder
✔ Create a shortcut key for a program
✔ Arrange the icons on your desktop
✔ Set up icons for DOS programs

Making a Shortcut Icon

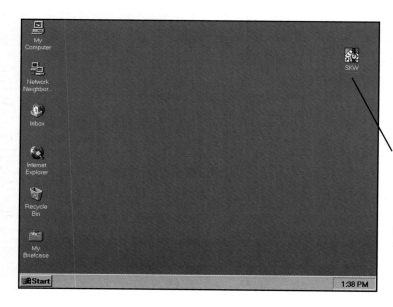

Instead of having to go through the Start menu to get to a frequently used program, you can install an icon on your desktop that will open the program with a simple double-click.

This is an example of a shortcut icon for Sidekick, a time/contact management program. In this section, you will create a shortcut icon for one of your favorite programs and install it on your desktop.

1. Double-click on the **My Computer icon**. The My Computer window you see here will appear.

2. Double-click on the **C drive icon**. The C drive window will appear.

Notice that in this example, the drive is labeled "C (C:)." Your label may be different.

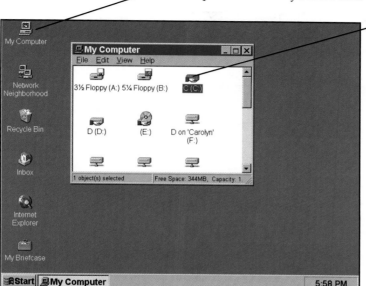

Note: If the view in the window is not like the one you see here, click on View in the menu bar, then click on Small Icons. The specific view doesn't really matter, however. Use the view with which you feel most comfortable.

3. Click repeatedly on the ▶ on the **scroll bar** to scroll to the folder (formerly called directory) where your favorite program is located.

4. Double-click on the **folder icon** where your program is located. The folder will open. In this example, we clicked on our Sidekick (Skw2) folder.

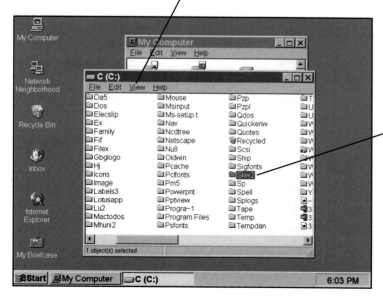

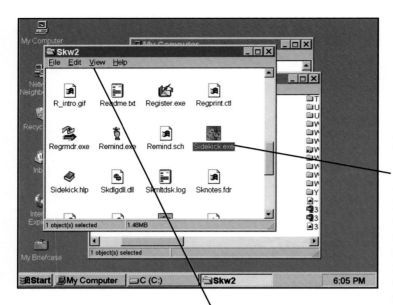

5. Click repeatedly on the ▼ on the **scroll bar** to scroll down to the icon that opens your program. In this example, it is the Sidekick.exe icon.

Note 1: If you don't know what the program icon looks like, here's how to identify it:

❶ The program startup icon usually has an "exe" extension. If your icons don't show file extensions, you may want to set the My Computer view to show the DOS extensions in the folder as shown here. (See Chapter 13) Or, see the next item below.

❷ Click on View in the menu bar, then click on Details. Look for an item that says, "Application" in the Type column. Some programs have multiple subprograms, each with its own "Application" designation. If you're not sure which one is the main program, double-click on each in turn. If the wrong component of the program opens, simply close it and go on to the next "Application" listing. After you have opened the main program, close it and go on to step 6 on the next page.

❸ The program startup icon usually has the program's name (e.g., Sidekick).

❹ Some program startup icons look like the logo on the software box (e.g., Quicken).

❺ The Microsoft Office products can be subfolders (subdirectories) within a folder labeled "MSOffice" or in separate folders labeled "Winword," "Excel," etc., depending on whether they were installed as part of a suite or separately.

Note 2: You can create a shortcut icon that goes directly to a specific file. Just browse to the file listing, and then complete the following steps (even, if appropriate, the one for fine-tuning a shortcut icon for a Windows 3.1 program).

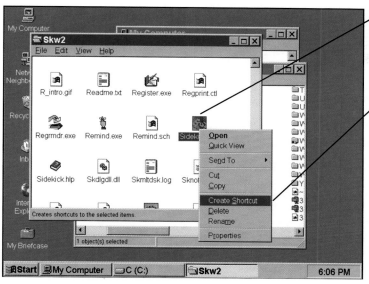

6. Click the **right mouse button** on the program icon (or Application listing if you're in the Detail view). A pop-up menu will appear.

7. Click on **Create Shortcut**. A duplicate icon will appear highlighted at the bottom of the folder or list. Please notice that the original icon is still there. The shortcut is simply a copy of the original and has a curved arrow in the bottom-left corner to identify it as a shortcut icon.

The highlighted icon will be named "Shortcut to ..." Go on to the next section to make the icon name shorter.

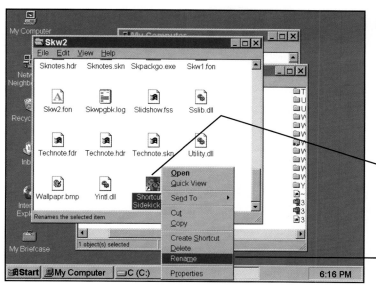

Renaming the Shortcut Icon

If you've been following along with this chapter, you've created a shortcut icon and it is now highlighted. Let's give it a shorter name.

1. Click the **right mouse button** on the highlighted **icon** (or highlighted Application listing). A pop-up menu will appear.

2. Click on **Rename**. A box will appear around the highlighted name.

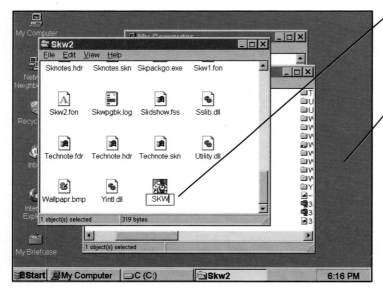

3. Type a **new name** for the icon. It will replace the highlighted "Shortcut to ..." In this example, we typed "SKW," short for Sidekick for Windows.

4. Click anywhere on the **desktop** to remove the highlighting and complete the naming process.

Moving the Shortcut Icon to the Desktop

Now that you've made and renamed a shortcut icon, let's move it to the desktop.

1. Click on the new **shortcut icon** to highlight it.

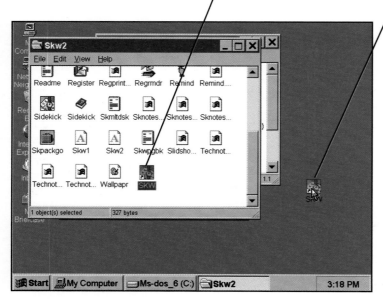

2. Drag the **icon** to the desktop. If it doesn't stay where you put it but flies over to the other desktop icons on the left, see the section, "Arranging Icons on the Desktop" later in this chapter.

When you want to open the program, double-click on this shortcut icon. The shortcut icon doesn't replace any of the other methods of opening the program. It simply gives you a more direct option.

Note: If this shortcut icon is for a Windows 3.1 program, be sure to read "Fine-tuning a Shortcut Icon for a 3.1 Program" on the next page.

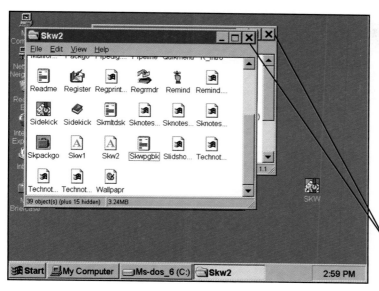

Closing All Open Windows

Closing all the windows is the "clunky" part of the process.

Note: you can set up NT so that it closes the first window when you open the next one in a series. See "Opening One Window at a Time" in Chapter 14.

1. Click on the **Close button** (■ of each open window.

Fine-tuning a Shortcut Icon for a Windows 3.1 Program

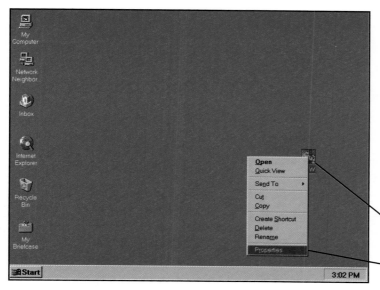

Windows NT 4.0 and its 32-bit operating system use memory differently than Windows 3.1. In order to make a "legacy" program (a program from an older operating system like Windows 3.1) work well in NT 4.0, you have to tell NT to run it in its own space – literally a virtual computer inside NT that is set to handle its specific memory requirements.

1. Click the **right mouse button** on the shortcut icon.

2. Click on **Properties**. The Properties dialog box for the icon will open.

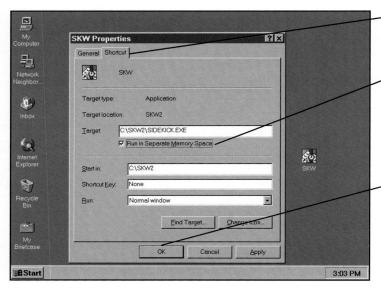

3. Click on the **Shortcut** tab to bring it to the front of the dialog box.

4. Click on **Run in Separate Memory Space** to put a ✔ in the box. This will run the 3.1 program in its own virtual computer configured for its memory needs.

5. Click on **OK**.

Putting a Folder on Your Desktop

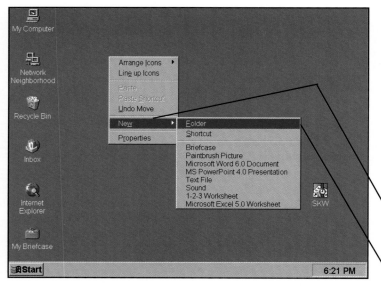

Windows NT does not retain the Group icons that you had in Windows 3.11. No problem. You can recreate group folders and place them on your desktop.

1. Click the **right mouse button** on a blank part of the desktop. A pop-up menu will appear.

2. Move the mouse pointer to **New**. Another menu will appear.

3. Click on **Folder**. A folder icon will appear on your desktop.

Naming and Moving a Folder

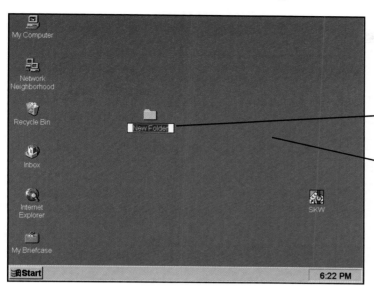

If you've been following along with the steps to put a folder on the desktop, the name of the folder is highlighted and has a box around it.

1. Type a **name** for the folder. In this example, it is Tasks.

2. Click anywhere on the desktop to remove the highlighting and complete the renaming process.

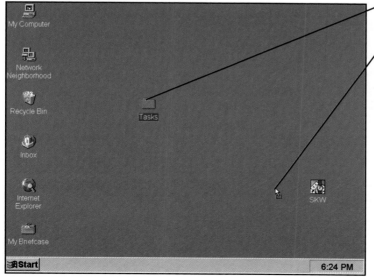

3. Click on the **folder** to highlight it.

4. Drag the **folder** to a new location on your desktop. Once again, see "Arranging Icons on the Desktop" later in this chapter if the folder doesn't stay where you put it.

Go on to the next section to learn several ways to populate the folder with shortcut icons.

Putting Shortcut Icons in a Desktop Folder

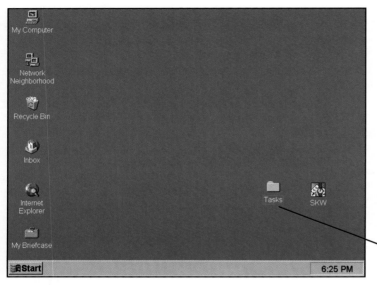

In the previous sections of this chapter, you created a folder and placed it on the desktop. The next step is to populate the folder with the programs you use most often.

If you already have a shortcut icon on your desktop, it's really easy to move it into the new folder. However, you can also add shortcut icons directly to the folder without first putting them on the desktop.

1. Click twice on the **folder** (in this example, Tasks). The Tasks window will appear.

Moving a Shortcut Icon from the Desktop to the Folder

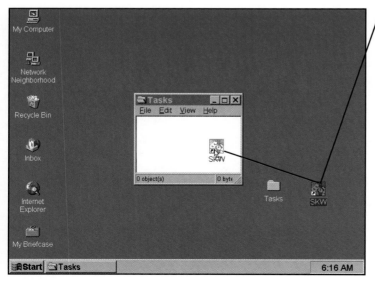

1. Click on the new **shortcut icon** and **drag it** to the folder.

2. Click on an **empty space** in the folder window to remove the highlighting from the icon.

Adding a Shortcut Icon Directly to the Folder

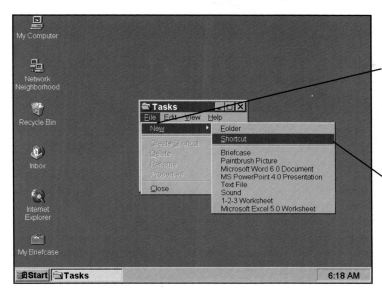

First, make sure that no icons are highlighted in the folder.

1. Click on **File** in the menu bar. A menu will appear.

2. Move the mouse arrow to **New**. A second menu will appear.

3. Click on **Shortcut**. The Create Shortcut dialog box will appear.

There are two ways to add a shortcut icon directly to the folder: (1) Type the path, or (2) Browse through folders until you locate the program. Even if you haven't got a clue about the path of the program you want to add to the folder, see the section at the top of the next page about the path for a bonus program.

Method #1: Typing the Path

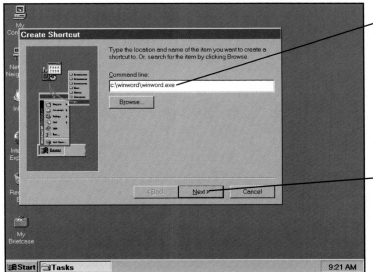

1. If you know the location, or path, of the program, **type** the **path** here. For example, type c:\winword\winword.exe if your Microsoft Word is located in the Winword folder on your C:\ drive. (If you don't know the path, skip on to Method #2: Browsing.)

2. Click on **Next**. The Select a Title for the Program dialog box will appear. Go to step 3 at the bottom of the next page.

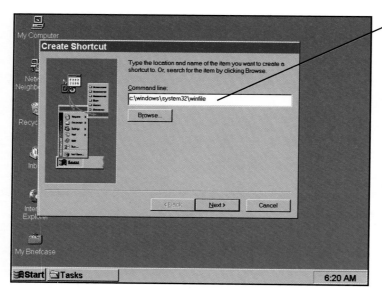

This example shows a bonus program! If you prefer File Manager over Windows Explorer, you'll be delighted to discover that the new File Manager in NT 4.0 is faster (32-bit) and can read long file names! The location of the new File Manager is: c:\windows\system32\winfile if NT 4.0 was installed over Windows 3.x or was a new installation.

If NT 4.0 was installed over Windows 95, try: c:\winnt\system32\winfile

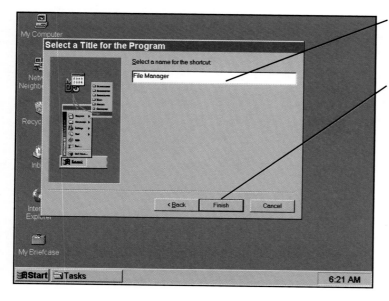

3. Type the name that you would like to appear under the icon.

4. Click on **Finish**. The shortcut icon will appear in the folder window.

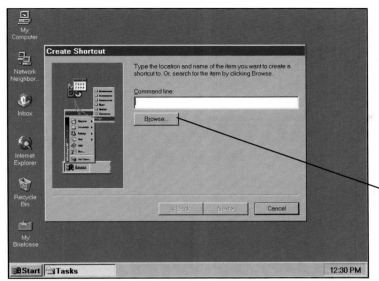

Method #2:

Browsing for the Program Path

If you don't know the path of the program you want to install as a shortcut icon, follow these steps:

1. Click on **Browse**. The Browse dialog box will appear.

Note: The Look in box will show the drive on which you are currently working. If the program for which you want to create a shortcut icon is on another drive, click on the ▼ to locate the correct drive, or see "Saving a File on Another Drive or in Another Directory" in Chapter 12 if you're not comfortable with the folder concept.

2. This example shows a list of small icons. If you want to show details rather than folders, **click** on the **Details icon**.

3. Double-click on the **folder** icon or listing for the program for which you want to create a shortcut icon. The screen will change to a detailed view of that specific folder (directory).

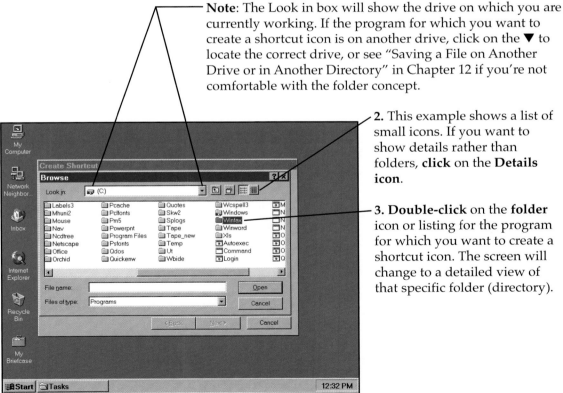

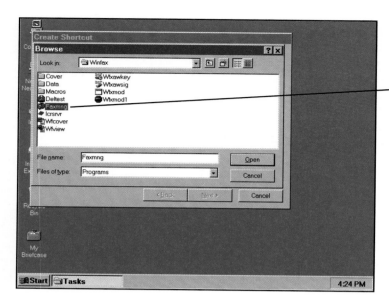

Notice that the folder now showing in the Look in box is the Winfax folder.

4. Double-click on the **file** that opens the program. In this example the executable file for WinFax PRO is Faxmng.

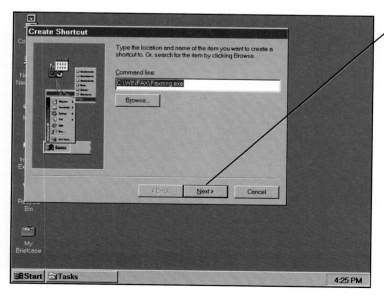

5. Click on **Next** and follow steps 3 and 4 in Method #1 a few pages back.

Note: If the program for which you are making the shortcut icon is a Windows 3.1 program, remember to go to the Properties dialog box and run it in a separate space. See "Fine-tuning a Shortcut Icon for a Windows 3.1 Program" earlier in this chapter for details.

Removing an Icon from a Folder

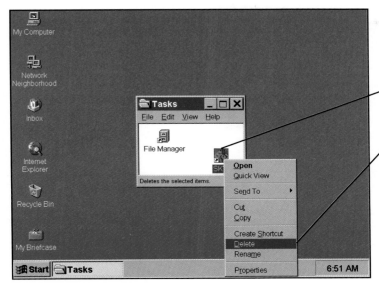

Getting rid of an icon couldn't be easier in NT.

1. Open the **folder**.

2. Right-click on the **icon** you want to remove. A menu will appear.

3. Click on **Delete**. The Confirm File Delete dialog box will appear (not shown here).

4. Click on **Yes** to delete the icon.

5. Click on the **Close button** (☒) to close the Tasks folder window.

Setting Up a Shortcut Key for a Program

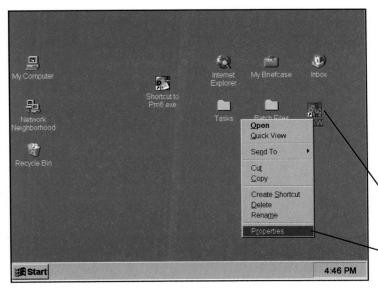

A shortcut key is actually a combination of keystrokes that will open a specific program. If you're in and out of a program several times a day but don't want to leave it running, a shortcut key can be just the thing you need.

1. First, **create** a **shortcut icon**.

2. Click the **right mouse button** on the shortcut icon. A pop-up menu will appear.

3. Click on **Properties**. The Properties dialog box will appear.

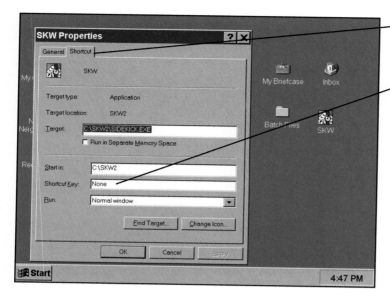

4. Click on the **Shortcut** tab to bring it to the front of the dialog box.

5. Click in the **Shortcut Key text box**. The cursor will appear after the word "None."

At this point, think of a letter (or number) that you want to represent this particular program. In this example, we chose "s" to represent Sidekick.

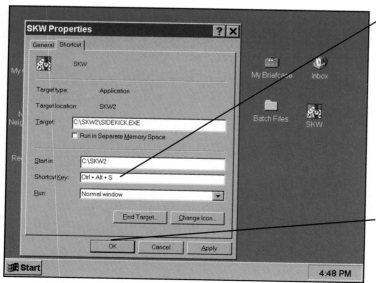

6. Type s (or the letter or number you chose for the shortcut key). As you type the letter, "Ctrl + Alt + *s*" will replace None in the text box. Notice that the "s" appears as a capital letter even though you typed it as a small letter. (You cannot use standard editing procedures to highlight None and replace it with Ctrl + Alt + s.)

7. Click on **OK**.

Any time you want to start Sidekick or switch back to it once its open, type Ctrl + Alt + s.

Arranging Icons on the Desktop

You can position your desktop icons in a variety of ways. In this section, we'll show you several options.

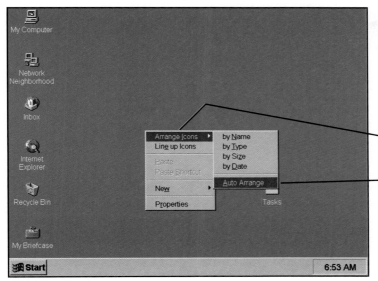

Using the Auto Arrange Feature

1. Click the **right mouse button** anywhere on the desktop. A menu will appear.

2. Click on **Arrange Icons**. A second menu will appear.

3. Click on **Auto Arrange** to put a ✔ before Auto Arrange. The menu will close and all of the icons will be lined up flush left. (If you had trouble manually placing icons earlier in the chapter, a ✔ was already present. See the next section.)

Turning Off Auto Arrange

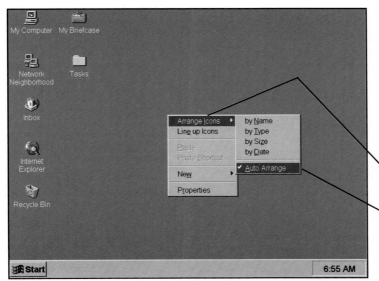

If Auto Arrange already has a ✔ in front of it, you need to follow the steps below before you can place an icon where you want it.

1. Click the **right mouse button** anywhere on the desktop. A menu will appear.

2. Click on **Arrange Icons**. A second menu will appear.

3. Click on **Auto Arrange** to remove the ✔. The menu will close.

Making Your Own Arrangements

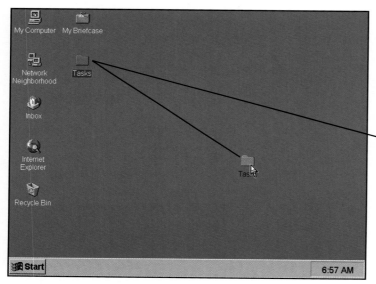

When the Auto Arrange feature is turned off (see the previous section), you can meet your own artistic or organizational needs by dragging various icons to different locations and then lining them up.

1. Click on the **icon** you want to relocate and **drag** it to another location on the desktop.

2. Repeat step 1 to reposition My Computer or any of the other icons on your desktop.

Lining Them up Neatly

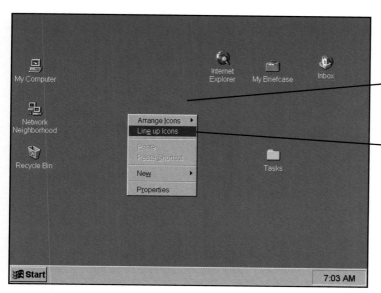

1. Click the **right mouse button** anywhere on the desktop. A menu will appear.

2. Click on **Line up Icons**. The menu will close.

Notice the icons are lined up neatly!

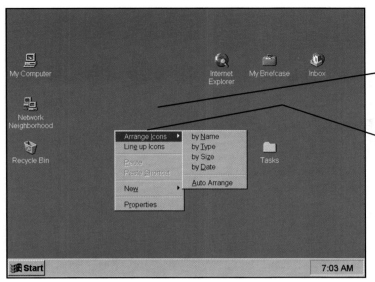

Exploring Arrangements

1. Click the **right mouse button** on any clear spot on the desktop.

2. Click on Arrange icons. Another menu will appear.

Notice you can line up by: Name, Type, Size, and Date

Setting up your own special view is limited only by your creativity and patience!

Setting Up Icons for and Running DOS Programs

You may have problems running DOS programs. Some DOS programs will work, others will not. In most cases, they will behave erratically. If you are going to run a DOS program in Windows NT 4.0, you should set up a shortcut icon. This process automatically creates a PIF file for the program. Do not run a DOS program from the Run menu or from the Command Prompt window because you will not be running the program from a PIF program setup. You can set up icons for DOS programs using the same procedures in this chapter. However, please note the following:

❖ Only programs written for DOS 5.0 or higher can be used.

❖ The Properties dialog box is different from the Windows version and more complicated. You need to be technically knowledgeable about "PIF" files and such to make modifications.

❖ You cannot set up the program's memory to run in a separate space as you can with Windows 3.x programs. For more information, go to Help and type "DOS."

Customizing the Start Menu

In Chapter 2 you learned how to start programs using the Start menu. Once you get the hang of it, the Start menu is a handy way to open programs. You can customize the Start menu by adding icons and folders to it. In this chapter, you will:

✔ Add a program icon to the Start menu
✔ Add a folder icon to the Start menu
✔ Populate a folder in the Start menu with program icons
✔ Remove a folder from the Start menu

Making the Start Menu Work for You

In addition to putting a shortcut icon on your desktop as you did in Chapter 9, you can add icons and even folders to the Start menu so that they actually appear on the menu itself.

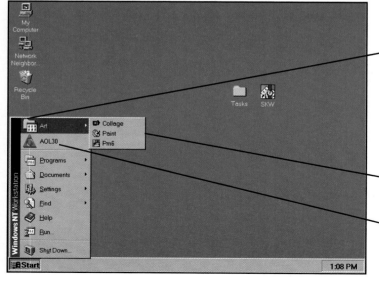

This example shows the following:

A folder added to the Start menu. Notice that it appears in a section above the standard, or default, items on the Start menu and that it has a ▶ to the right to indicate that there are programs in this folder.

Icons added to the new folder in the Start menu.

An icon added to the Start menu.

Adding an Icon
to the Start Menu

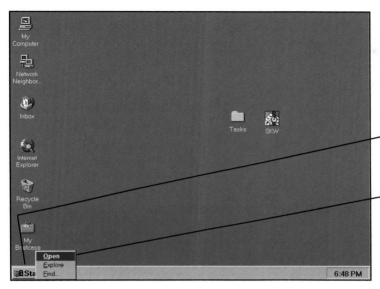

In this section, you'll add a program icon to the Start menu. In the example that follows, we chose AOL because we use it constantly. However, you can add any program icon you select.

1. Click the **right mouse button** on the **Start** button. A pop-up menu will appear.

2. Click on **Open**. The Start Menu window will appear.

Note: Most applications designed to work in Windows NT 4.0 automatically add an icon to the Start menu or one of its subfolders (such as Programs) during installation.

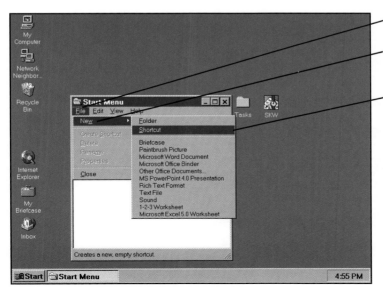

3. Click on **File** in the menu bar.

4. Click on **New**. A second menu will appear.

5. Click on **Shortcut**. The Create Shortcut dialog box will appear.

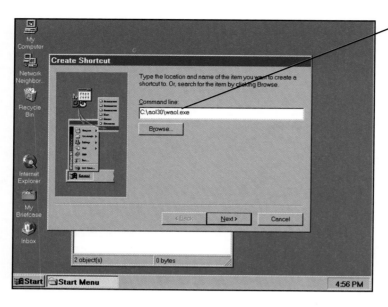

6. Type the **path** to the program icon. If you don't know the path, browse to the folder where the program is located. (See "Adding a Shortcut Icon Directly to the Folder" in Chapter 9.)

7. After you have the path, **repeat** the **steps** in Chapter 9 to create a desktop icon.

Note: Remember, if the icon is for a Windows 3.1 program, complete the steps to run it in a separate space.

Adding a Folder to the Start Menu

In this section, you will add a folder to the Start menu and populate it with programs. The example shows a folder called "Art."

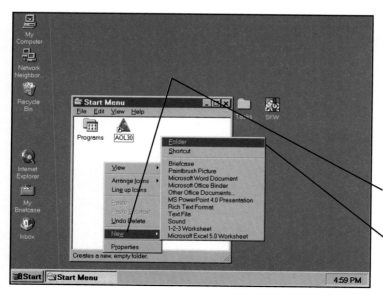

1. Repeat steps 1 and 2 on the previous page if the Start menu window is not already open.

2. Click the **right mouse button** on any clear space in the Start menu window. A menu will appear. (Make sure that nothing is highlighted when you click.)

3. Click on **New**. A second menu will appear.

4. Click on **Folder**. A new folder icon will appear in the window.

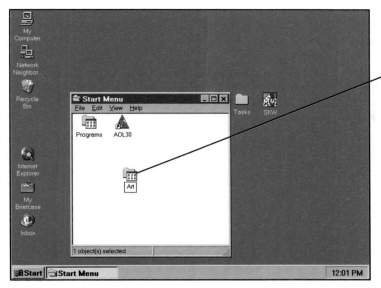

Naming the Folder

1. Type a **name** for the folder. In this example, we typed "Art."

2. Click anywhere in the window to complete the naming process.

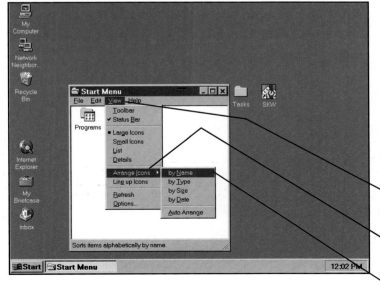

Arranging Icons in a Window

You can arrange icons in a window, as well as on the desktop. See "Arranging Icons on the Desktop" in Chapter 9 for a detailed discussion. In this section, we'll arrange the icons alphabetically by name.

1. Click on **View** in the menu bar.

2. Click on **Arrange Icons** Another menu will appear.

3. Click on **By Name** to arrange them alphabetically by name.

Populating a Folder in the Start Menu

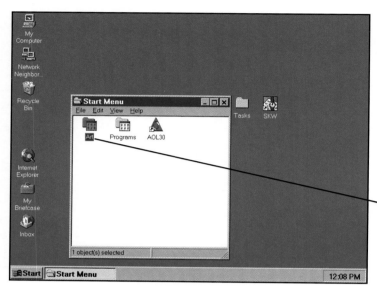

There are several ways to place program icons in a newly created folder in the Start menu. You can drag any icon that is visible on the Desktop or is in the Start menu window to the folder (see Chapter 9 if you need help.) Or, as shown below, you can create an icon from scratch in the open folder window.

1. Double-click on your **new folder icon**. The folder will open and, in this example, it will be empty.

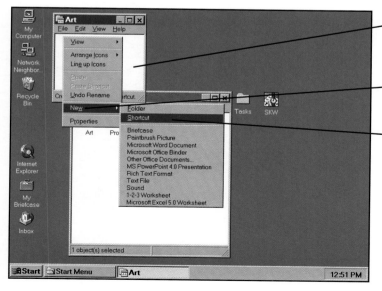

2. Click the **right mouse button** anywhere in the Art window. A menu will appear.

3. Click on **New.** A second menu will appear.

4. Click on **Shortcut**. The Create Shortcut dialog box will appear.

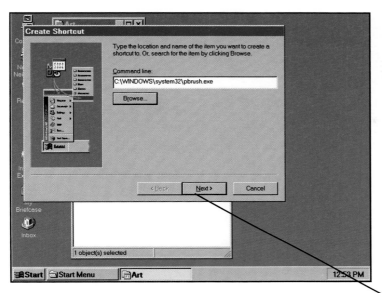

5. If you know the location, or path, of the program, **type** the **path** here. For example, type c:\windows\system32\pbrush.exe to make an icon for the *new* Paint program. If NT was installed over 3.1, you may have *two* Paint programs. The one in the windows\system32 directory is a 32-bit program and is faster than the one that came with Windows 3.1.

If you don't know the path of the program you want to add, browse through folders to locate the program.

6. Click on **Next**. The Select a Title for the Program dialog box will appear.

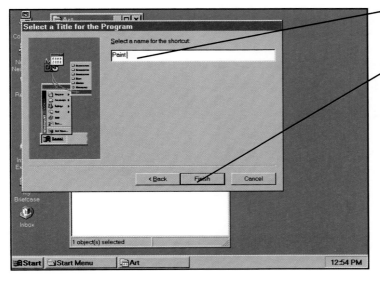

7. Type a **name** for the shortcut icon. In this example, it is "Paint."

8. Click on **Finish**. The dialog box will close and the Paint icon will appear in the Art window, as you see in the next example.

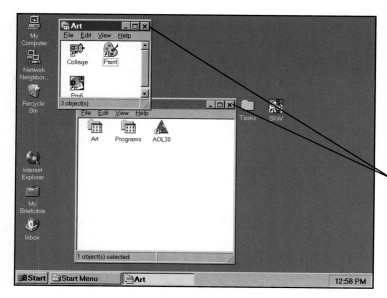

Notice the Art window with, in this example, three shortcut icons.

Notice also the Start menu window with the Programs folder that came with NT, the new Art folder, and the AOL30 shortcut icon.

9. Click on the **Close buttons** ⊠ of both windows to close them and check your results.

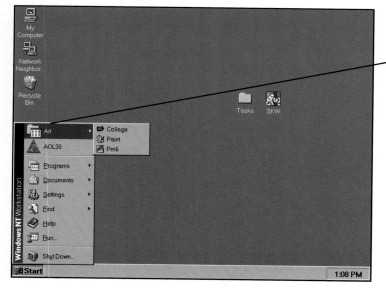

10. Click on the **Start button**. The Start menu will open.

11. Click on the new folder you created. In this example, it's the **Art Folder.** A menu will appear containing the icons you created.

12. Click anywhere on the desktop to close the Start menu.

Deleting a Folder or Icon from the Start Menu

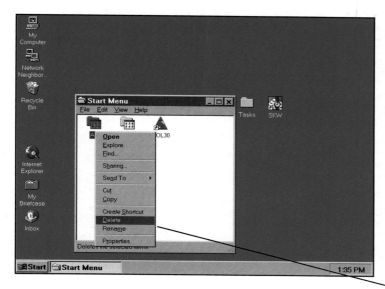

Deleting folders and icons that you have created is easy. The process deletes only the short-cut icons. It doesn't delete the original program.

1. Open the **Start menu** window. See steps 1 and 2 in "Adding an Icon to the Start Menu" at the beginning of this chapter if you need help.

2. Click the **right mouse button** on the program icon or folder icon you want to delete. A menu will appear.

3. Click on **Delete**. A message box will appear. **Click** on **OK**.

Note: You can also drag and drop the unwanted icon into the Recycle Bin.

Using the Automatic Startup Feature

If you typically start a certain program first thing in the morning, consider adding it to the Startup menu so that it opens automatically when you turn on your computer.

If you recently converted from Windows 3.x to NT 4.0, you may have noticed that you no longer have a Startup group window at the bottom of your screen. The feature is still in 4.0. It's just hidden behind a couple of layers of windows in the Start menu. In this chapter, you will do the following:

✔ Add a program to the Startup folder
✔ Remove a program from the Startup folder
✔ Override the Startup feature when booting up your system

Putting a Program Icon in the Startup Folder

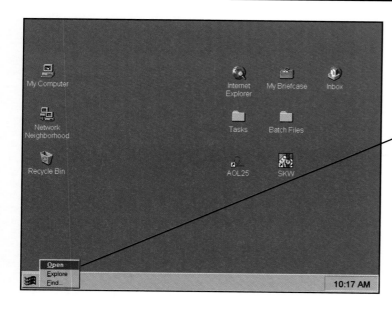

The Startup folder is hidden in the Start menu.

1. Click the **right mouse button** on the **Start** button. A pop-up menu will appear.

2. Click on **Open**. The Start Menu window will appear.

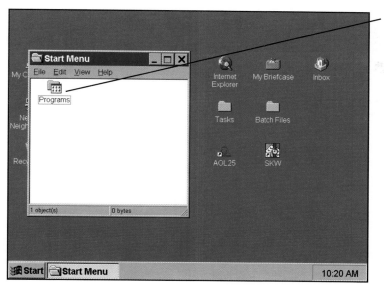

3. Double-click on the **Programs icon**. The Programs folder will open.

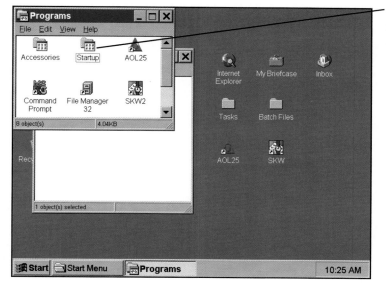

4. Double-click on the **Startup** icon. The Startup folder will open.

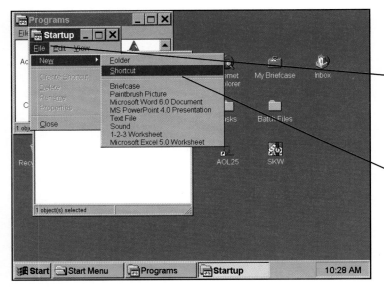

You're now ready to add the shortcut icon to the Startup folder.

5. Click on **File** in the menu bar.

6. Click on **New**. A second menu will appear.

7. Click on **Shortcut**. The Create Shortcut wizard will appear.

If you've gone through Chapter 9 or 10, you know the drill from here. Just follow the directions in the Wizard and either type the path for the program or browse to its location. Then type a name for the shortcut.

Removing a Program from the Startup Folder

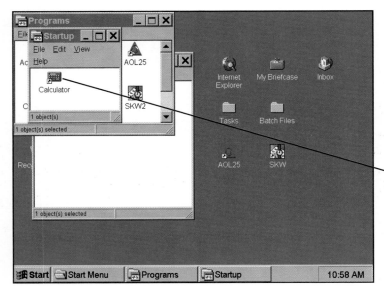

If you change your mind and you don't want a program to start up automatically, it's a simple task to remove it from the Startup folder.

1. Repeat steps 1-4 at the beginning of the chapter to open the Startup folder.

2. Click the **right mouse button** on the **program** you want to remove from the Startup folder. A menu will appear.

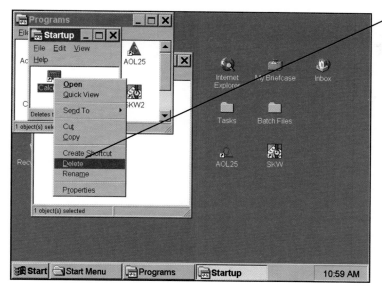

3. Click on **Delete**. The menu will close. A Confirm File Delete message box (not shown here) will appear asking whether you are really sure you want to delete the item. **Click** on **Yes** to delete the shortcut icon. Remember to empty the Recycle Bin.

Overriding the Startup Feature

It takes longer to boot up your system when you have programs in the Startup menu. There may come a day when you want to boot up as quickly as possible and not wait for the automatic startup programs. Hold down the Shift key as your system boots to override the automatic startup feature. When you're ready to use a program from the Startup menu, you'll have to start it manually. This is only a temporary override, however. The next time you boot up, the programs in the Startup menu will open automatically.

Managing Your Files

Part II is written for the person who upgraded from a Windows 3.x environment, as well as the person who is new to networking. Managing files can be a chore on a single machine. When you have access to other machines it can be daunting. Windows NT 4.0 gives you lots of options for managing your files including its unique "My Briefcase" program.

PART

I

PART

II

PART

III

PART

IV

PART

V

PART

VI

PART

VII

Using Files Over the Network

Your ability to open folders and files on other computers depends on your level of authorization and on whether the folders and files are shared or not shared. See Chapter 29, "Controlling Access to Workstations," for a discussion of authorization levels and shared versus not shared files and folders. This chapter shows you how to do the actual opening and saving of shared files. In this chapter, you will do the following:

✔ Open a shared file on another machine
✔ Create a shortcut to a shared folder or file
✔ Mark a file as Read Only
✔ Protect a file with a password
✔ Open a folder and a file on a restricted access machine

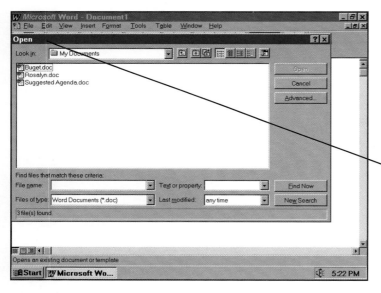

Opening a Shared File

In this section, you'll open a shared file on another computer to which you have access.

1. Open your **word processing program** to the Open dialog box as shown here. In this example, we used Microsoft Word 7.

If you're using Word 6, see the example at the bottom of the next page.

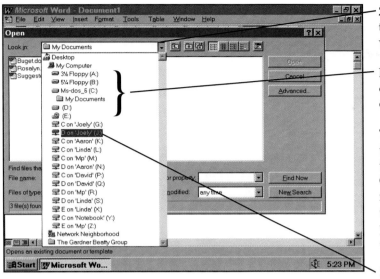

2. Click on the ▼ to the right of the Look in box. A list of drives will appear.

Drives A through E are the drives on this particular computer.

The drives shown below E are the network drives to which this computer is connected. Our list is set up to show the name of the person using the computer. The drives in your list may be identified differently.

3. Click on the **drive** to which you want to connect. You'll be connected to that drive and a list of the folders on that drive will appear. Go on to step 4 at the top of the next page. If you're using Microsoft Word 6, see steps 2a and 3a below for directions on locating the drive on another computer.

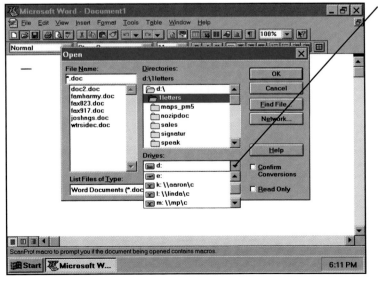

2a. Click on the ▼ to the right of the Drives box. A list of drives will appear.

3a. Scroll through the **list** to locate the drive to which you want to connect. Since you're familiar with the directory tree setup of Word 6, we won't show any more examples of Word 6 screens. However, the information presented later in this chapter on protecting a file with a password and marking a file as Read Only will apply even though the screens look different.

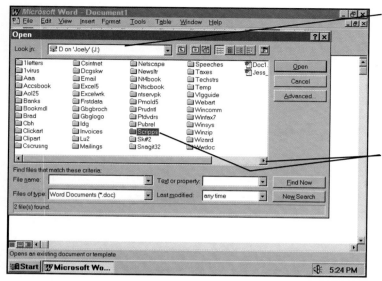

Notice that the Look in box now shows that you are on the D drive of Joely's computer and that your computer considers this to be its J drive. (See Chapter 31, "Mapping Network Drives," for a discussion of how this is done.)

4. Click on the ▶ to scroll through the list of folders. **Double-click** on the **folder** you want to open. A list of the files in that folder will appear in the window.

Note: If you want to see the details on each file, click on the Details button. If you want the file names to show the "doc" extension, as they do in this example, see Chapter 13, "Using Windows NT Explorer."

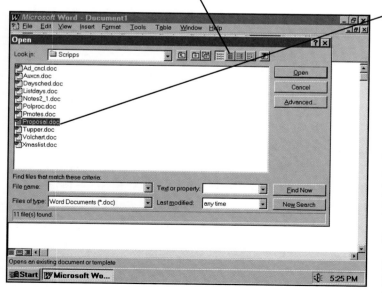

5. Double-click on the **file** you want to open. It will appear on your screen. You can work on the file as if it were physically located on your own computer.

6. Click on the **Save** button in the toolbar to save it back to the original computer/folder. Or, use the Save As command on the File menu to save it to your own computer or to another drive on the network. Use the steps shown above to go to the appropriate drive.

7. Click on the ☒ (Close button) to close the file. See the next section for steps on creating a shortcut to a network file.

Creating a Shortcut to a Network File

If you regularly use a file on another drive, it's a pain in the neck to navigate through drives and folders every time you open it. You can create a shortcut icon to go to a file on another drive. (See Chapter 9, "Working Smarter with Shortcut Icons and Desktop Folders." Or, you can use the Documents list on the Start menu. (See Chapter 2, "Starting a Program or Document.") But wait ... there's a third way!

If you're working with Microsoft products designed for Windows 95 or NT 4.0, you can make use of a handy feature, called the Favorites Folder, located in the Open dialog box or the Save As dialog box. In this example, we're using the Open dialog box in Microsoft Word 7.

1. If you haven't been following along with this chapter, **do steps 1-4** in the previous section of this chapter and use the Open dialog box to go to a network drive and folder you use regularly. Don't open an individual file just yet.

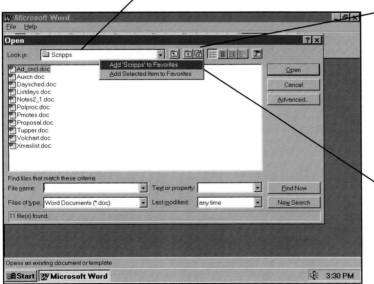

2. Click on the **Add to Favorites** button. A menu like the one you see in this example will appear. If you're not sure which is the Add to Favorites button, place the mouse arrow on top of the button (but don't click). A balloon, called a ToolTip, will pop up with the button's name.

Notice that you can add the entire folder to your list of favorites, or you can add specific files. Click on the file you want to add to highlight it, or use the Ctrl key as you click on multiple files to highlight more than one.

3. Click on the appropriate **choice** in the menu.

Using the Favorites Folder to Open or Save a File

Using the Favorites Folder is a big time saver! If you've been following along with this chapter, the Open dialog box is on your screen and you have added a folder to the Favorites list.

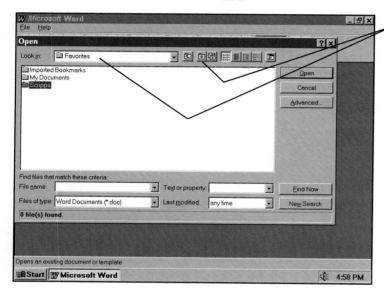

1. Click on the **Look in Favorites** button. The folder in the Look in box will change to show "Favorites," and the folder or files you added to Favorites will appear in the list. This example shows three folders in the Favorites list.

2. Double-click on the **folder** or **file** you want to open.

This example shows the Open dialog box. The Look in Favorites button is also in the Save As dialog box, so you can use it to save a file to a specific folder on your own machine or across the network.

Marking a File as Read-Only

If you want others to be able to open a file but not be able to change it without permission, you can mark the file with a password.

This section assumes you have a file open and have opened the Save As dialog box.

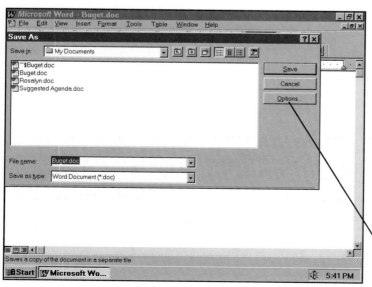

1. Click on the **Options** button. The Options dialog box will appear.

2. Type a **password** in the Write Reservation Password box.

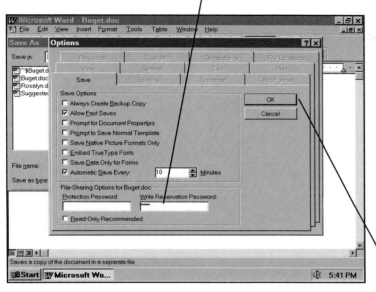

A password can have up to 15 characters, including letters, numbers, and symbols. It is case sensitive, which means that if you use a capital letter when you first type the password, you must use it every time. If you forget the password, you won't be able to open the file because this process marks the file with a password on *your* computer, as well as for anyone in the network trying to open the file.

3. Click on **OK**. The Confirm Password dialog box will appear.

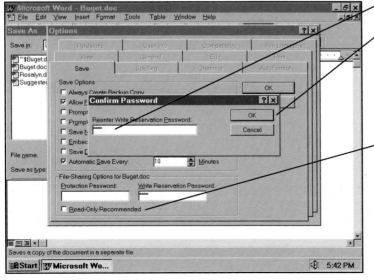

4. Reenter the **password**.

5. Click on **OK**.

6. Click on **OK** in the Save As dialog box (not shown here) to accept the password and close the file.

Note: We don't recommend the Read-Only Recommended option. It is a *recommendation* and the person opening the file can choose to ignore it, click on NO when the message appears, and proceed to make changes after the file has opened.

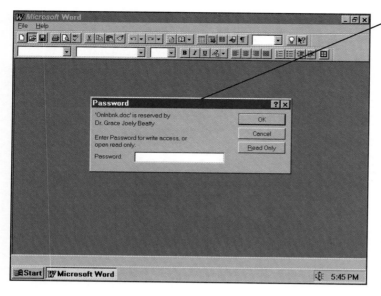

When this file is opened by you or anyone else, this message appears.

The person opening the file must type the password or click on Read Only. The Read Only option means that if changes are made to the file, it must be saved under a different name. The original file will remain unchanged.

If you don't want anyone to be able to open the file, even with a password, it must be in a folder that is "not shared." See Chapter 29, "Controlling Access to Workstations."

Protecting a File with a Password

You can set up a file so that it needs a password to be opened by you or anyone else. *Once opened, however, it can be changed.*

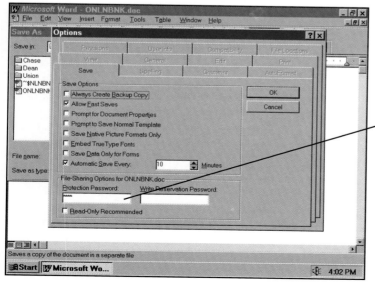

1. Repeat steps 1-4 in the section above to open the Options dialog box. Also, read the Notes and the information about passwords. They apply to this section as well.

2. Type a **password** in the Protection Password box.

You'll be asked to re-enter the password as in the previous example.

As soon as you click on OK in the Save As dialog box, the file cannot be opened at all without the password.

Changing or Deleting a Document Password

Here's how to change or delete the password assigned to a document.

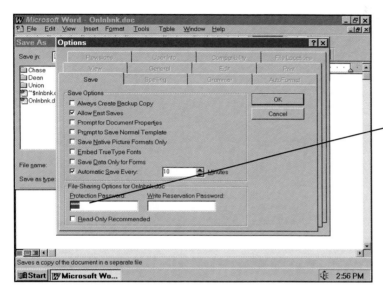

1. Open the **document** in question.

2. Open the Save As dialog box, then the **Options** dialog box you see here.

3. Double-click on the **password** to highlight it.

4. If you're changing the password, **type** the new one. You'll be asked to reconfirm.

5. If you're removing the password, **press** the **Delete** key.

6. Click on **OK** in both dialog boxes.

Being Denied Access to a Drive

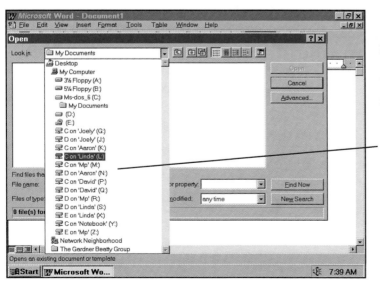

You may be able to see a network drive but not be able to access it.

In this example, you've double-clicked on Linda's C drive.

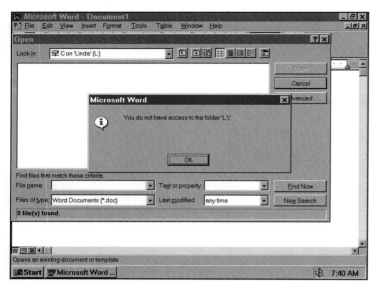

If you receive this message, you have been denied access. **Click** on **OK** to close the message box.

So what happened? Your system administrator (or Linda) has restricted access to the C drive. (See Chapter 29, "Controlling Access to Workstations" for directions on marking drives and folders "not shared.") However, a specific folder can be shared even though the rest of the drive is off limits. See the section below.

Opening a Shared Folder when Access to the Entire Drive Has Been Denied

Look again at the list of drives in this window. You will notice that Linda's C and D drives are listed, as well as a folder named Budget. This means that the Budget folder is available exclusive of other folders on Linda's C drive.

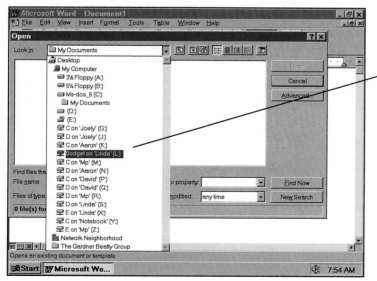

1. Click twice on the **name** of the specific **folder** that you want to access. The folder will appear in the Open window.

You're all set to cruise around the network, but if you'd like more information, see Chapter 13, "Using Windows NT Explorer," or Chapter 14, "Using My Computer and My Briefcase."

Using Windows NT Explorer

Explorer is the new and improved version of File Manager. It uses folders to organize your programs and files instead of directories, but the concept is the same. One specific difference between File Manager and Explorer is that you can't format disks in Windows NT Explorer; you have to go to My Computer (see Chapter 14, "Using My Computer and My Briefcase"). Because Explorer and My Computer do most of the same things, you'll find topics covered in Chapter 14 that are not covered in this chapter and vice versa. In this chapter, you will do the following:

✔ Learn how to browse through drives and folders
✔ Show file extensions and the file path
✔ Copy, paste, delete, and move folders and files
✔ Rename folders and files and create a new folder
✔ Use Quick View to preview a file
✔ Open files and start programs from Explorer
✔ Map network drives
✔ Send e-mail from Explorer
✔ Add a destination to the SendTo menu

Opening Windows NT Explorer

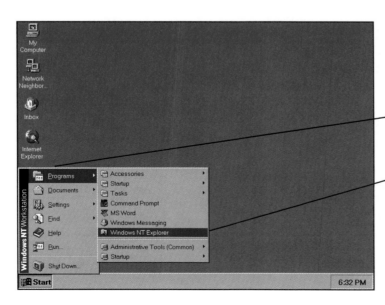

You open Explorer through the Start menu.

1. Click on the **Start** button to open the Start menu.

2. Move the mouse pointer up to **Programs** to highlight it. A second menu will appear.

3. Click on **Windows NT Explorer**. It will probably be the last program on the list, just above Administrative Tools.

Showing File Details

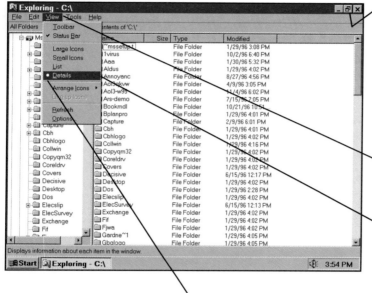

1. If Explorer doesn't appear in its maximized view, as you see here, **click** on the **Maximize**  button to the right of the toolbar.

This screen shows the Details view. There are three more views from which to choose.

2. Click on **View** in the menu bar. The View menu will appear.

3. Click on **Details** to make your view look like this one. Try experimenting with different views to see which one you prefer.

In this example, the circle beside Details shows that it is the current view. To show file extensions, see "Showing File Extensions and the File Path" later in this chapter.

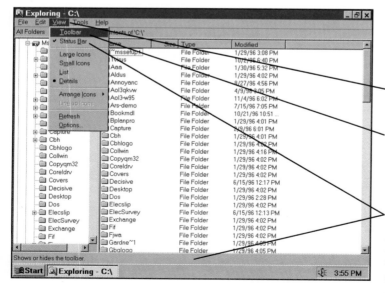

Adding a Toolbar and Status Bar

1. Click on **View** in the menu bar.

2. Click on **Toolbar** if it doesn't have a ✔. The menu will close and a toolbar will appear below the menu bar.

Notice that you can add a status bar to the bottom of the Explorer window. The option on the menu is checked in this example because the status bar already shows.

Browsing Through Drives and Folders

Although Explorer uses folders instead of directories, the hierarchical relationship between drives, folders, and files is the same as it was in Windows 3.1; that is, folders reside on a specific drive and files reside within folders. What is different is the addition of two more layers in the hierarchy. Windows NT 4.0 has added a Desktop layer at the top of the hierarchy. Just below the Desktop is My Computer and all drives, both local and network, reside on My Computer.

1. Drag the **scroll button** up to the top of the scroll bar.

Notice that Desktop is at the top of the hierarchy, My Computer is indented under Desktop, and the drives are indented under My Computer.

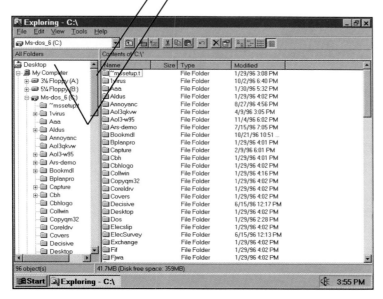

Folders are indented under the drive they are on.

Explorer, like File Manager, has two sections. The left section, or pane, shows the drive and folders. The right section shows the contents of the highlighted drive.

The contents of the C: drive will be displayed in both panes because, in this example, it is the drive on which you were working when you opened Explorer. Our C: drive is labeled, "Ms-dos_6 (C:)." Your C: drive may have a different label.

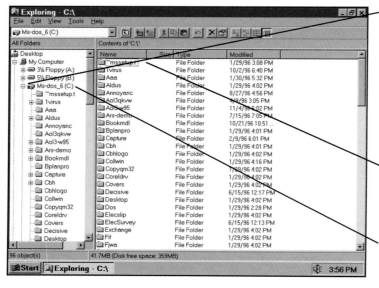

Notice the minus sign to the left of the C: drive icon. This indicates that the drive is "open" and fully expanded because, in this example, it is the drive you were working on when you opened Explorer. All of the folders on the C: drive are listed below C:.

The folders are also listed in the contents pane. Notice the "Contents of C:\" label that appears above this pane.

2. Double-click on the **C:** drive. It will close and folders will no longer appear under it. They will, however, still be shown in the contents pane as long as the drive is highlighted on the left.

Notice that the C: drive now has a + sign to its left to indicate that it contains folders that are not showing in a list below the drive even though they do show in the pane on the right.

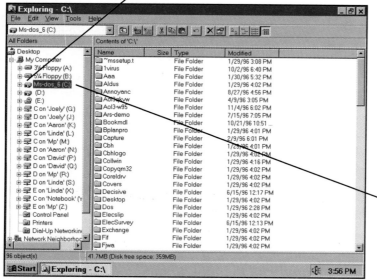

Take a look at the icons beside each item.

Indicates that C: and D: are local hard drives, meaning they're on your computer.

Indicates a network drive.

Notice the icons beside other items.

3. Double-click on the **C:** drive to open it again.

Notice that the highlighted drive is also shown in the Look in box.

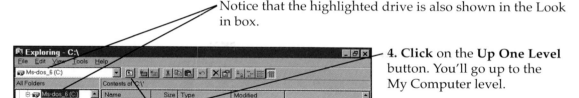

4. Click on the **Up One Level** button. You'll go up to the My Computer level.

Note: If you're at the file level, clicking on the Up One Level button will take you to the next folder up, or to the drive level if there are no folders. At the drive level, it will take you to My Computer. From My Computer, you'll go to the Desktop.

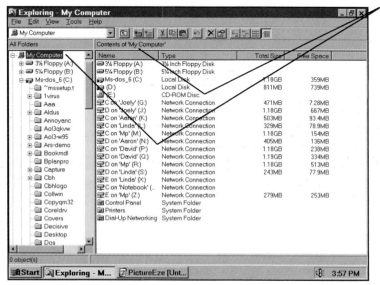

When My Computer is highlighted, the contents are shown in the right pane. Notice that it shows all the local drives, as well as all the network drives. You can double-click on one of the network drives to open it, but we'll show you another way to open a network drive in the next section.

Going to a Different Drive

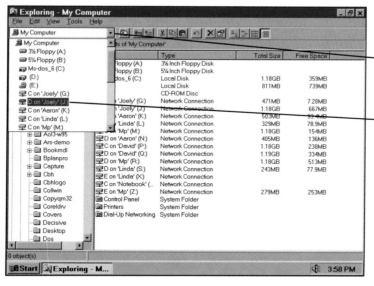

The Look in box contains a list of all drives.

1. Click on the ▼ to the right of the Look in box. A list of drives will appear.

2. Click on the **drive** to which you want to go. In this example, it's D on Joely, which is the J: drive on your machine.

Note: There is a Go To command on the Tools menu. Simply type j:\ to open the J: drive, or type j:\letters to open the Letters folder on the J: drive. Be sure to label a network drive with the letter that identifies it on your computer, not its letter on the computer where the drive actually resides.

The folders on the J: drive will be shown in the "Contents of" pane on the right.

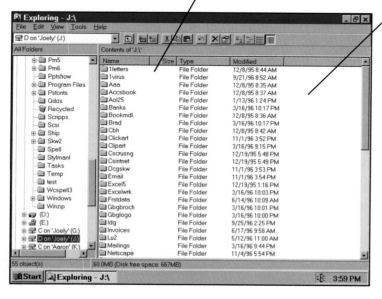

3. Double-click on a **folder** to open it and see the files. This will automatically expand the drive folder on the left so that all the folders on the new drive appear in a list under it.

4. Go back to the **C: drive**. You can scroll up to see your C: drive, use the Look in box, or use the Go To command on the Tools menu.

Now that you know how to move around, it's time to get acquainted with Explorer.

Showing File Extensions and the File Path

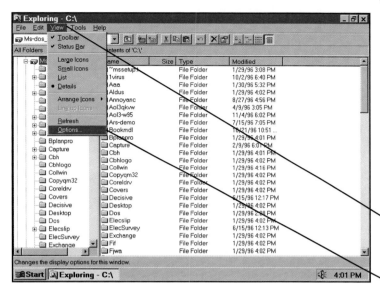

The file extension identifies the type of file. For example, "doc" identifies Microsoft Word documents and "xls" identifies Microsoft Excel files. It helps to see extensions when you keep files of more than one type in a folder. You can also set your computer to show the full path, or location, of a file. If you work on lots of different drives, this can be helpful.

1. Click on **View** in the menu bar. The View menu will appear.

2. Click on **Options**. The Options dialog box will appear.

3. Click on **Display the full path in the title bar** to put a ✔ in the box if you want this option.

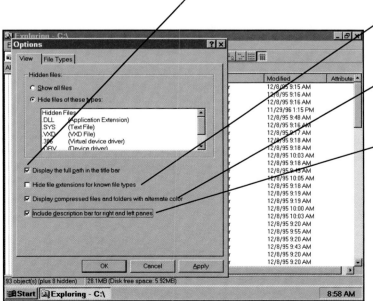

4. Click on **Hide file extensions...** to *remove* the ✔ if you want the extensions to show.

5. Click on **Display compressed files...** to put a ✔ in the box, if you'd like this option.

6. Leave the ✔ beside **Include description bar contents**. This is the "Contents of..." line above the details pane. It's nice to be reminded of the drive you're on, especially if you jump around between drives and computers.

7. Click on **OK**.

Housekeeping with Explorer

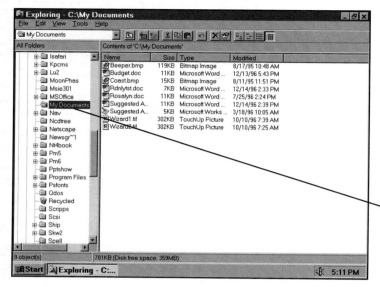

You'll like the ease with which you can copy and paste, move, delete, and rename folders and files.

First, we'll do a quick review of selecting folders and files because these steps apply to all housekeeping functions.

Selecting Folders

1. Click on a **folder** to highlight it. This selects the folder and all of its contents.

To select files within the folder, see the next section.

Selecting Files

1. Click on a single **file** to highlight it.

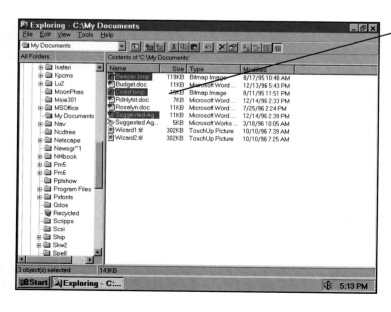

2. To select, or highlight, non-contiguous files, such as the ones in this example, **press and hold** the **Ctrl** key as you **click** on each file.

3. To select contiguous files, **click** on the **first file** in the sequence. **Press and hold** the **Shift** key, and then **click** on the **last file** that you want to select. All files between clicks will be highlighted.

4. To select the entire contents of a folder without selecting the folder itself, **click** on **Edit/ Select All** in the menu bar.

Copying Files Between Drives

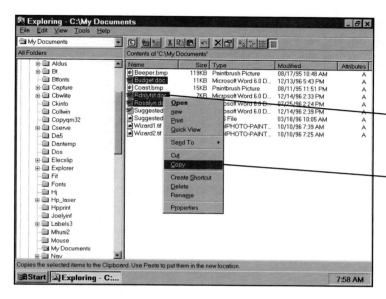

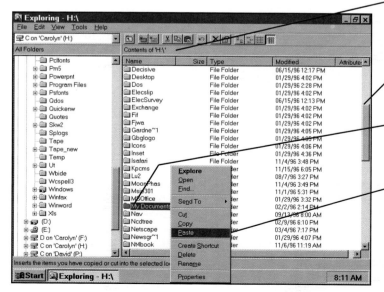

1. Go to the **drive** and **folder** that have the original files.

2. Select the **file(s)** you want to copy.

3. Click the **right mouse button** on one of the highlighted files. A menu will appear.

4. Click on **Copy**. You won't see anything happen, but the files are now copied to the Clipboard, a temporary storage area on your computer.

Note: If Copy is grayed out on the menu, your mouse pointer was not on top of one of the highlighted files. Repeat steps 2 and 3 and try again.

5. Go to the **drive** where you want to paste the copied file(s). Be sure the name of the drive appears here.

6. Scroll to the **folder** where you want to paste the file(s).

7. Right-click on the **folder** where you want to paste the file(s). A menu will appear.

8. Click on **Paste**. If the files have the same names as files already in this folder, you'll see the message on the next page. Otherwise, you won't see anything, but when you open the folder the copied file(s) will be there.

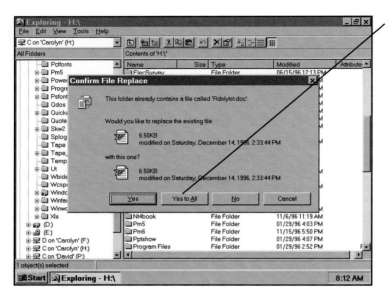

9. **Click** on **Yes to All** if you know that you want to write over each file. If you want to check each file before you decide to write over it, click on Yes.

Moving Files Between Drives

Use the Cut/Paste commands to move files between drives.

1. **Go to** the **drive** that has the files you want to move.

2. **Select** the **files**.

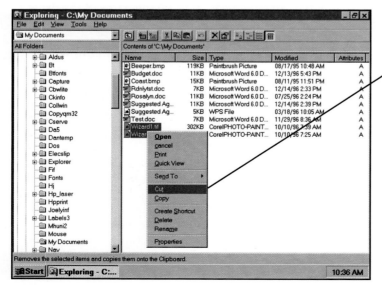

3. **Right-click** on one of the **highlighted files**. A menu will appear.

4. **Click** on **Cut**. You'll still be able to see the files but the file icons will be grayed out. When you paste them into another folder, they will move to the other drive.

5. **Go to** the **drive** to which you want to move the files.

6. **Right-click** the **folder** to which you want to move the files and **click** on **Paste** in the menu that appears.

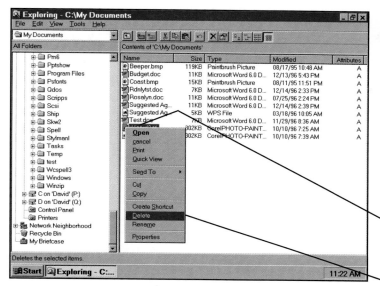

Deleting Folders and Files

When you want to "throw away" a folder or file, be sure to use the Delete command, which sends it to the Recycle Bin. The Cut command, on the other hand, does not remove a file from a folder until you actually paste it into another folder.

1. Right-click on the **folder or file(s)** you want to delete. A menu will appear.

2. Click on **Delete**. A Confirm Delete dialog box will appear (not shown here). **Click** on **Yes** to send the folder or file(s) to the Recycle Bin.

Rescuing a Deleted Folder or File

Even after you confirm that you want to delete a folder or file and it is sent to the Recycle Bin, you have three ways to restore it.

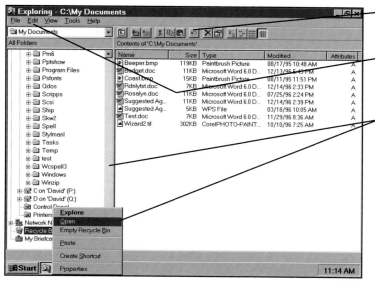

1. Click on the **Undo** button in the toolbar.

2. Click on **Edit** in the menu bar, and then **click** on **Undo Delete** on the Edit menu.

3. Drag the **scroll button** to the bottom of the scroll bar. **Right-click** on **Recycle Bin** and then **click** on **Open** on the menu. See "Restoring an Item from the Recycle Bin" in Chapter 15.

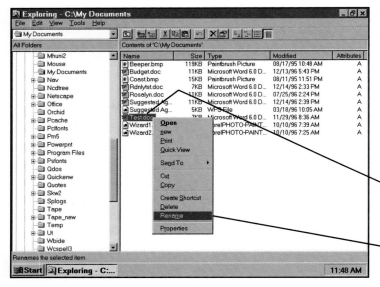

Renaming Folders and Files

You'll love the ease with which you can rename folders and files in NT 4.0. A file must be closed before you can rename it. If it's not closed, you'll get an "Access denied" message.

1. Right-click on the folder or **file** you want to rename. A menu will appear.

2. Click on **Rename**. A box will appear around the name and the name will be highlighted.

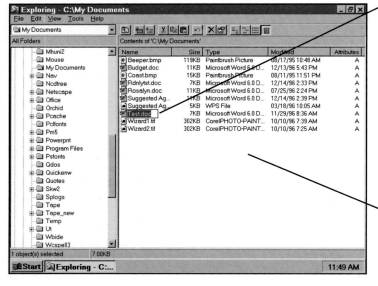

3. Type a **new name**. It will replace the highlighted text.

Note: If you chose to show the file extension, be sure to type the file extension in the new name or NT won't be able to recognize the file type.

You can also use standard editing procedures to edit part of the name.

4. Click anywhere in the window to complete the naming process.

Creating a New Folder

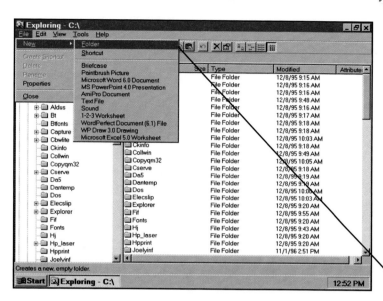

1a. Click on the **C: drive** if you want the new folder to be a main folder on that drive. In this example, C: is hidden by the File menu. Or,

1b. Click on the **folder** in which you want to create a subfolder.

In this example, we're creating a main folder on the C: drive.

2. Click on **File** in the menu bar. The File menu will appear.

3. Highlight New. A second menu will appear.

4. Click on **Folder**. A folder labeled "New Folder" will appear at the bottom of the list of folders in the right pane. "New Folder" will have a box around it and be highlighted.

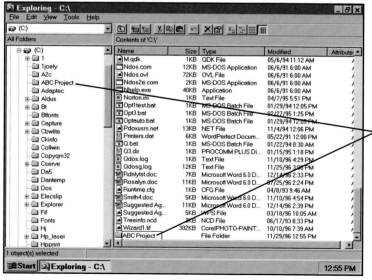

5. Type the **name** of the new folder. In this example, it's the ABC Project.

6. Click anywhere in the window to complete the naming process.

Notice that the ABC Project folder already appears in the correct alphabetical order in left pane. It will stay at the bottom of the right pane until you go to another folder or drive. When you come back to the C: drive, ABC Project will appear in the correct alphabetical order in the right pane.

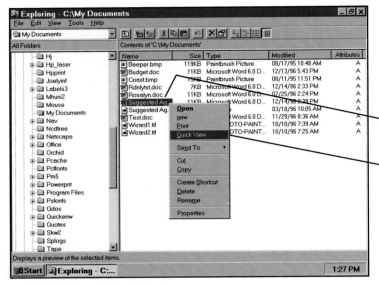

Using Quick View

NT 4.0 has a nifty Quick View command that lets you preview a file from Explorer.

1. Right-click on the **file** you want to view.

2. Click on **Quick View**. The file will appear in a special Quick View window. You can edit the file by clicking on File/Open File for Editing in the Quick View window. This will open the file in its application program.

Opening a File and Starting a Program from Explorer

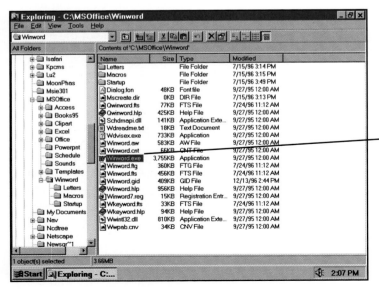

You can open files and start programs directly from Explorer.

1. Double-click on a **file**. This will open the file and its application program.

2. Double-click the **application file** for a program to open it. In this example, it's the application file for MS Word. See Chapter 9, "Working Smarter with Shortcut Icons and Desktop Folders," for a discussion on identifying application files for programs.

Mapping Network Drives from Explorer

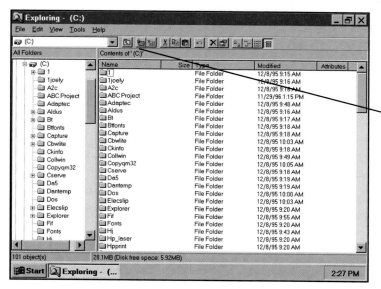

If you know you have authorization to connect to a specific drive, but it is not listed in the Look in box, you can connect to it from Explorer.

1. Click on the **Map Network Drive** button in the toolbar. The Map Network Drive dialog box will appear.

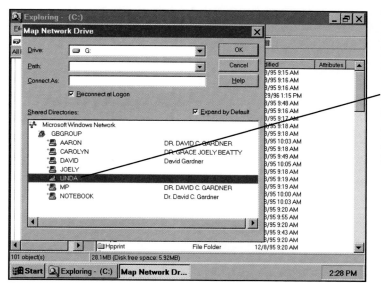

Notice the + sign to the left of each machine. This means that you can double-click on the machine to get a list of drives.

2. Double-click on the **machine** to which you want to connect. In this example, it's Linda. A list of drives on that machine will appear.

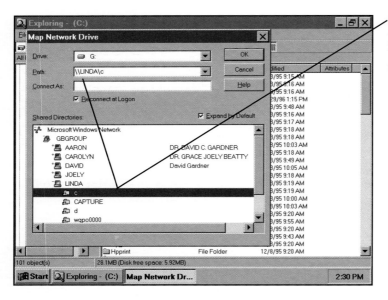

3. Click on the **drive** to which you want to connect. Its name will appear in the Path box at the top of the dialog box.

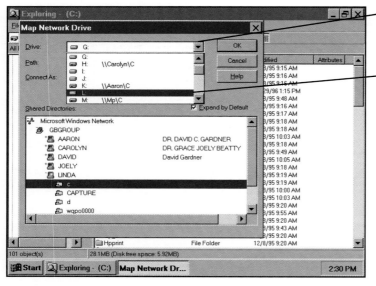

4. Click on the ▼ to the right of the Drive box. A list of drives will appear.

5. Click on the **letter** you want to give to this drive on your machine. In this example, it's L. See Chapter 31, "Mapping Network Drives," for a discussion of naming drives.

Sending E-Mail from Windows NT Explorer

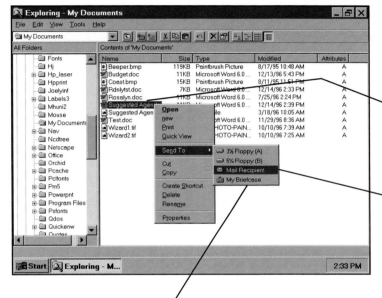

If you have set up Windows Messaging (See Chapter 26, "Using Windows Messaging"), you can send a file directly from Explorer.

1. Right-click on a **file**. A menu will appear.

2. Click on **SendTo**. A second menu will appear.

3. Click on **Mail Recipient**. Windows Messaging will open and the file will be inside an e-mail message. See Chapter 26, "Using Windows Messaging," for directions on completing the e-mail message.

See Chapter 14, "Using My Computer and My Briefcase," for an introduction to My Briefcase.

Adding a Destination to the SendTo Menu

The title of the SendTo menu that you see in the example above is a little deceiving because it doesn't move the files to the specified destination, it copies them there. If you regularly copy files or folders to a specific destination, you can customize the SendTo menu by adding the destination to the menu. For example, we added our optical drive (E:) to our SendTo menu. You can create a destination for a drive or folder on your own machine or on a network machine.

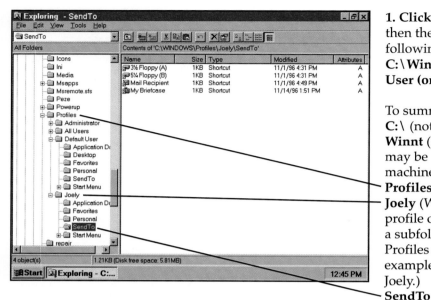

1. **Click** on the **C:** drive and then the folders shown in the following path:
C:\Winnt\Profiles\Default User (or your name)\SendTo.

To summarize:
C: (not shown here)
Winnt (not shown here, but it may be Winnt 4.0 on your machine)
Profiles
Joely (When you create a user profile on a machine, it creates a subfolder for that name in the Profiles folder, so in this example, there's a folder for Joely.)
SendTo

Note: We set up our machines with a dual boot, so our Default User folder was in the Windows\Profiles folder. If you can't locate the Default User folder, do a search on Default User (see Chapter 16, "Finding Files, Folders, and Other Computers"). There will be lots of matches. Look for the Profiles folder in the path.

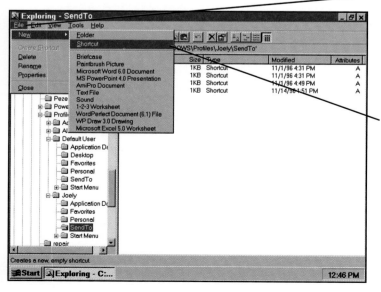

2. While the SendTo folder is highlighted, **click** on **File** in the menu bar. The File menu will appear.

3. **Highlight New**. A second menu will appear.

4. **Click** on **Shortcut**. The Create Shortcut wizard will appear.

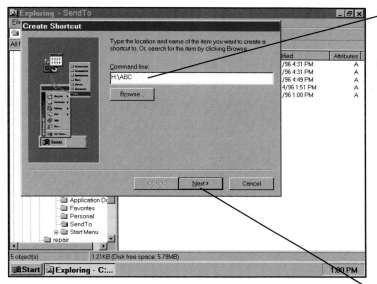

5. Type the **exact path** of the folder. You can use the Browse button to go there, but it won't work to copy the path to this text box because it's set up to copy only file names. Browsing will help you record the exact path, and then you can type it here.

Note: We had trouble getting NT to complete this process with a folder labeled "ABC Project" (with a space between ABC and Project). When we renamed the folder "ABC," we had no problems.

6. Click on **Next**. The Select a Title for the Program wizard window will appear.

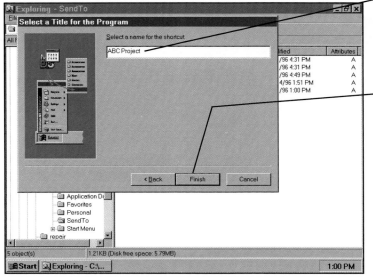

7. Type the **name** you want to appear on the SendTo menu. In this example, it's ABC Project. (A space in the destination name was no problem.)

8. Click on **Finish**. A shortcut will appear in the SendTo folder.

Now it's time to test this new destination on the SendTo menu. Go to a file you want to send to your new destination. Right-click on it and then click on SendTo. Your new destination will be on the SendTo menu.

Resizing Explorer Window Panes

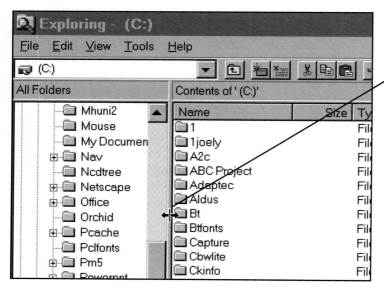

You can change the size of the left and right window panes in Explorer.

1. Place the **mouse pointer** on the line between the panes. It will change to the shape you see in this close-up view of the Explorer window.

2. Drag the **separator** to the left or right to give more space to a particular side. Or, **double-click** the **separator line** to automatically adjust the view to show all details on the right.

3. If the file name does not show completely in the right pane as you see in this example, **double-click** the **mouse pointer** on the dividing line between Name and Size. The mouse pointer will change to the shape you see here and the column will automatically adjust to show the longest file name. Or, drag the dividing line to the right if you want to manually control the width of the column.

Note: If after trying Windows NT Explorer, you decide you're a dyed-in-the-wool File Manager user, see the section entitled, "Adding a Shortcut Icon Directly to the Folder," in Chapter 9 to learn how to get a 32-bit version of File Manager onto your desktop!

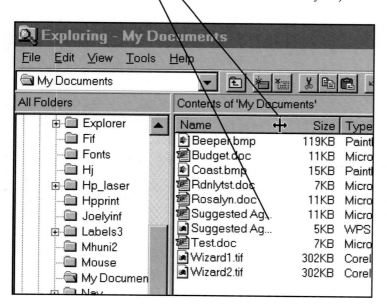

CHAPTER 14

Using My Computer and My Briefcase

Inside the My Computer window you can do everything that you can do with Windows NT Explorer, and it's really a matter of personal preference which one you use. The one exception is formatting disks, which must be done in My Computer. Because My Computer and Windows NT Explorer (Chapter 13, "Using Windows NT Explorer") do most of the same things, some topics are covered in more detail in the Explorer chapter. You may want to check it out. When you have files in more than one location, such as a laptop or another network drive, you must be very careful that you don't copy an older version of the file over the most recent version. My Briefcase is a program that will help manage this process. In this chapter, you will do the following:

✔ Reconnect network drives
✔ Copy, paste, cut, and delete folders and files
✔ Format a disk
✔ Change the view and add a toolbar
✔ View only one window at a time
✔ View drive properties
✔ Use My Briefcase to update files

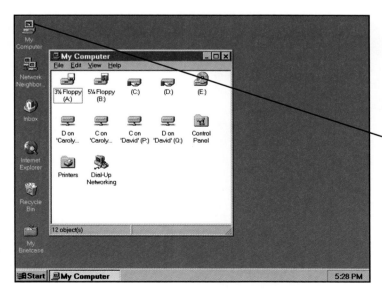

Opening My Computer

My Computer is an icon on your desktop.

1. Double-click on **My Computer**. The My Computer window will open as you see here.

Reconnecting Network Drives

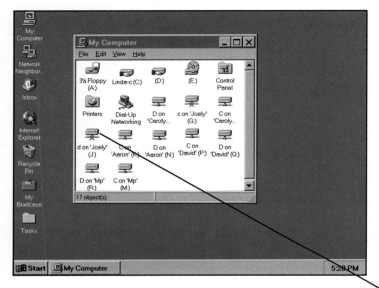

Although NT should be able to locate network drives even when they are booted up at different times, sometimes it can't or doesn't locate them. NT will continue to boot up the rest of your connections, but the unavailable drive will have a red X in My Computer.

Note: If a drive to which you know you have access authority is not listed, see the section, "Changing the View in My Computer," for directions on adding a toolbar and mapping network drives.

1. Double-click on the **drive** with the X. The drive window will open on your screen.

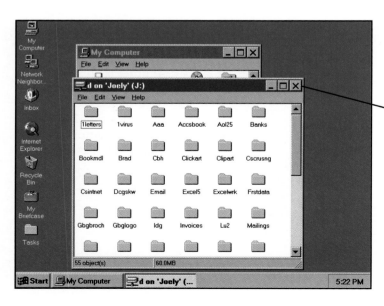

2. If a password is required for you to access this drive, a dialog box will appear (not shown here). **Enter** your **password**.

3. Click on the **Close** button (☒) to close the drive. When you go back to the My Computer window, the X will be gone.

4. Repeat this process for each drive that has an X.

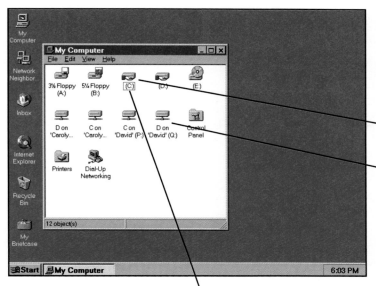

My Computer shows each of the local drives on your machine and each network drive to which you have access. Notice that the icons for each type of drive are different.

🖳 Identifies a hard drive on your machine.

🖳 Identifies a network drive. D on David (Q) means that the D: drive on David's machine is considered by your machine to be its Q: drive. See Chapter 31, "Mapping Network Drives," for a discussion of naming drives.

1. Double-click on the **C: drive** icon to open the window for your C: drive.

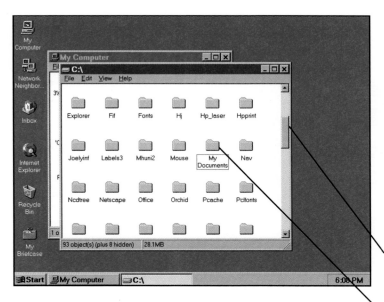

The default view in My Computer is the large icons you see here. Although large icons are easy to see, a disadvantage in our minds is that you have to *know* that a folder contains subfolders because you can't tell by looking at the icon. If you know your own computer and are familiar with the computers on your network, you may like this view. It's purely a matter of personal preference.

2. Scroll through the **window** until you see a folder you want to open.

3. Double-click on a **folder**. In this example, it's My Documents.

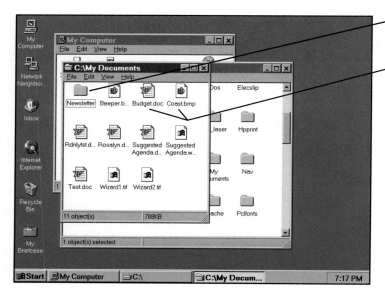

This example shows a subfolder (subdirectory).

With the large icon view that you see in this example, it's easy to see that the icons for each file type are different, so you may not find it especially helpful to see extensions on the file names. However, setting your computer to show file extensions will show them in all instances. If you show them in Explorer, you cannot choose not to show them in My Computer. See the section entitled, "Changing the View in My Computer," later in this chapter for information on file extensions.

Managing Files in My Computer

All of the housekeeping functions, such as cut, copy, paste, move, delete, and rename are available in My Computer. They are described in detail in Chapter 13, "Using Windows NT Explorer."

1. Right-click the **folder or file** with which you want to work. A menu will appear.

2. Click on the **command** you want to use.

Notice that you can use Quick View to preview a file. You can even send the file with e-mail from a My Computer window.

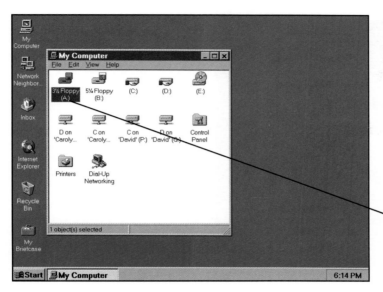

Formatting a Disk

1. Double-click on the **My Computer** icon on your desktop to open the window you see here.

2. Insert a **disk** into your A: (or B:) drive.

3. Click on the **A: drive** icon to highlight it.

4. Click on **File** in the menu bar. The File menu will appear.

5. Click on **Format**. The Format A: dialog box will appear.

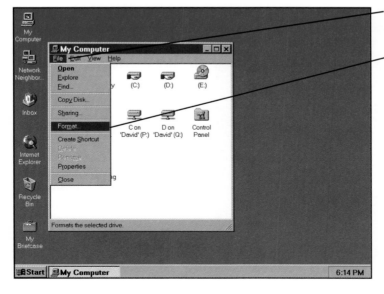

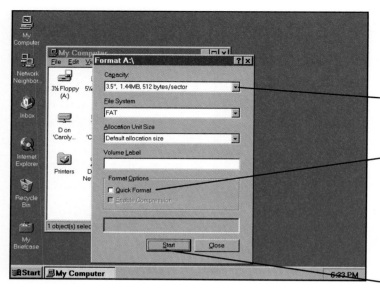

Today most disks are 1.44KB. If you are formatting one of those annoying 720KB disks, go to step 6.

6. Click on the ▼ to the right of the capacity box and choose the 720KB size.

Note: Quick Format is best used only if you know for a fact that the disk contains no bad sectors, it has been formatted previously, and you only want to remove files from the disk. Otherwise, don't click here.

7. Click on **Start** to begin the formatting process.

Changing the View in My Computer

There are numerous ways to change what you see in My Computer.

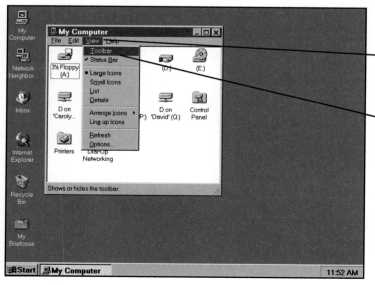

Adding a Toolbar

1. Click on **View** in the menu bar. The View menu will appear.

2. Click on **Toolbar**. The menu will close and a toolbar will appear under the menu bar. The toolbar won't show completely in this size window. Enlarge the window manually or click on the Maximize button (□) on the title bar.

Opening One Window at a Time

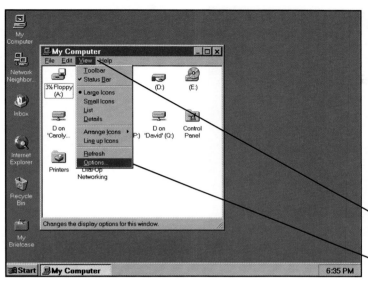

My Computer is set to show large icons and to open each new window without closing the previous one. If you want to change to the details view or add a toolbar (see Chapter 13), it has to be done in each window! You can change the view to show only one window at a time. This will also allow you to make changes to the view that apply to all windows.

1. Click on **View** in the menu bar.

2. Click on **Options**.

3. Click on the **Folder** tab if it's not already in front.

4. Click on **Browse folders by using a single window...** to put a dot in the circle. When you apply this option, you can go back to the previous window simply by pressing the Backspace key.

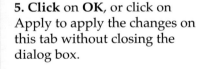

5. Click on **OK**, or click on Apply to apply the changes on this tab without closing the dialog box.

Note: To show file extensions, click on the View tab. See Chapter 13 for more details on selecting this option. There is one less option on the View tab in My Computer than you'll see in Windows NT Explorer, but showing file extensions is an option in both places.

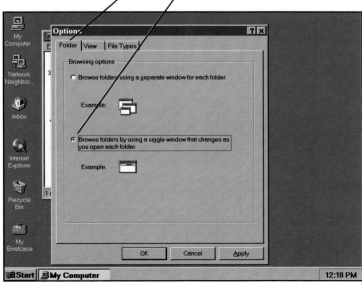

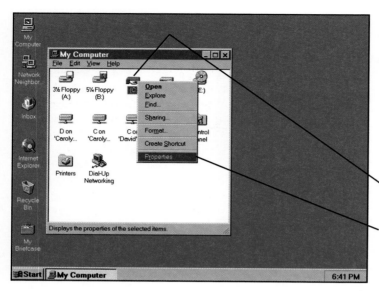

Viewing Drive Properties

You can check the used versus free space on a drive, check for errors, and mark a drive as shared or not shared in the Properties dialog box.

1. Right-click on the **C: drive**. A menu will appear.

2. Click on **Properties**. The Properties dialog box will appear.

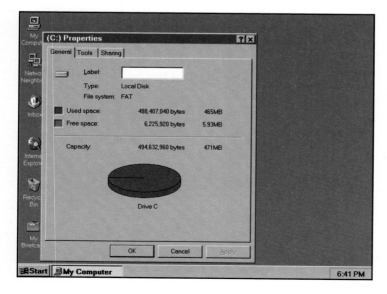

The General tab shows used versus free space.

See Chapter 17, "Scanning Hard Drives for Errors," and Chapter 20, "Backing Up Your Workstation," for detailed discussions of the options available on the Tools tab.

The Sharing tab allows you to mark drives as shared or not shared. See Chapter 29, "Controlling Access to Workstations," for more details.

Using My Briefcase

If you do work at home, use a laptop when you travel, or share a folder with others, you have a document control problem in the making. When you copy a file from a disk to your hard drive or from one folder to anther, it's too easy to lose the most recent copy by writing over it with an older version of the file. The My Briefcase icon on your desktop helps manage the updating process.

My Briefcase will update files over the network. You can also use My Briefcase with a laptop if the laptop is part of the network through a docking station or its own connection, or if there is a physical cable connection between your computer and the laptop. If there is no physical connection between the computers, you can put your files on a floppy disk and "sneaker net" (meaning "carry") it to the A: drive of the laptop (or home computer). This is the option we'll show you in this chapter. The process is the same, in any event, whether it's over the network or by disk.

Sending Files to My Briefcase

Double-click on the My Computer icon, and then double-click on the C: drive icon in the My Computer window. Double-click on a folder (in this example, the ABC folder) to open it.

The view in the My Computer window shows the toolbar, and the window has been manually enlarged to show all the buttons on the toolbar. An option to see one window at a time was also selected. See the previous sections in this chapter for a discussion of these issues.

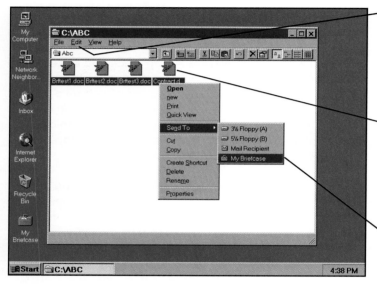

1. **Click** on **Edit** in the menu bar, and then **click** on **Select All** to highlight all the files in the folder. (Or, select the individual files you want to use.)

2. **Right-click** on **one of the highlighted files**. A menu will appear.

3. **Move** the pointer to **SendTo**. A second menu will appear.

4. **Click** on **My Briefcase**. An animated graphic of flying documents will appear as the files are *copied* to the Briefcase.

5. **Close My Computer**. You won't need it for the rest of the process.

Moving My Briefcase to a Floppy Disk

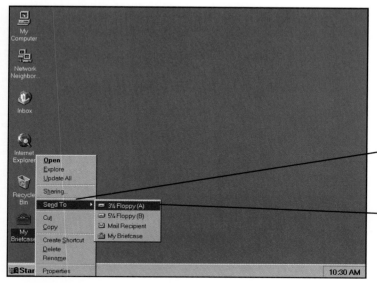

Now that the files are in My Briefcase, it's time to move My Briefcase to a floppy disk.

1. **Insert** a **disk** in the A: drive.

2. **Right-click** on **My Briefcase**. A menu will appear.

3. **Move** the mouse pointer to **SendTo**. A second menu will appear.

4. **Click** on **A: drive**. In this instance, the SendTo command will *move* My Briefcase to the floppy disk.

Moving My Briefcase from a Floppy Disk Back to the Desktop

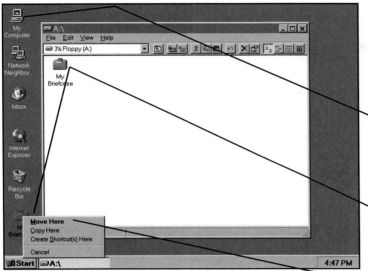

On the road, work on the files as you normally would. When you bring the disk back to the office, you're ready to see how My Briefcase facilitates the transfer and updating process.

1. Double-click on the **My Computer** icon, and then **double-click** on the **A: drive** icon to open the window you see here.

2. Press and hold the **right mouse button** on **My Briefcase** and **drag** it to the desktop. A menu will appear.

3. Click on **Move Here** to move My Briefcase back to your desktop.

Opening My Briefcase

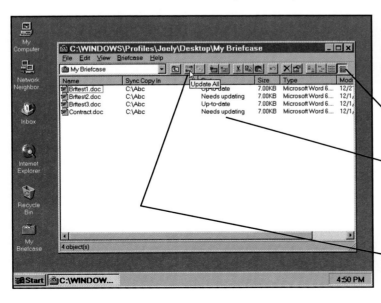

1. Double-click on **My Briefcase**. The first time you do this you'll see a Welcome Window. **Click** on **Finish** and it will go away forever.

2. Click on the **Details** button to see file details.

When you open My Briefcase, it scans the original files on your computer and compares them with its files. You then see a status report on each file.

3. Click on the **Update All** button in the toolbar.

Updating Files

My Briefcase keeps track of which files have been updated on the disk versus the hard drive and shows you graphically which way the updating copying process will go.

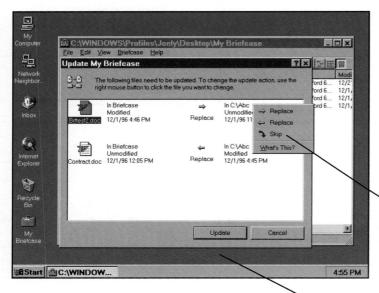

In this example the file, contract.doc, has been modified on the hard drive by the legal department. Obviously, you want the latest version of the contract, and My Briefcase lets you know that you need to update it.

You can, however, choose *not* to update a specific file.

1. Right-click on the **file** you don't want to update. A menu will appear. **Click** on **Skip**. When you update the files, the modified version of this file in My Briefcase will not be written over the original file on the hard drive.

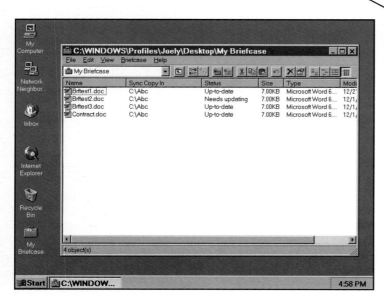

2. Click on **Update**. The files in My Briefcase, as well as the original files on the hard drive, have been updated.

Notice the resulting status of each file in the My Briefcase window. The file you skipped in step 1 shows that it needs updating because My Briefcase recognizes that it is a different version from the one on the hard drive.

Splitting a Briefcase File from the Original

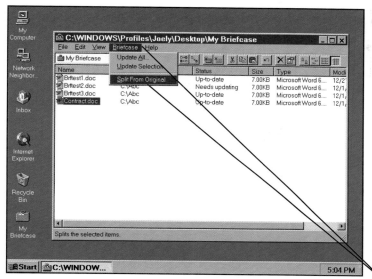

If you have a file in the Briefcase for a contract that has been accepted by your customer, you don't want that file updated by any changes made to the contract document on the hard drive. You can split the Briefcase version from the original and make it an "orphan." As an orphan, it is immune from the updating process.

1. In My Briefcase, **click** on the **file** you want to split from its original.

2. Click in **Briefcase** in the menu bar. **Click** on **Split From Original**.

Notice that it is now labeled "Orphan" and will not be involved in the updating process.

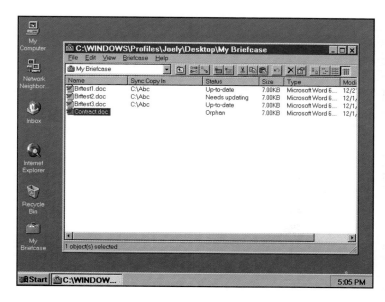

Notes on using My Briefcase:

Make sure both computers are set for the same date and time before you make copies to use or the updating process will get confused.

You can rename My Briefcase if the name is a little too cute for your tastes.

Sharing files under any conditions, even with a program like My Briefcase, requires a document control policy. Don't wait until it's too late to establish one.

Using the Recycle Bin

When you use Windows NT Explorer or My Computer to delete a file or folder, it is not actually deleted. It is sent to the Recycle Bin where it will stay forever until you clear the Bin. This is good in that it prevents the accidental deletion of items. However, if you don't clear the Bin periodically, you get what we call "hard drive buildup;" that is, all the "deleted" files that you thought were dead and gone will live on in the Recycle Bin and continue to take up space on your hard drive. In this chapter, you will:

✔ Empty the Recycle Bin
✔ View the contents of the Recycle Bin
✔ Restore an item from the Recycle Bin
✔ Permanently Deleting Files
✔ Disable the Recycle Bin

Emptying the Recycle Bin

If you just deleted some files or folders and you know there is nothing else in the Recycle Bin, you can empty it without viewing the contents. Go to the next page if you want to check the contents first.

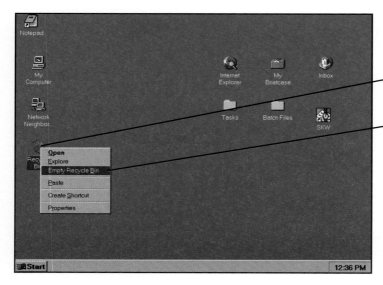

Notice that the Recycle Bin icon shows there is "trash" in the Bin.

1. Right-click on the **Recycle Bin** icon. A menu will appear.

2. Click on **Empty Recycle Bin**. The Confirm File Delete window will appear.

3. Click on **Yes** in the Confirm File Delete window (not shown here) to empty the Bin and close the window. Notice that the "trash" is now gone from the Recycle Bin icon.

Viewing the Contents of the Recycle Bin

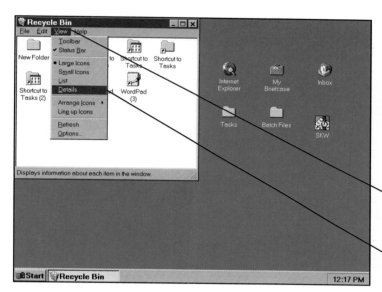

You can check on the contents of the Recycle Bin.

1. Double-click on the **Recycle Bin** icon on your desktop. The Recycle Bin window you see here will appear. The default view shows large icons, but you can change the view to see file details.

2. Click on **View** in the menu bar. The View menu will appear.

3. Click on **Details**. A detailed description of each item in the Recycle Bin will appear.

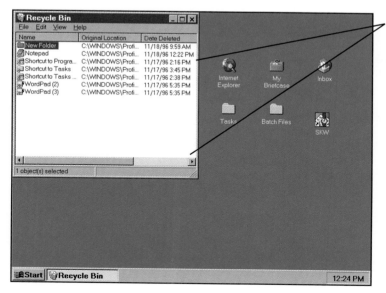

Notice that you now have more information about the contents of your Recycle Bin. Use the ▶ on the bottom of the dialog box to scroll over to view the rest of the details, or click on the Maximize button (□) on the right of the title bar to enlarge the window.

Restoring an Item from the Recycle Bin

If you accidentally deleted a file or folder, you can easily restore it. In this example, we will restore a Notepad shortcut icon that was deleted from the desktop (sent to the Bin).

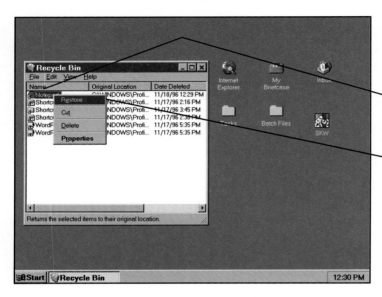

1. Repeat steps 1 through 3 on the previous page to open the Recycle Bin and view the contents.

2. Click the **right mouse button** on the item you want to restore. A menu will appear.

3. Click on **Restore.** The item will be returned to its original location.

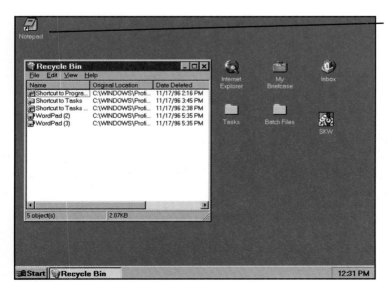

In this example, a shortcut icon has been restored to the desktop.

Note: You never know where the restored icon might show up on your desktop, so you may have to move the Recycle Bin window or close it to see the icon.

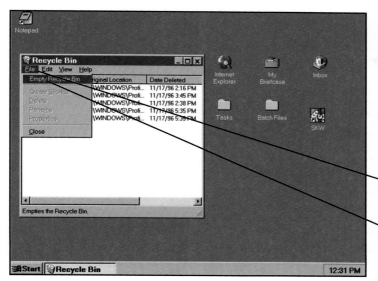

Permanently Deleting Files

After you have reviewed the list of items in the Bin and restored any that you accidentally deleted, you can permanently delete the remaining items.

1. Click on **File** in the menu bar. The File menu will appear.

2. Click on **Empty Recycle Bin**. The Confirm Multiple File Delete dialog box will appear.

3. Click on **Yes**. The entire contents of the Recycle Bin will be permanently deleted, and the dialog box will close.

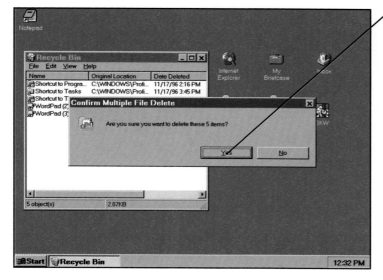

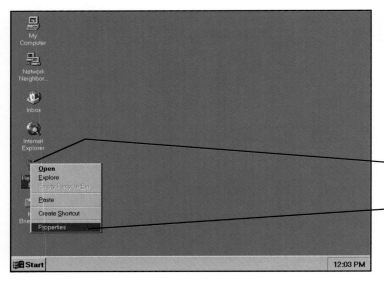

Disabling the Recycle Bin

If you don't want to use the Recycle Bin or can't afford the disk space, you can disable the Recycle Bin.

1. Right-click on the **Recycle Bin** icon. A menu will appear.

2. Click on **Properties**. The Properties dialog box will appear.

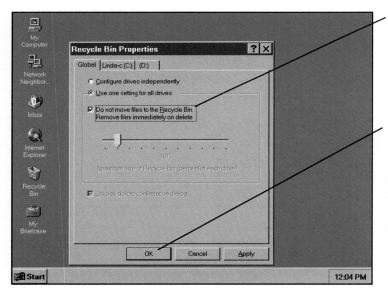

3. Click on **Do not move files to the Recycle Bin** to put a ✔ in the box. With this option the files will be deleted and you won't be able to use the Recycle Bin to restore them.

4. Click on **OK**. The Recycle Bin has been turned off. The icon will remain on your desktop even though it is inactive. You can reactivate it at any time by reversing the steps shown above.

Note: Files deleted through File Manager do not go to the Recycle Bin. Files on a network drive that are deleted over the network also don't go to the Recycle Bin (even if they are deleted through Explorer or My Computer). In both these situations, the files are simply deleted.

Finding Files, Folders, and Other Computers

You may have experienced the frustration of forgetting the eight-character abbreviated file name you had to create for a Windows 3.1 file. The long file names in Windows NT 4.0 help to solve this problem, but if you're like us, you probably will have more than one occasion when you forget where you saved the silly thing. (We blame it on the stress of deadlines. If you've come up with a better excuse, please share it with us.) You'll be pleased to know that NT 4.0 has an excellent Find function that works across the network, so you can even search on another computer. This chapter will show searching for a file using the Start menu, but the same process works in Windows NT Explorer by clicking on Tools/Find (see Chapter 13) or by right-clicking on My Computer (see Chapter 14). In this chapter, you will do the following:

✔ Search for a file on another drive
✔ Search for specific text within a file
✔ Search for another computer

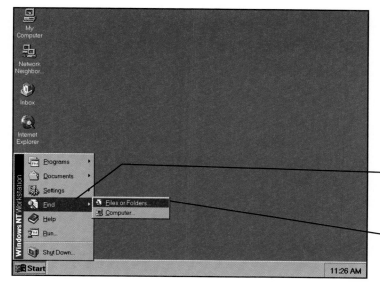

Finding a File

This example will show a search for a file, but the process also works for folders.

1. Click on the **Start** button. The Start menu will appear.

2. Move the mouse arrow to **Find**. A second menu will appear.

3. Click on **Files or Folders**. The Find: All Files dialog box will appear.

4. Click on the **Name & Location** tab if it's not already in front.

Searching for a File Name

You can search for specific file names.

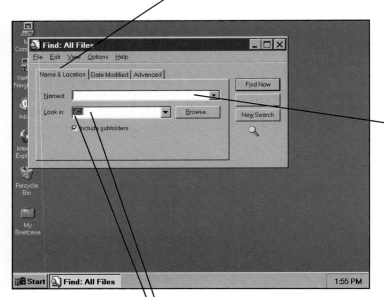

1. Type the **name** of the file if you know it. If you don't remember the name, leave this text box blank. We'll show you other ways to search.

Note: The Find function is not case sensitive, but it will search for the *exact* spelling you specify here. If you're not sure of the exact name, don't put anything here. We'll show you how to use identifying text and file type as search parameters a little later in this chapter.

You can use the wild-card symbol (*) to broaden the search. For example, if you know your file starts with "bank" but you think it could be "banks" or "banking," type bank*. The * tells the computer to search for everything beginning with "bank" no matter what the rest of the letters may be.

Notice that by default, the search will be folders and subfolders on the C drive. If you want to search another drive on your machine or on the network, go on to the next section.

2. If you know the exact name of the file for which you are searching and you're certain it's on the C drive, go to the section entitled, "Viewing the Results of a Search" later in this chapter. Otherwise, read on for suggestions on defining your search.

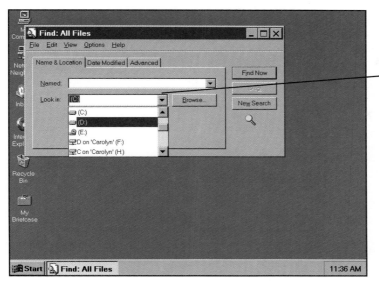

Searching a Specific Drive

1. Click on the ▼ to the right of the Look in box. A list of drives will appear.

2. Scroll through the list and **click** on the appropriate **drive** letter. Notice that you can search other drives on the network as well as your own drives. (Choose My Computer to search all drives on your computer as well as all drives to which you are connected. Be prepared to wait; it will take a while.)

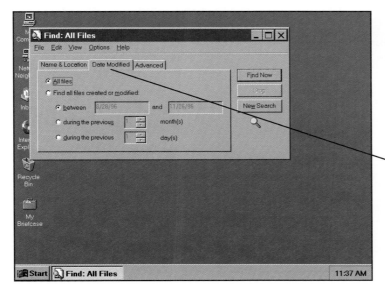

Searching Within a Specific Time Period

You can limit the search to files created or modified within a specific time period.

1. Click on the **Date Modified** tab to bring it to the front.

2. Make the appropriate **changes** based on the information you know about the file.

Limiting the Search to a File Type

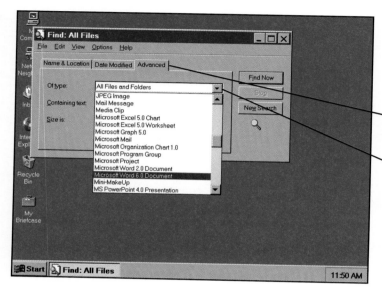

You can help the search progress more quickly by limiting it to a specific type of file, such as a Microsoft Word document or a JPEG image.

1. Click on the **Advanced** tab to bring it to the front.

2. Click on the ▼ to the right of the type box. An extensive list of application programs and file types will appear.

3. Click on the appropriate **file type**.

Searching for Specific Text

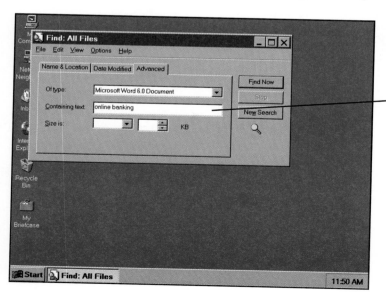

You may not remember the file name, but you may remember specific words or names in the file.

1. Type the **text or name** in the Containing Text box.

Viewing the Results of a Search

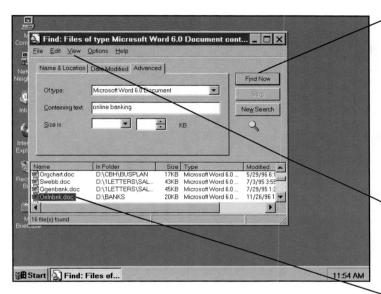

1. Click on **Find Now**. The magnifying glass will move around while the search is ongoing and a list of matches (if any) will appear in the bottom part of the window. If you recognize your file in the list, click on Stop to halt the search. Notice that the number of files found is shown at the very bottom of the window.

2. This example shows the Details view of the files. If you want another view, click on View in the menu bar and choose the view you prefer.

3. Click on a likely **file** to highlight it.

4. Click on **File** in the menu bar.

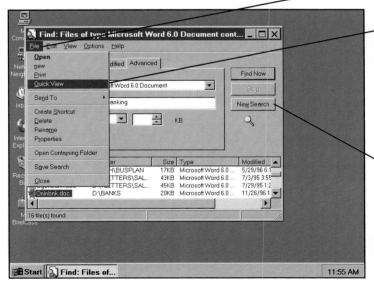

5. Click on **Quick View**. After a pause, the file will appear in a window. Or, right-click on the file and choose Quick View.

You can maximize the window or close it and choose another file to view.

6. Click on **New Search** to clear the current results and start over.

7. If you're certain that a specific file is the one you want, **double-click** on it and the file and its application program will open.

Finding a Shared Computer

If you can't locate a shared computer on the list of available drives, you can search for it with Find.

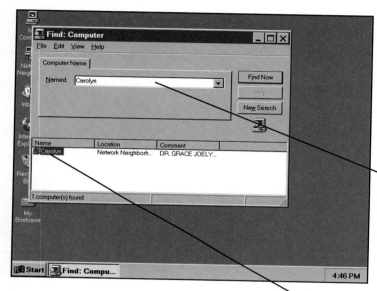

1. Click on the **Start** button. The Start menu will appear.

2. Highlight Find. A second menu will appear.

3. Click on **Computers** to open the Find: Computer dialog box you see here.

4. Type the **name** of the computer in the Named box. In this example it's Carolyn, but it could be Marketing, for instance.

5. Click on **Find Now**. The results of the search will be shown in the bottom part of the window.

6. Double-click on the **computer** to open it.

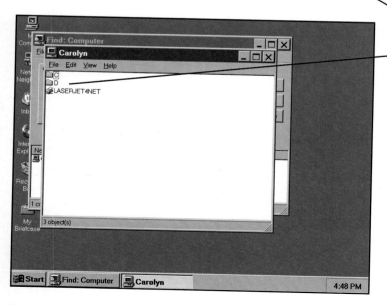

You can now open a particular drive on that computer or map the network drive. See Chapter 31, "Mapping Network Drives," for more details.

Keeping Your Workstation Humming

In many ways, a computer is like a fine automobile. It can be a lot of fun and can get you to where you want to go quickly. However, it does require periodic maintenance, fine-tuning, and sometimes the addition of accessories that did not come with the car right out of the show room. In the following chapters we show you how to maintain your workstation at peak performance by fixing errors and fine-tuning the memory. We also show you how to add new programs and accessories and how to back up your work.

PART

I

PART

II

PART

III

PART

IV

PART

V

PART

VI

PART

VII

Scanning Hard Drives for Errors

In the normal course of computing, little electronic blips and glitches cause errors. Use the scandisk utility that comes with NT 4.0 to look for the errors on your drives and fix them. If you are an old hand with Windows 3.1, no doubt you have used Scandisk to find and fix errors. Windows NT has a primitive scandisk utility (compared to Norton Utilities Disk Doctor for Windows 3.x and Windows 95). However, it does the job. In this chapter, you will:

✔ Scan a hard drive for errors and fix any that are found automatically
✔ Learn about how and when NT will automatically scan

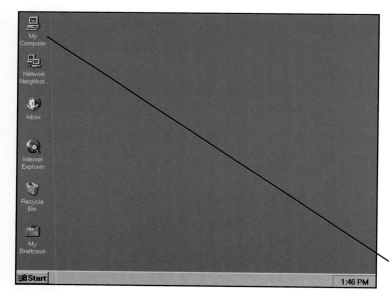

Scanning for Errors

As part of good preventive maintenance, it is important to keep your computer as healthy as possible. Scanning for errors on a frequent basis will help keep your computer in optimum working condition.

1. Close all files and programs before you start this process!

2. Double-click on the **My Computer icon**. The My Computer window will appear.

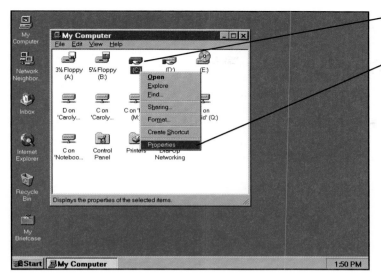

3. Right-click on the **C: drive** icon. A menu will appear.

4. Click on **Properties**. The C: Properties dialog box will appear.

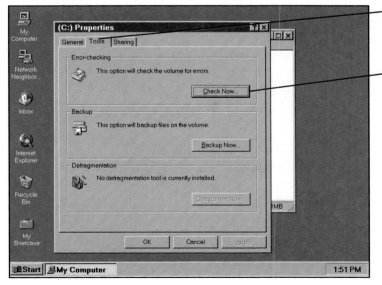

5. Click on the **Tools tab** to bring it to the front of the window.

6. Click on **Check Now**. The Check Disk C:\ window will appear.

7. Click on **Automatically fix file system errors**. Errors in the file system can be caused by power failures or shutting off your machine without going through the appropriate steps shown in Chapter 3. This option will cause NT to check that files are recorded properly and completely, and fix those that are not.

Note: NT 4.0 recommends that you do *not* automatically fix file system errors if you have a dual boot. We tried it and NT would not let us proceed!

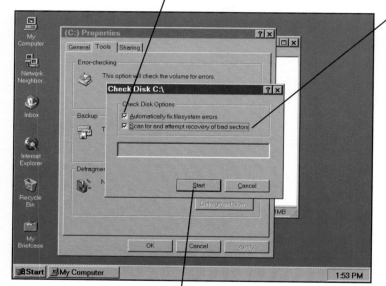

8. Click on **Scan for and attempt recovery of bad sectors**. There is no rhyme nor reason to when and why bad sectors occur, but banging on your hard drive, especially when it's running, is not a good idea. Seriously, these types of errors occur in the best of families despite the most diligent care on your part. All you can do is check the disk, as you are doing in this chapter. If NT discovers bad sectors, you'll get a message window giving you the option of fixing the error, ignoring it, or cancelling the process. If you have a system or network administrator you can call, now would be a good time to do so. If you choose to fix the error, NT will mark the cluster as bad and attempt to move the data to a good cluster, but you may lose data. Hopefully, you've backed up critical files. (See Chapter 20, "Backing Up Your Workstation.")

9. Click on **Start**. The program will begin checking for errors. A status bar will inform you of the progress.

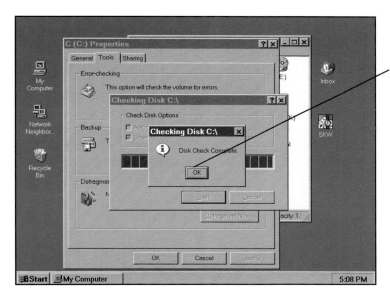

When the process is complete, this message will appear.

10. Click on **OK**. The dialog box will close.

11. Repeat the process for your D: drive (if you have one.)

Scanning Automatically on Crashes

One of the built-in features of NT is that when it crashes, it will automatically scan the disk and fix errors as it reboots. However, if allocation errors are created that do not crash the system, it will not fix them automatically and you must follow the procedures in this chapter.

Defragging is a Chore

Unfortunately, NT 4.0 does not come with a built-in defragmentation program. NT's suggestion in the Help menu is to back up your disk to tape, reformat the disk, and then restore your files. Ugh, what a chore! Whatever you do, do not go to DOS and defrag with a program that is not made for NT 4.0. We did that and had to reinstall NT 4.0. (We have a dual boot on our machines with the choice of being either Windows NT or Windows 3.11 with DOS 6.22. Believe us when we say that the DOS 6.22 defragmentation program is an NT killer!) See Chapter 33 for some defrag suggestions.

Installing a Tape Device

NT 4.0's backup program works only with tape devices. Therefore, you cannot use it to back up to hard drives, optical drives, or floppies. Moreover, NT 4.0 does not support all brands of tape devices, and, unlike Windows 95, it will not automatically recognize and install the tape device. In this chapter, you will do the following:

✔ Install a tape device

Opening the Control Panel

To install the driver for an internal tape drive, assuming the hardware part is handled, you must go to the Control Panel to start the process. In this example, you will install the NT driver for a Colorado Jumbo 250 tape drive. This drive was already set up for Windows 3.11 for Workgroups when we upgraded the machine to Windows NT 4.0. If you have a different type of tape drive, your process may differ from the one shown here. Also note that, as of this writing, NT 4.0 does not support external tape drives.

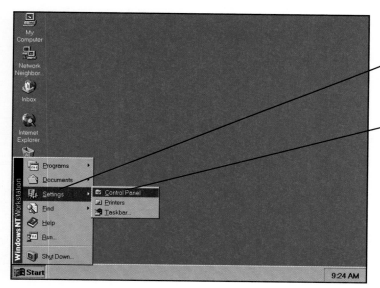

1. Click on the **Start Button**. A menu will appear.

2. Slide the **mouse pointer** up to **Settings.** Another menu will appear.

3. Click on **Control Panel**. The Control Panel window will appear.

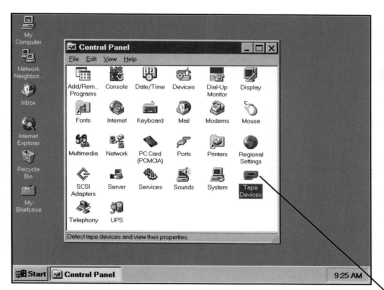

Detecting the Tape Device

Unlike Windows 95, Windows NT 4.0 does not automatically find the tape device on a machine when you install it. In this section, you will ask NT 4.0 to find the tape device. If NT doesn't find your tape device, you must contact the manufacturer for assistance. You only have to do this once (unless, of course, you put in a different tape device).

1. Double-click on the **Tape Devices icon** in the Control Panel window. The Tape Devices dialog box will appear.

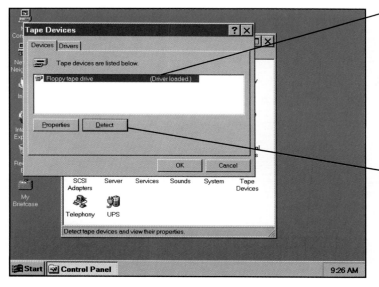

Note: You may or may not see this message. It will depend on whether or not you had previously installed a tape device and are changing to a new one or you are rescanning because the first scan failed to install the proper drivers or detect the device (as in our case).

2. Click on **Detect**. The Rescanning for Tape Devices message box will appear while NT looks for your tape device.

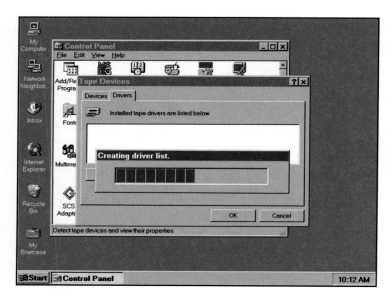

A message box will show the progress of the scan for the tape device (installed hardware). It will be followed by the Creating Driver List message box you see here.

Once this message box finishes, the New Floppy Tape Device Found dialog box will appear.

Installing the Tape Driver

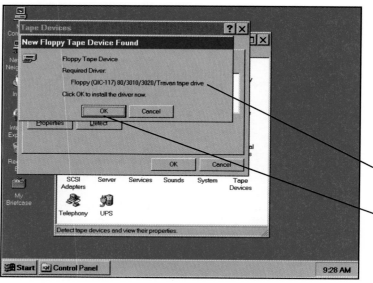

Once NT has detected your tape device, the next step is to install a tape driver that will allow NT to run the tape device. In this section, you will install the latest NT tape driver for this tape device from your NT installation CD-ROM. So have it handy!

Notice that NT has found your tape device!

1. Click on **OK**. A Devices dialog box will appear.

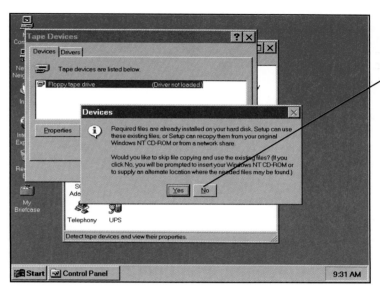

2. Insert the **NT 4.0 Installation CD** into the your CD-ROM drive.

3. Click on **No** to install the *latest* driver from your NT CD. Next, the Systems Settings Change dialog box will appear.

Note: If you click on Yes, NT may install an older driver already on your machine. The chances are that this older driver was used with a previous version of Windows before you upgraded to NT. In that case, the tape won't work with that driver.

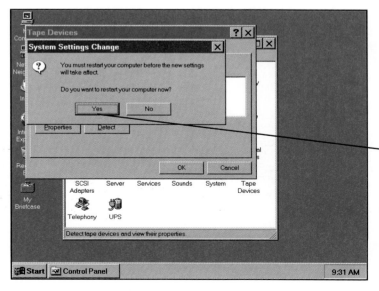

Rebooting the Computer

You must reboot your computer to complete the tape and driver installation process.

1. Click on **Yes**. The computer will reboot.

You are now set up to use NT's backup program with you tape device (see Chapter 20, "Backing Up Your Workstation," for details).

Installing Software

NT 4.0's installation program has simplified the installation and removal of software programs. If you have a CD-ROM drive, it couldn't be faster or easier. In this chapter, you will do the following:

✔ Install a program
✔ Start a newly installed program
✔ Learn how to uninstall programs

Installing a Program from a CD

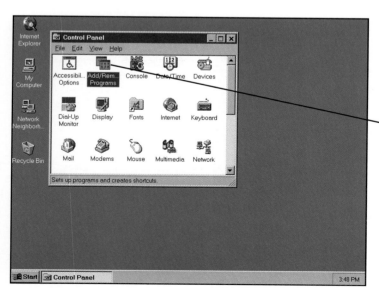

To install a program, you must first open the Control Panel.

1. Click on the **Start button, move** the **mouse pointer** to **Settings,** and then **click** on **Control Panel** to open it.

2. Double-click on the **Add/ Remove Programs icon**. The Add/Remove Programs Properties dialog box will appear.

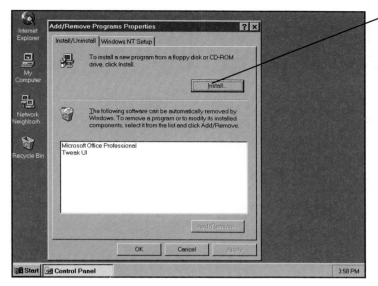

3. Click on **Install**. The Install From Floppy Disk or CD-ROM dialog box will appear.

4. Insert the **CD** of the program you want to install into your CD-ROM drive.

5. Click on **Next**. NT will:

❖ Search for an installation program in your floppy drive(s).

❖ If NT doesn't find an installation program in a floppy drive, it will look for it in your CD-ROM drive.

❖ When NT finds an installation program, the Run Installation Program dialog box will appear.

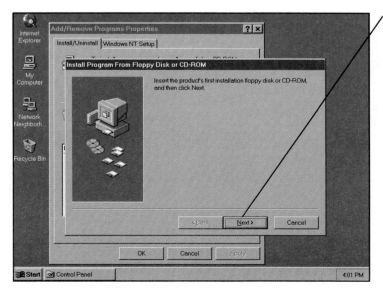

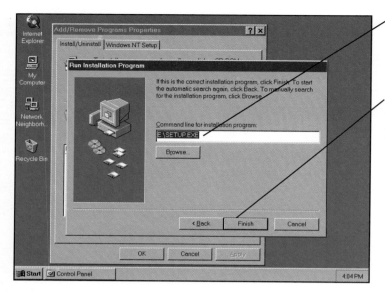

Notice that NT found the installation program on the CD-ROM drive (on this machine, the CD is drive E).

6. Click on **Finish** and follow the directions as they appear on your screen.

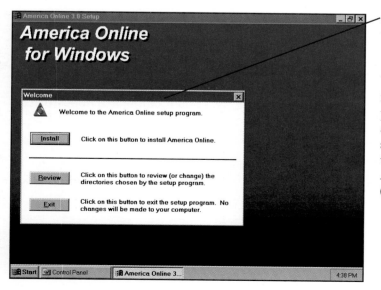

As you can see, each program will have its own version of "install."

When the installation is finished, the new folder for the program you installed will appear on the desktop, as shown on the next page. In this example, we installed America Online, version 3.0 (16-bit).

Here's the folder for the new program you just installed.

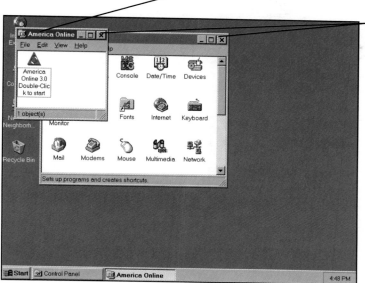

7. Click on the **Close boxes** (☒) to close the windows.

Starting the Newly Installed Program

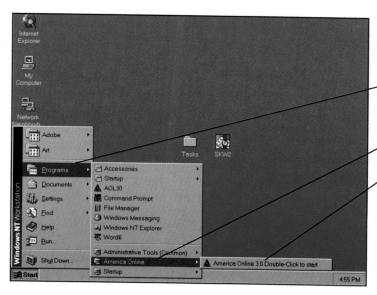

1. Click on the **Start button**. A menu will appear.

2. Move the **mouse pointer** to **Programs**. Another menu will appear.

There's the new folder!

3. Click on the **program** if you want to start it. Otherwise, click anywhere on the desktop to close the menus.

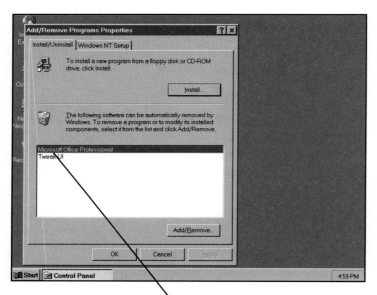

Removing a Program

Removing software programs that have been designed to work with NT's uninstall feature is great. This is in contrast to the problems of uninstalling programs from Windows 3.11. Unfortunately, if you install a program that is not designed for NT, then you will have to punt and go back to the old way of uninstalling.

1. Repeat steps 1 to 3 in the section in this chapter entitled "Installing a Program from a CD" to open the Add/Remove Programs Properties dialog box.

2. Click on the **program** you want to remove to highlight it.

Note: The programs listed here can be uninstalled by Windows NT's uninstall feature. Notice that the AOL 3.0 program that we just installed is not listed. That's because only programs that are set up for NT 4.0 will appear here. Other programs, like this 16-bit version of AOL 3.0, cannot take advantage of the built-in uninstall program. Had we installed the 32-bit version of AOL, it would be listed here. Because the AOL program is not listed, we will be removing a different program as an example of the uninstall process.

3. Click on **Add/Remove**. A message box will appear.

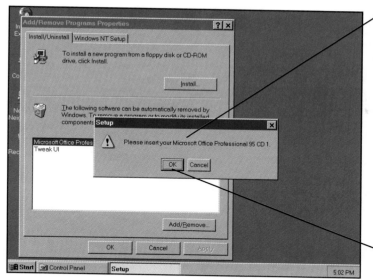

Notice that you need the CD for the program to uninstall it. (Actually, this is the only pain in the neck part of this otherwise simple uninstall process. In the older versions of Windows, you did not need the installation CD or disks to uninstall, but what can you do?)

4. Insert the **program CD** into the CD-ROM drive (in this example, the Microsoft Office Professional CD).

5. Click on **OK** to start the uninstall process.

When the program is uninstalled, you will get a message box telling you that NT has successfully completed the process. You will then have to close the Add/Remove dialog box and remove the CD from the CD-ROM drive.

Backing Up Your Workstation

The NT 4.0 backup program is designed to work only with tape drives. If your systems administrator has not already done so, it's a fairly simple thing to install the NT 4.0 driver for your model tape drive (see Chapter 18). If you do not have a tape drive, skip this chapter. Backup will not work with other drives or floppies. In this chapter, you will:

✔ Back up several files to tape
✔ Restore several files from the tape to your hard drive

Opening the Backup Program

1. Insert a **tape** into the tape drive.

2. Click on the **Start button**. A menu will appear.

3. Move the **mouse pointer** to **Programs**. Another menu will appear.

4. Move the **mouse pointer** to **Administrative Tools (Common)**. Another menu will appear.

5. Click on **Backup**. The Backup dialog box will appear.

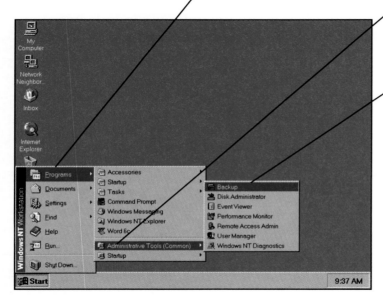

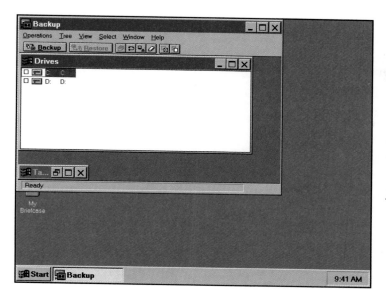

Notice that there is a waiting period while NT 4.0's backup program looks for the tape drive and determines the type of tape in it.

Note: If NT finds a "Foreign Tape," the message box shown below will appear. *A Foreign Tape is a tape that is not formatted for NT 4.0.*

If this is your first time using the tape backup program in NT, and you have recently upgraded, you will get this message since no doubt your tape is formatted for a previous version of DOS or Windows.

6. Click on **OK** to close the message box.

Preparing the Tape for Backup

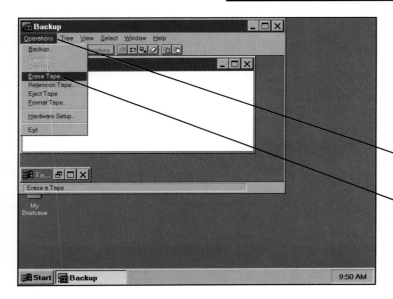

In this section, you will erase a "foreign tape." *A foreign tape is a tape that has not been formatted for NT 4.0's backup program.* By erasing the tape, you automatically convert it to work with NT.

1. Click on **Operations**. A menu will appear.

2. Click on **Erase Tape**. An Erase Tape dialog box will appear.

Notice the message "The tape in the drive is not recognizable." Ignore the commentary. We already know that the tape is a "foreign tape."

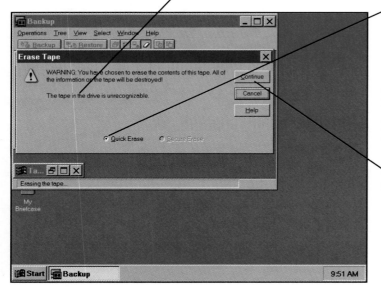

Notice that the Quick Erase option has been selected automatically. The Secure Erase option is grayed out, and we were unable to click on it. It's just as well because a "secure erase" takes forever! For most people, the Quick Erase is the only way to go.

3. Click on **Continue**. An Erase Status dialog box will appear.

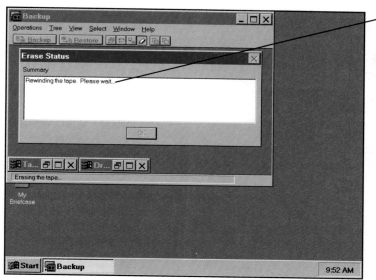

Note: This dialog box will be here for quite a while, so please don't think you've done something wrong because it is taking so long. Go have a cup of coffee or make a phone call. Eventually, the tape will be rewound and the Erase message box will appear as shown below. Tape drives can be so slow!

This message is just NT 4.0 warning you that the tape you are about to erase has data on it that was created for another application (e.g., the Colorado tape program for Windows 3.1, etc.). Make sure you want to erase this tape. Once you click on Continue, the formatting (erasing) will begin. Any data on the tape will be lost, and you will not be able to use this tape with 3.1 software.

4. **Click** on **Continue** to close the dialog box.

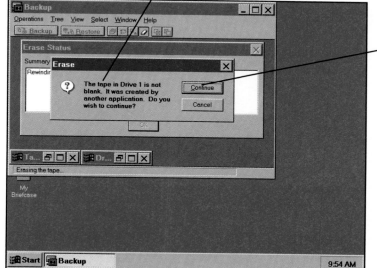

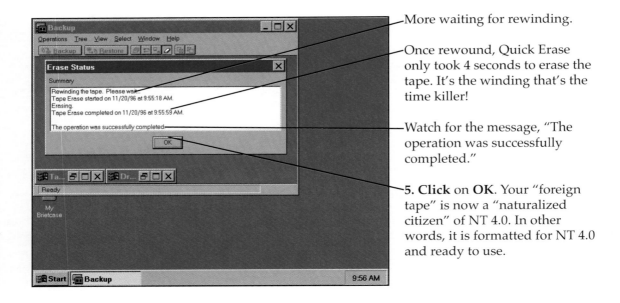

More waiting for rewinding.

Once rewound, Quick Erase only took 4 seconds to erase the tape. It's the winding that's the time killer!

Watch for the message, "The operation was successfully completed."

5. Click on **OK**. Your "foreign tape" is now a "naturalized citizen" of NT 4.0. In other words, it is formatted for NT 4.0 and ready to use.

Backing Up to Tape

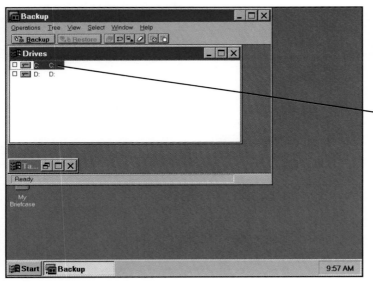

You can back up your entire system, one or more folders, or just a file or two in a specific folder. In this example you will back up specific files in a folder.

1. Double-click on **C** to open the C Drive list of folders.

Notice that the Backup screens look a little like File Manager screens.

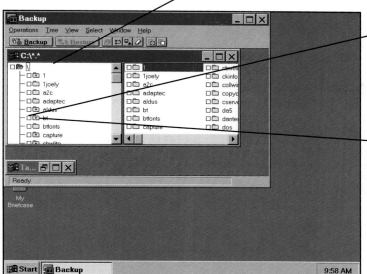

Note: If you want to back up all of the files in the folder, you can skip steps 2 and 3. Just click on the check box to the left of the folder to put an X in the box, and go on to step 4.

2. Click on the **folder icon** of the folder containing the files you want to back up. A list of the files contained in the folder will appear in the right window frame. In this example, we clicked on our BT folder icon.

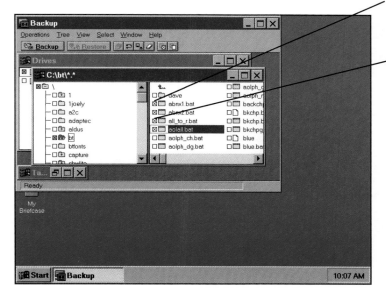

3. Click in the **check box** next to the file(s) you want to back up to **put** an X in the **box**.

Note: Only files that have X's in the boxes will be backed up.

4. Click on **Backup**. The Backup Information dialog box will appear as shown here.

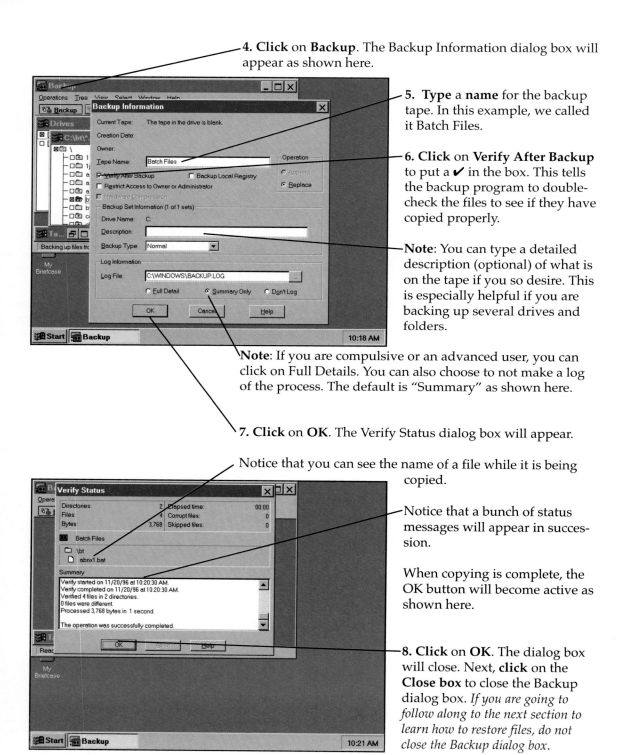

5. Type a **name** for the backup tape. In this example, we called it Batch Files.

6. Click on **Verify After Backup** to put a ✔ in the box. This tells the backup program to double-check the files to see if they have copied properly.

Note: You can type a detailed description (optional) of what is on the tape if you so desire. This is especially helpful if you are backing up several drives and folders.

Note: If you are compulsive or an advanced user, you can click on Full Details. You can also choose to not make a log of the process. The default is "Summary" as shown here.

7. Click on **OK**. The Verify Status dialog box will appear.

Notice that you can see the name of a file while it is being copied.

Notice that a bunch of status messages will appear in succession.

When copying is complete, the OK button will become active as shown here.

8. Click on **OK**. The dialog box will close. Next, **click** on the **Close box** to close the Backup dialog box. *If you are going to follow along to the next section to learn how to restore files, do not close the Backup dialog box.*

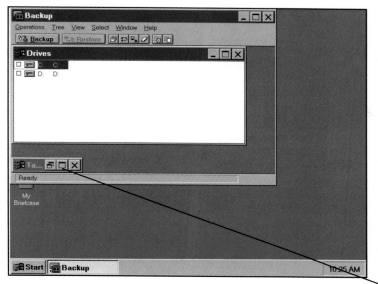

Restoring Files to Your Hard Drive

Putting copies of files that you have backed up onto your hard drive is a piece of cake.

1. Insert the **tape** containing the files you want to restore into your tape drive.

2. Repeat steps 2 to 5 in the first section of this chapter to open the Backup dialog box as shown here if it is not already open.

3. Click on the **Expand Window button** to open the Tapes window.

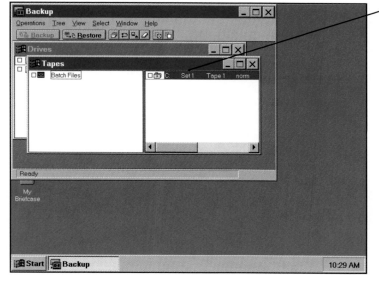

4. Double-click on **Set 1 Tape** to open the Batch Files Set 1 window.

Note: If you chose to back up files in a folder with many subfolders, your screen will look different from this one.

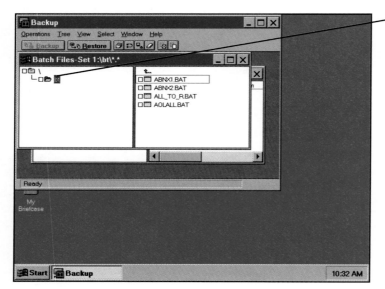

5. Click on the **folder** to display the backup files in the folder that you saved to tape.

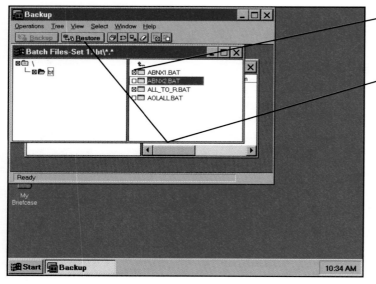

6. Click on **each file** that you want to restore in succession to **put** an ✕ in each **box**.

7. Click on **Restore**. The Restore Information dialog box will appear.

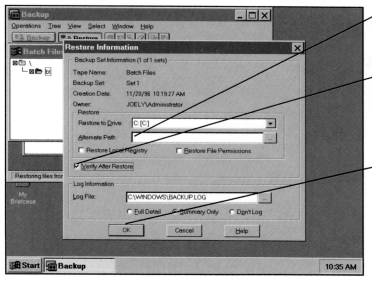

Notice that you can specify an alternate folder and/or drive by typing the path here.

8. Click on **Verify After Restore** to put a ✔ in the box. This tells the restore program to double-check the files to see if they have copied properly.

9. Click on **OK**. The Restore Status dialog box will appear.

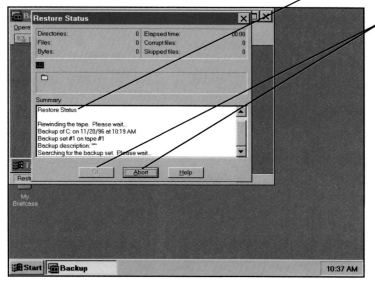

Notice that the Restore Status dialog box will keep you informed of its progress.

Notice that the OK button is grayed out and that you can cancel at any time before completion by clicking on the Abort button.

Note: If you are writing over files on your hard drive with the copies on the tape drive, the Confirm File Replace dialog box will appear like the one on the next page.

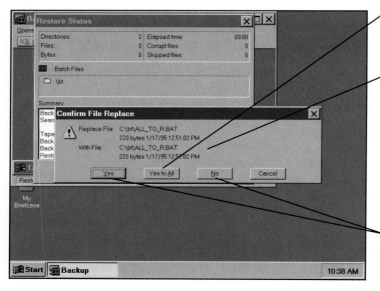

10. Click on **Yes** to **All**. The Verify Status dialog box will appear.

If you think some of the files on your hard drive, are newer than the ones on the tape drive, you may want to compare dates as shown here.

If there is a difference in the dates of two files with the same name–the one on the tape and the one on your hard drive– click on Yes or on No, depending on which version of the file you want on your hard drive. Remember that you will always have a copy of one version of the file on the tape unless you erase the tape. The next file being copied will appear in the dialog box for a similar comparison.

Notice that as each file is restored to your hard drive, it appears here during the restoration process.

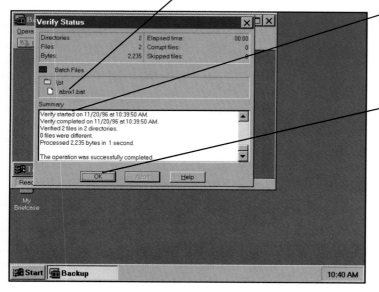

The status of the process is continuously updated here. When the restoration is complete, the OK button will become active.

11. Click on **OK**. The dialog box will close.

12. Click on the **Close Box** (☒) on the Backup dialog box title bar to close the program.

Managing Virtual Memory

Windows NT Workstation 4.0 requires a great deal of Random Access Memory (RAM). In fact, it uses much more than the 16MB of RAM that is recommended for it. To do this, NT creates a *swap file* on your workstation's hard disk that it uses the same way that it uses the RAM chips in your computer. That is, it temporarily writes program data to the swap file then reads the data back as needed while running the program. A new copy of the swap file (and *paging file* or virtual memory) is created each time the workstation boots up, and it is expandable. NT makes the file bigger as it requires more memory and smaller when less is needed. NT allows you to make changes to the virtual memory setup, but there are only a few circumstances under which it makes any sense to do so. Be sure to read the guidelines on the next two pages before making any changes to your virtual memory. In this chapter, you will:

✔ Find out when virtual memory changes may be in order
✔ Check on your workstation's virtual memory
✔ See how to make changes to the virtual memory

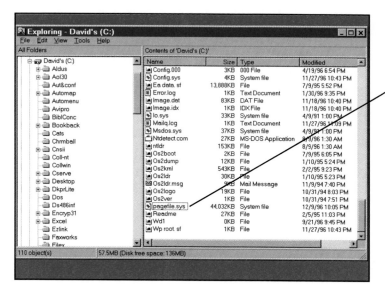

Finding the Swap File

The swap file is named *pagefile.sys* by NT. You can use File Manager, My Computer, Windows NT Explorer (as in this example), or the Find utility on the Start menu to see where and how big the pagefile.sys file is. It's usually in the root directory, but if you have more than one hard disk, there could be swap files on each one.

Deciding Whether to Make Changes

Unless you are receiving "Out of Memory" error messages, you should not have to make changes to the virtual memory settings that NT determined for your computer during installation. The only other reason to change the settings would be to try to improve the system's overall speed.

Note 1: You can only make changes to the virtual memory if you are logged on as Administrator or as a member of the Administrators group. If you're on a corporate network, consult with your systems administrator before making any changes.

Note 2: If you decide to make any memory changes, be sure to make a record of the original settings first so that they can be restored if the changes do not have the desired effect on your computer.

"Out of Memory" Error Messages

You may be receiving the error message because your hard disk is so crowded that NT can't expand the swap file when it needs to. The solution may be as simple as freeing up as much space as possible by deleting old or unused files or storing files on floppy disks or backup tapes. If you have more than one hard disk, you may want to try setting up swap files on both disks to see if this solves the problem. If you continue to get the error messages after making the changes, you should consider having your computer serviced or upgraded so that it is better able to run NT without this problem.

Improve Speed of Performance

Another reason to change virtual memory settings would be to try to improve your system's overall speed. However, the improvement you can get by doing this will be slight. Generally, these changes may improve performance:
  1) If the swap file was set up on a slow hard disk and your computer has another hard disk that is faster, or
  2) If the swap file was set up on a hard disk that is very fragmented.

Changes You Can Make

Use a Faster Hard Disk

A hard disk's speed affects the speed of the entire system. If you have more than one hard disk, compare their speeds by referring to the manuals that came with the computer or disks. Although you can use NT's Performance Monitor to check disk speed, it isn't easy. There are much more user-friendly programs, such as Norton Utilities, that can give you this information. If one disk is faster than the other, it should be the one that holds the swap file.

Put Swap Files on Both Hard Disks

As noted before, NT tries to expand the swap file when needed. If the disk with the swap file is too crowded, this can't happen. With swap files on both disks, if the swap file on one disk fills up and NT needs more, instead of giving you an "Out of Memory" message, it can use the file on the other disk. Of course, NT won't necessarily use the faster disk first.

"Defrag" and Set Minimum and Maximum Size

As files are written to and deleted from your hard disk, pockets of free space start to develop. At some point, when new files are being added or old ones are being expanded, the operating system won't find enough space for the entire file. Instead, the file will be fragmented—split into several pieces and put wherever room exists. If this happens to the swap file, which is in almost constant use by NT, your hard disk has to use a lot of time looking for all the pieces.

To see whether your disk is fragmented, you have to use a "defrag" program, such as the ones discussed in Chapter 33. A defrag program can also create more contiguous free space by putting the fragmented files back together. After "defragging" your hard disk, you can set up virtual memory to take advantage of the contiguous space.

By default, NT sets a minimum size for the swap file and expands or contracts it as needed. A maximum size can also be set. You can make NT keep the file the same size all the time by setting the minimum and maximum sizes to the same number. That way it won't get fragmented. Each time the workstation reboots, it will use the same free space for the swap file that it used the last time.

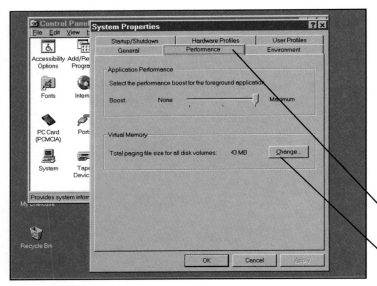

Checking Virtual Memory

1. Right-click on the **My Computer icon** and **click** on **Properties**, or **open** the **Control Panel window** and **double-click** on the **System icon**. The System Properties dialog box will appear.

2. Click on the **Performance tab** to bring it to the front.

3. Click on the **Change button**. The Virtual Memory dialog box will appear.

The upper section of the dialog box shows you what disks are present, how big they are, and how much space is in use for the swap file.

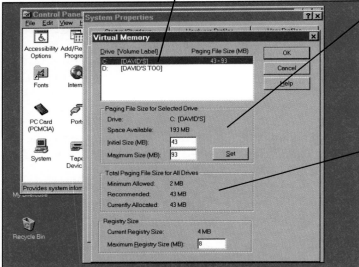

Minimum and maximum file sizes can be changed in the section labeled "Paging File Size for Selected Drive." If you want to set the minimum and maximum to the same size to avoid fragmentation, this is where you'd do it.

The section labeled "Total Paging File Size for All Drives" shows the total size NT recommends for a swap file. A file of this size can be set up on either disk, or the total can be split between the two disks. For example, if a total size of 43 MB is recommended, you could set a 43 MB initial file size, as is shown here, or set a 20 MB initial file size on one disk and a 23 MB initial size on the other hard disk.

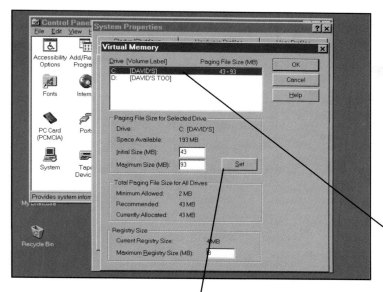

Making Changes

Based on the guidelines earlier in this chapter, and the space available and recommended size in this dialog box, decide how big you want to make the file and whether to use one disk or the other, or both. If you're setting both a minimum and maximum size, be sure to "defrag" the hard disk(s) first.

1. Click on a **hard drive** to highlight it.

2. Click in the **Initial Size box** and **type in** a **number** for the minimum file size.

3. Click in the **Maximum Size box** and **type in** a **number**.

4. Click on **Set**.

5. Repeat steps 1 through 4 for the other hard disk if you are setting up two swap files.

6. Click on **OK**. The dialog box will close.

7. Click on **OK** in the System Properties dialog box. The dialog box will close and a message will appear telling you that you need to reboot the workstation for changes to go into effect.

8. Click on **Yes** in the message box to reboot the workstation.

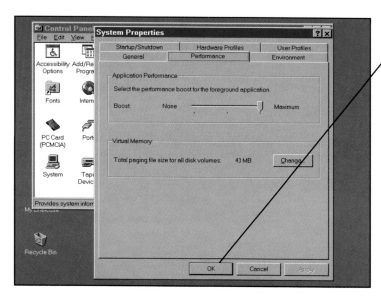

Communicating

Windows NT includes several services that let you connect to the outside world. To use these you need to install Remote Access Services, Dial Up Networking, and, most importantly, your modem. This section takes you through the steps of getting your equipment and NT set up for going online. It's best to follow the chapters in sequence. Even if the setup in a chapter has already been done, it's worth your while to read through it for background information. Online communication with NT is rather complicated, and there are many things about setting it up that can easily be overlooked.

PART

I

PART

II

PART

III

PART

IV

PART

V

PART

VI

PART

VII

Setting Up Your Modem

The first step in getting connected to the outside world is setting up your modem. Windows NT calls this "installing" the modem, though most people would probably consider "installing" a task that involves actually handling hardware. If you are in an office that has technical support, your modem will probably have been set up when Windows NT was installed in your computer. However, since modem setup is not automatic during Windows NT's installation, you may have to do this yourself. You'll certainly have to do it if you are setting up your own workstation or installing a new modem in your computer. Before you start, ask your systems administrator what model and speed the modem is in your computer and what *COM port* it is attached to. If you're on your own, look for this data in the manuals that came with your computer and modem. In this chapter, you will do the following:

✔ See if a modem has been set up on your computer
✔ Use the Install New Modem Wizard to set up a modem
✔ Learn how to check or change your modem's properties
✔ Set up any outside line access codes or phone card numbers that you may need to use

Looking for Your Modem

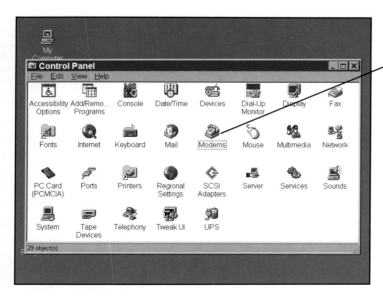

1. Open the **Control Panel window**.

2. Double-click the **Modems icon**.

If your modem has already been set up, the Modems Properties dialog box will appear. (The Modems Properties dialog box is shown later in this chapter.)

If your modem has not been set up, the Location Information dialog box (shown on the next page) will appear.

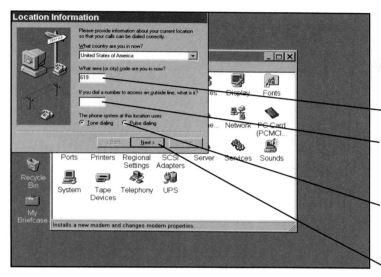

This is where you tell NT where you're dialing from. See "Setting Dialing Properties," later in this chapter, for more on locations.

3. Type in your **Area Code**.

4. Type in the outside line **access code** (such as 9) if you have to use one.

5. Click on **Pulse** if you do **not** have tone (push button) dialing.

6. Click on **Next**. The Install New Modem Wizard will appear.

Working with the Install New Modem Wizard

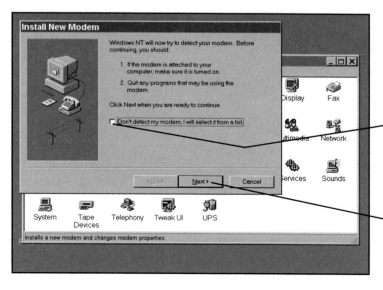

The Install Wizard walks you through the modem setup process. If your computer has an external modem, make sure that it is turned on. First, the Wizard will try to detect your modem by itself.

Note: You can bypass the automatic modem detection and choose from a list of supported modems by clicking in this square to place a ✔ there.

1. Click on **Next**. A dialog box showing COM ports and what the Wizard finds there will appear as the Wizard looks for modems.

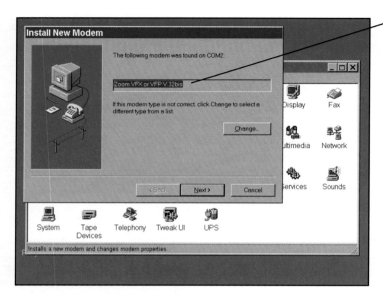

After a few moments, the results will be displayed here. Check the modem model against the information in your computer or modem owner's manual to be sure that it is accurate.

2a. If the modem is correct, **click** on **Next** and skip to step 5 in the next section, "Selecting a Modem."

OR

2b. If the modem is incorrect, **click** the **Change button**. Another Install New Modem dialog box will appear.

Selecting a Modem

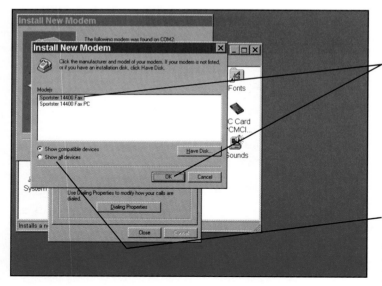

The Wizard shows you a list of modems that it thinks are similar to yours.

1a. If the correct modem is in the list, **click** on **it** to highlight it and then **click** on **OK**. The screen shown at the top of this page will reappear, and you can click on the Next button to proceed to step 5.

OR

1b. If your modem isn't in the list, **click** on **Show all devices**. The dialog box will change to list all modems that NT supports.

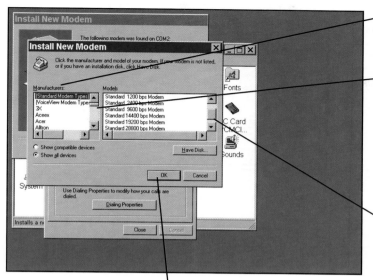

The left side of the list shows modem manufacturers' names below two generic categories.

2. Scroll through the list to find your modem's manufacturer, then **click** on **it** to highlight it. If the manufacturer isn't listed, use the top category, "Standard Modem Types." A list of modem models will appear in the right side of the dialog box.

3. Scroll through the list of models until you see yours and **click** on **it**. If you are selecting a generic ("standard") type, select the highest speed your modem will support.

Note: If you have a modem that is not on these lists, but it came with a diskette that contains drivers for NT 4.0, you can click on the "Have Disk" button in this dialog box. A series of dialog boxes will appear prompting you to insert the diskette and guiding you through the process of installing the drivers. When this process is completed, the screen shown at the top of the previous page will appear listing your modem, and you can click on the Next button to proceed to step 5.

4. Click on **OK**. The screen shown at the top of the previous page will appear, and you can click on the Next button to proceed to step 5.

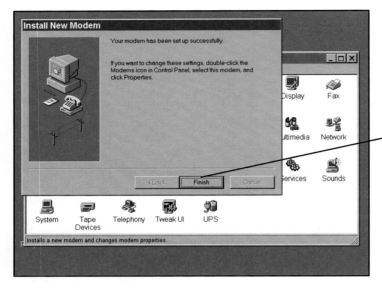

It will take a few moments for the Wizard to finish recording information about your modem so that Windows NT can use it correctly. Once it's done, the dialog box that you see here will appear.

5. Click on **Finish**. The Modems Properties dialog box will appear.

At this point you could close the Modems Properties dialog box and Control Panel window and be done with it. However, you may want to continue to the end of the chapter to see how you can customize and automate your modem's use.

Checking or Changing Your Modem's Properties

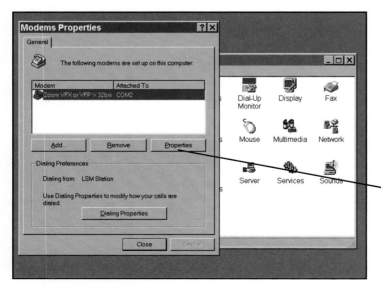

Once a modem has been set up, the Modems Properties dialog box will open when you double-click on the Modems icon in the Control Panel. Your modem and the COM port for which it's set up will be listed. If more than one modem was installed, click the one you want to check to highlight it.

1. Click on **Properties**. A Properties dialog box for the selected modem will appear.

Note: If you need to add another modem, click the Add button and the Install Wizard will start up again.

On the General tab, you can set the volume of your modem's speaker. Set it toward Off to tone down the volume so that the noises the modem makes during a connection are off or barely audible. Set it toward High to hear every detail.

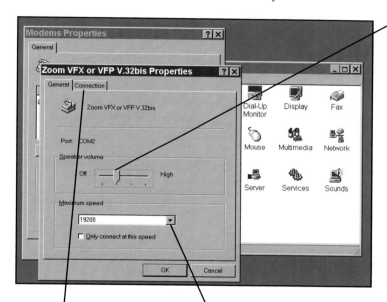

2. Drag the **volume button** to the left or right to adjust the modem's volume down or up.

Your modem's speed will have been set by the Wizard, but can be changed here. Generally, this should be set to a speed just a bit higher than what your modem's manual says it will support. For example, set a 14,400 modem to 19,200. Nearly all modems will automatically adjust their speed down if necessary when connecting to another system. Don't set the speed too high or the modem may not function correctly.

3. Click on the ▼. A list of speeds will appear. You can scroll up or down through the list until you see the speed you want to select. Click on the speed you want to set the modem to.

4. Click on the **Connection tab** to bring it to the front.

You shouldn't have to adjust the Connection properties (Data Bits, Parity, and Stop Bits, shown at the top of the next page) unless the only system you dial into specifies other settings. Nearly all dial-up systems can work with the "8-None-1" settings. One exception is CompuServe's network. However, Windows NT comes with a connection script that will make changes to the connection properties for you automatically when you dial into CompuServe, then set them back to "8-None-1" when you disconnect. We'll point out the script later, in Chapter 24, "Using Dial-Up Networking." These settings can also be set individually for each entry in your Dial-Up Networking phonebook (see Chapter 24).

The Install Wizard automatically selects "Wait for dial tone..." and sets the "Cancel..." time to 60 seconds. If your calls take longer to connect, click on the 60 to highlight it and type in a higher number.

If you are often called away from your computer, you may want to set the automatic disconnect time on this tab to keep from running up connection costs.

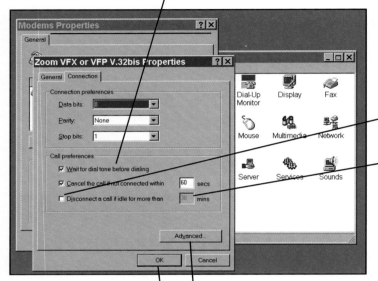

5. Click in the **square** next to "Disconnect..." to select it.

6. Click in the **minutes box** to highlight the number in it and type in the number of minutes you want.

Note: Setting the disconnect time may cause problems if you download large files from remote systems, including the Internet. For example, if you have set the disconnect time to 15 minutes and the file would take 20 to download, the call will disconnect before the download is completed.

The Advanced button brings up a window where you can specify hardware or software flow control and error control for your modem. Unless you are advised by your system administrator or dial-up system to change these, you should not have to.

7. Click on **OK** to save any changes you have made and close the modem's Properties dialog box.

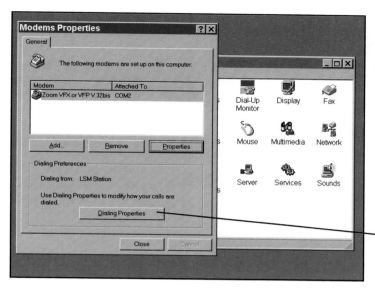

Setting Dialing Properties

Windows NT has added a new feature that it calls "telephony dialing properties." This lets you specify such things as outside line access codes and phone credit card numbers that will be entered automatically each time you make a call using your modem.

1. Click on **Dialing Properties**. The Dialing Properties dialog box will appear.

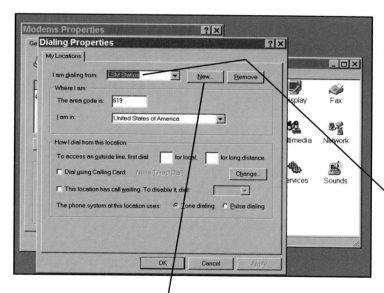

You can create more than one set of dialing properties. NT calls these sets of properties "locations." For example, you may use a credit card for some calls, so you could make one location that uses the credit card and another location that does not. You can name the location anything you want.

The location is shown in this list box. We've already made a location that we called "LSM Station." You can switch between locations by clicking on the ▼ at the time you make a call. We'll demonstrate this in Chapter 24, "Using Dial-Up Networking."

2. Click on **New**. A message will appear telling you that a location has been added.

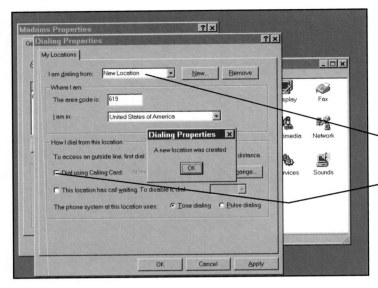

3. Click on **OK** and the message will disappear.

When the message is gone, "New Location" will be highlighted in the "I am calling from" list box.

4. Type in a new **location name**. We used "Calling Card."

5. Click in the **square** next to "Dial using Calling Card" to place a ✔ in it if you use one.

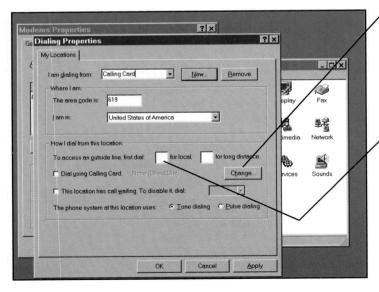

6. Click on **Change**. A dialog box will appear in which you can select a calling card, enter the account number, etc.

You can also specify outside line access codes for each location.

7. Click in the appropriate space and type in any numbers that may be needed for your outside calls.

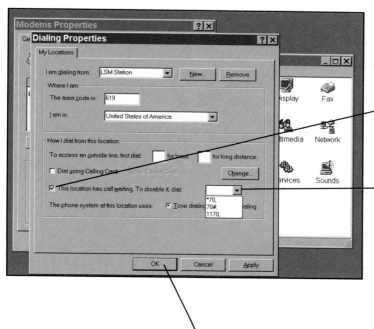

If you have call waiting, you'll want to disable it when you use your modem. Call waiting can cause your modem to disconnect during a call.

8. Click in the **square** next to "This location has call waiting" to place a ✔ in it if you have call waiting.

9. Click on the ▼ to open the drop-down list of call waiting disable codes.

10. Click on the **disable code** for your call waiting system to select it. If you aren't sure what the code is, it should be in your local phone book.

11. Click on **OK** to save your selections and close the Dialing Properties dialog box.

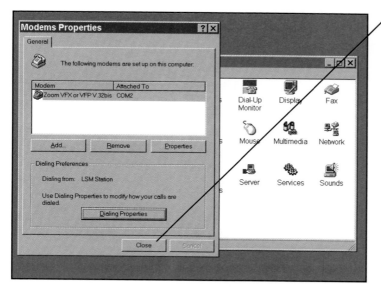

12. Click on **Close**. The Modem Properties dialog box will disappear.

That's it! Your first step in connecting to the outside world is complete. In the next two chapters, you'll add or configure the other two vital components: Remote Access Service and Dial-Up Networking.

CHAPTER 23

Adding Remote Access Service

Remote Access Service (RAS) must be installed for your workstation to connect to an outside network, or for you to connect to your workstation from another location. In order to install RAS, you must be logged on as Administrator or as a member of the Administrators group. RAS setup is quicker if your modem is installed first; see the previous chapter if it is not.

You will need the Windows NT Workstation installation CD or diskettes to install RAS and network protocols. You'll also need to know the phone number and what kind of protocol is in use for any network you want to dial into. If you will be dialing into an Internet Service Provider, you'll need to know their phone number, domain name, and the address of their Domain Name Server (DNS).

If you are on a network, consult with your systems administrator before adding RAS. He or she will have to provide you with lots of network information. This will include the address for your network card, your workstation's name, and whether the network has DHCP, a DNS, WINS, or LMHOSTS (these are files or servers that translate Internet names into numbers). If so, you'll need their addresses. Small, peer-to-peer networks generally don't use these. If you are your own network administrator, you'll know if you do. In this chapter, you will do the following:

✔ Add Remote Access Service to your workstation
✔ Configure TCP/IP for networking

Adding a Network Service

1. **Open** the **Control Panel**.

2. **Double-click** the **Network icon**. The Network dialog box will appear.

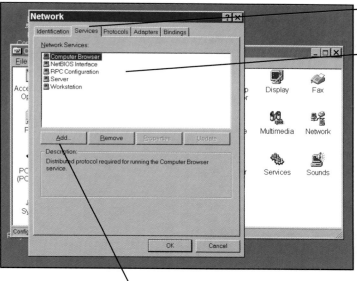

3. Click on the **Services tab** to bring it to the front.

Network services that are already installed for your workstation are listed here. Generally speaking, you shouldn't remove one unless you know it's superfluous. Some may seem to be, but are not. For example, your workstation uses some "Server" services in its routine network operations. A brief description of each one appears in the lower part of the dialog box if you click on the service name.

If Remote Access Service is listed, you don't need to install it. If it isn't listed, proceed to the next step.

4. Click on **Add**. The Select Network Service dialog box will open, and after a moment the services that can be added will be listed in it.

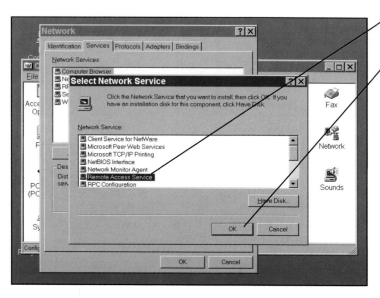

5. Click on **Remote Access Service** to highlight it.

6. Click on **OK**. A Windows NT Setup dialog box will appear and ask for you to insert the installation CD or diskettes.

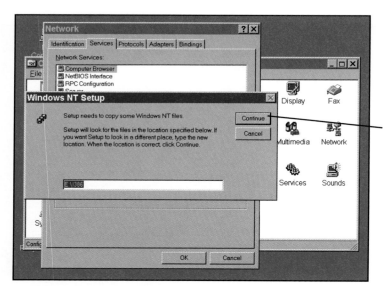

Note: To override the CD's "autorun" feature and keep the CD's startup menu from appearing, hold down the Shift key on your keyboard while you insert the CD.

7. Insert the **installation CD** into your CD drive and **click** on **Continue**.

Another message will appear while files are being copied, showing you its progress. When the files have been copied, the Add RAS Device dialog box will appear. You will need the installation CD again later if the network protocols you'll need haven't been installed, so leave it in your CD drive for now.

Adding a Remote Access Service Device

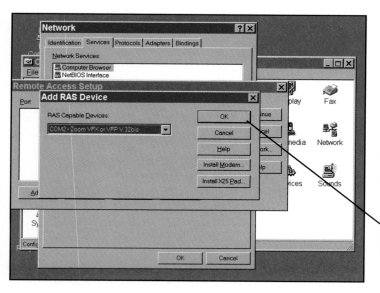

RAS needs to know what piece of hardware is going to be used with it for your remote connection. In nearly all cases, this "device" will be your workstation's modem. The Add RAS Device dialog box will list your modem if it is already installed. If it is not installed, click on the Install Modem button and follow the modem installation steps shown in the previous chapter.

1. Click on **OK** if your modem is listed. The Remote Access Setup dialog box will appear.

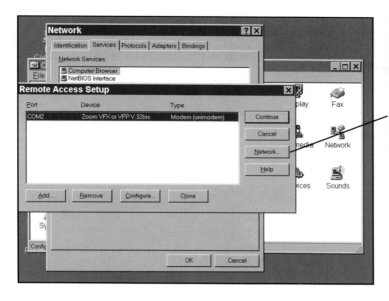

The device you selected will be highlighted. Now you have to tell RAS what network protocols you want to be able to use with the modem.

2. Click on **Network**. The Network Configuration dialog box will appear.

Selecting Network Protocols

RAS needs to know what network protocol is used for the network you want to connect to. You can install more than one, but don't install protocols that you don't need; they'll just use up valuable memory and make the connection process slower and more complicated than it has to be.

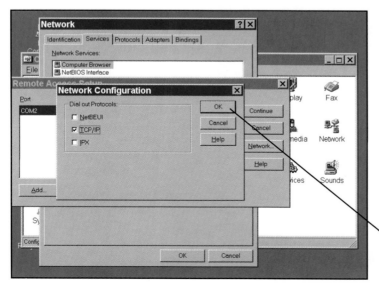

❖ If you're going to be dialing into the Internet or a UNIX network, you'll need to select TCP/IP.

❖ For interacting with Windows networks, you'll need NetBEUI.

❖ Novell networks use IPX.

1. Click on the **box** next to the protocol you need to place a check mark in it.

2. Click on **OK**. The Network Configuration dialog box will disappear.

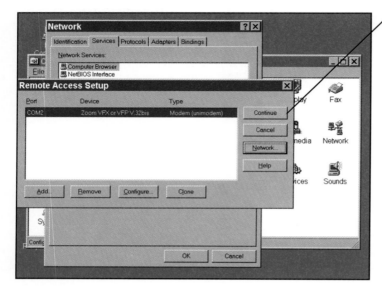

3. Click on **Continue**.

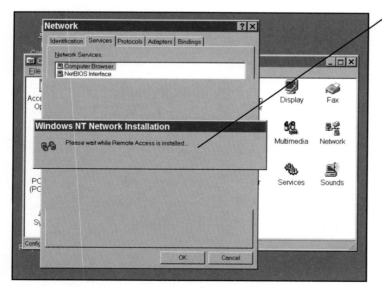

A Windows NT Network Installation message box asking you to "Please wait..." will appear for a few moments. Next, the Windows NT Setup dialog box (shown earlier) will appear again, asking for the NT installation CD.

Note: If the network protocol(s) you selected were previously installed, you will not be asked for the CD.

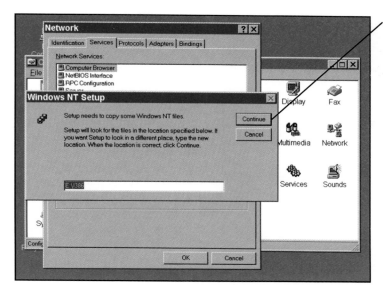

4. Click on **Continue**. The dialog box will change to show you the progress of file copying.

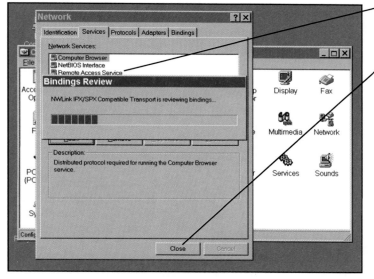

Once RAS is installed, it's added to the list of Network Services.

5. Click on **Close**. The message shown in this screen will appear as NT checks the network *bindings*. Bindings are the interrelationships between the network services, network protocols, and network adaptors that are installed.

If you didn't add the TCP/IP protocol, you'll be prompted to restart your computer; click on Yes to restart the workstation and complete the RAS installation.

If you installed TCP/IP, you'll receive a message (not shown here) telling you that you have to configure it. Click on the OK button in the message box and proceed to the next section.

Configuring TCP/IP

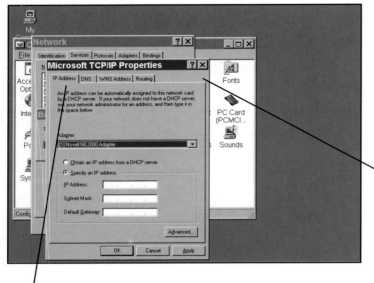

Note: Read through this section and collect the information you'll need before entering any data into this dialog box.

When TCP/IP is first installed, the TCP/IP Properties dialog box will come up automatically, unless you're on a network that has the Dynamic Host Configuration Protocol (DHCP) and DHCP has been enabled for your workstation. If your network has a DHCP server, you won't need to configure TCP/IP.

The IP Address tab has a space for your network card's address and subnet mask number. Fill them in if you have one. If your network has a DHCP server, select "Obtain an IP address from a DHCP server." If you're using a stand-alone workstation, you can ignore this tab.

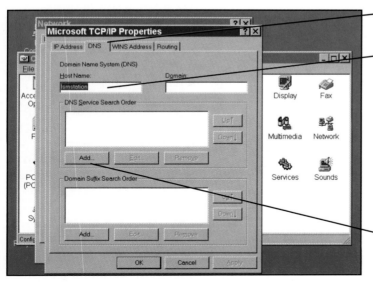

1. Click on the **DNS tab** to bring it to the front.

2. Type the **name of your computer** in the Host Name box. This is its name on your network, or the name you gave it during NT installation if it's a stand-alone workstation.

3. Type your **network or ISP's domain name** in the Domain box, or leave it blank (it's optional).

4. Click on **Add** in the DNS Service Search Order section. The TCP/IP DNS Server dialog box will appear.

5. Type in the **address** for your network's or your ISP's domain name server.

6. Click on **Add**. The address will be added to the dialog box.

7. Repeat this process to add Domain Suffixes if advised to do so by your network administrator. This isn't necessary for a stand-alone workstation.

If your network has a Windows Internet Name Server (WINS), add its address on the WINS Address tab and, if appropriate, enable LMHOSTS lookup.

Ask your network administrator if DHCP, the network's DNS, WINS, or LMHOSTS are set up on your network. These are servers or files that translate host names into numerical addresses. Also ask if IP Forwarding (enabled on the Routing tab) is available. Don't enable or try to configure these if they are not available on your network.

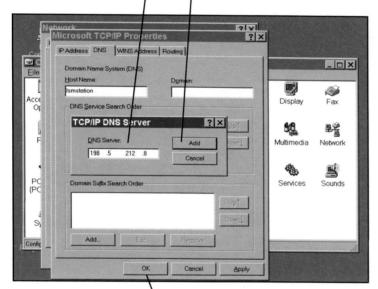

If you are using NT on a stand-alone workstation, a DNS server address is provided by your Internet Service Provider, and DHCP, WINS, LMHOSTS, and IP Forwarding won't apply.

8. When finished, **click** on **OK** to apply and save your settings.

Note: Clicking on OK has the same effect as clicking on Apply, except that OK also closes the dialog box.

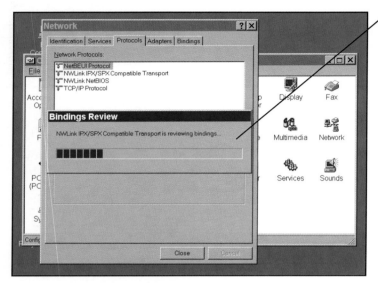

A couple of message boxes will appear as *bindings* are reviewed and stored. Bindings are the connections between adaptors, services, and protocols that let them work together so that your networking will work correctly. For example, RAS (a service), and TCP/IP (a protocol) have to be "bound together" for dial-up access to the Internet to work. Fortunately, NT takes care of bindings for you.

At this point, you may receive a message telling you that the WINS address was not set up for your adaptor card and asking if you want to continue. If your network has WINS and you forgot to enter it, click on No, go to the WINS Address tab and fill it in. If you have a stand-alone workstation or WINS is not set up for your network, ignore the message and click on Yes.

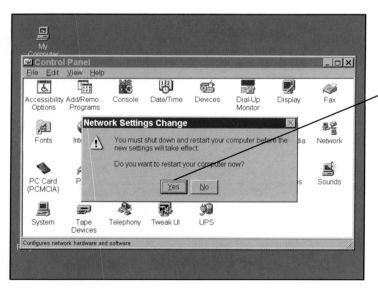

Eventually, the Bindings Review will be complete and you'll be asked to reboot your workstation.

9. Click on **Yes** to reboot your workstation.

Once it's back up and running, you can proceed to setting up Dial-Up Networking in the next chapter.

Using Dial-Up Networking

Dial-Up Networking (DUN) is the third vital component, after your modem and Remote Access Service, that is needed to connect your workstation to a remote network, or to dial in to a workstation from another location. DUN can be started before using network or Internet programs, or set to connect you automatically (autodial) whenever you start a program that requires the remote connection. DUN uses a phonebook entry for each network or Internet Service Provider (ISP) you connect to. To set one up, you'll need to know the phone number, whether to use PPP (Point-to-Point Protocol) or SLIP (Serial Line Internet Protocol), whether you have been assigned a permanent *IP address*, whether you need to specify a DNS or WINS address, and your user name and password. If the connection can be automated using a script file, your network or ISP should provide you with a copy of it. In this chapter, you will do the following:

✔ Add a listing to your Dial-Up Networking phonebook
✔ Customize a listing in your phonebook
✔ Create a desktop shortcut for a phonebook entry
✔ Check out the Dial-Up Networking Monitor

Starting Dial-Up Networking

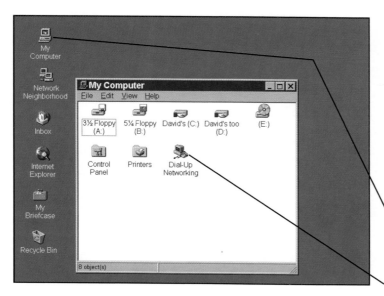

Dial-Up Networking (DUN) is started from its icon in the My Computer window. You can also create a shortcut for DUN on your desktop, or place one on your Startup menu for convenience. (See Chapters 9 and 10.) If you choose not to use auto-dial, you can always start DUN and make your connection this way.

1. Double-click the **My Computer icon**. The My Computer window will appear.

2. Double-click the **Dial-Up Networking icon**.

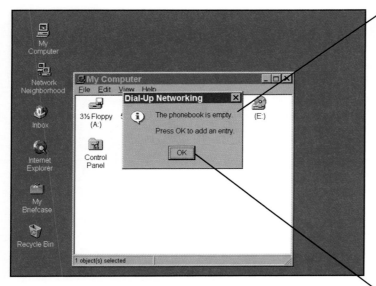

If you haven't used DUN before, this message appears. By clicking on OK, you can either use the New Phonebook Entry Wizard to create phonebook entries, or turn the Wizard off and make an entry by yourself. You can always get the Wizard back; we'll show you how later.

If an entry has already been set up in the phonebook, the DUN dialog box (see "Modifying Phonebook Entries and Settings" in this chapter) will appear.

3. Click on **OK**. The New Phonebook Entry Wizard will start.

Adding Phonebook Entries with the Wizard

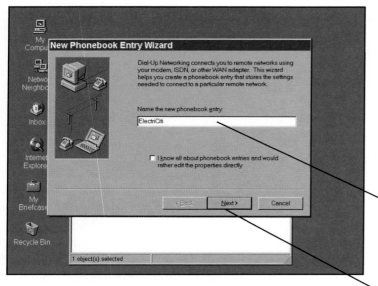

The Wizard makes setting up a new entry easy. Once it's there, however, our experience has been that an entry always needs some tinkering to get it to work exactly the way we want it to. First, we'll set up an entry with the Wizard, and in the next section, we'll show you how an entry can be made or modified without the Wizard.

1. Type a **name** for your phonebook entry. We've used the name of our excellent Internet Service Provider, ElectriCiti.

2. Click on **Next**. Another Wizard dialog box will appear.

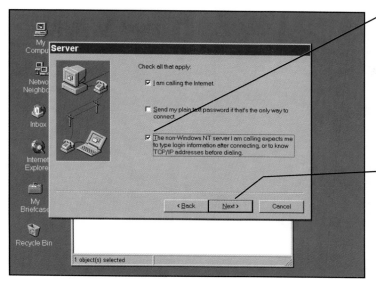

3. Click in the appropriate **boxes** to place ✔ in them. If you click one that turns out not to be necessary, it doesn't matter. The settings that the Wizard makes for the new entry can always be modified later if they don't work or don't work as well as they should.

4. Click on **Next**. Another Wizard dialog box will appear.

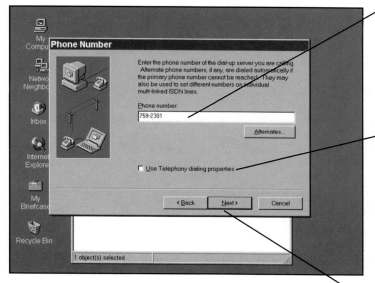

5. Type the **phone number**. If the network or ISP you're calling has more than one phone number, click the Alternates button and enter the other number(s) in the dialog box that appears.

If you have call waiting, need outside line access codes, are calling another area code, or want to use a credit card for your call to this number, select "Use Telephony dialing properties." Additional boxes for country code and area code will appear. We'll discuss this more later in the chapter.

6. Click on **Next**. Another Wizard dialog box will appear.

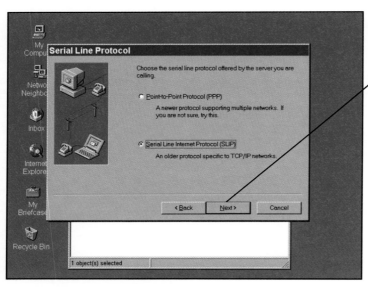

7. Click in the **box** next to the appropriate type of connection to select it.

8. Click on **Next**. Another Wizard dialog box will appear.

If a script can be used to automate your connection but you don't have it yet, it can be added later. If you don't need a script (most PPP connections do not), click next to "None." If you want to type in the logon information each time you make the connection, click next to "Use a terminal window."

We use a script for our ElectriCiti connection in this example, so we copied it to the WINNT\System32\ras\ directory in advance. This is the directory where NT looks for scripts. You may want to make a note of its name if you will be copying a script file to it later.

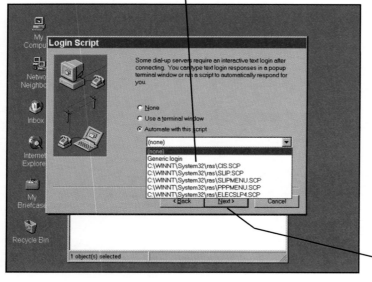

Several sample scripts are included with NT, including one that changes COM port settings for dialing into CompuServe's network and restores them when you disconnect. You can select one of these scripts now and edit it as needed. (The CompuServe script does not need to be edited.) There's more on editing scripts later in the chapter.

9. Click on a **script** to select it.

10. Click on **Next**. Another Wizard dialog box will appear.

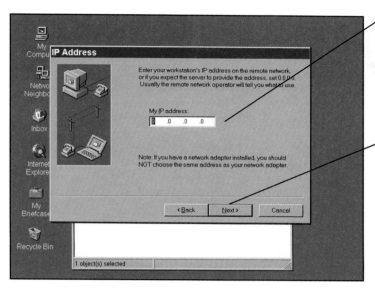

11. If your network or ISP has assigned a permanent IP address to you, enter it here. If a different IP address is assigned each time you connect, leave the "0.0.0.0" as it is.

12. Click on **Next**. Another Wizard dialog box will appear.

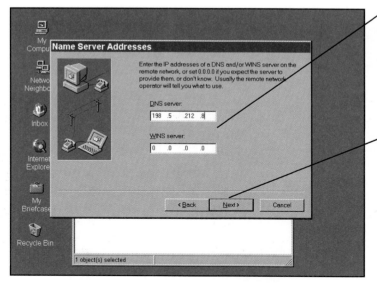

13. If your network or ISP has given you a DNS (Domain Name Server) or WINS (Windows Internet Name Server) address to use, enter it here. If not, leave the boxes as they are.

14. Click on **Next**. Another Wizard dialog box will appear.

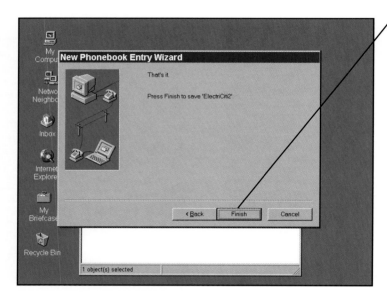

15. Click Finish. The Dial-Up Networking dialog box will appear.

Modifying Phonebook Entries and Settings

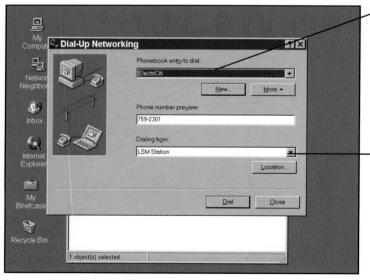

The entry you just added, if you've been following along, appears here. Other entries can be added by clicking on the New button. Then the new entry can be selected by clicking on the ▼ next to the "Phonebook entry" to dial box.

If you have set up different locations for using telephony dialing properties, such as an outside line access code or phone credit card, you can select the location you want to use by clicking on the ▼ next to the "Dialing from" box. (See "Setting Dialing Properties" in Chapter 22.)

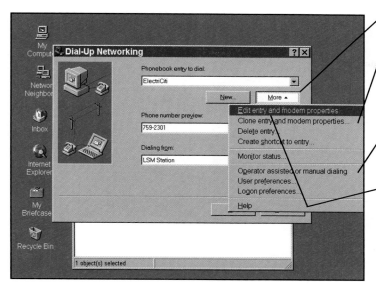

1. Click on **More**. A menu will appear.

The choices in this part of the menu apply only to the entry that is highlighted in the "Phonebook entry to dial" box.

Choices in this part of the menu apply to all entries.

2. Click on **Edit entry and modem properties**. The Edit Phonebook Entry dialog box will appear.

On the Basic tab, you can change the entry's name or phone number.

You can also select "Use Telephony dialing properties" if you have call waiting, need to dial an outside line, want to use a credit card, or use any of the other telephony options (see "Setting Dialing Properties" in Chapter 22).

Some systems that you dial into may tell you that you need settings for flow control, error control, or data compression that are different from the default settings. If so, click on the Configure button next to the box that lists your modem to make these changes for this entry only.

3. Click on the **Server tab** to bring it to the front.

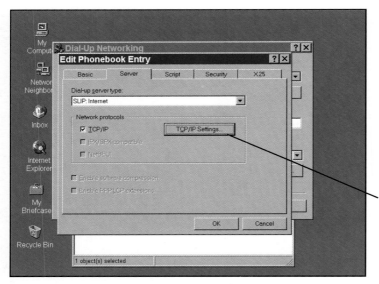

The Server tab lets you specify the server you will connect to using this list box. Types include SLIP, PPP, and Windows (for dialing into a Windows network).

If TCP/IP is used for connecting with this phonebook entry, you can make changes to its settings.

4. Click on **TCP/IP Settings**. A TCP/IP Settings dialog box will appear.

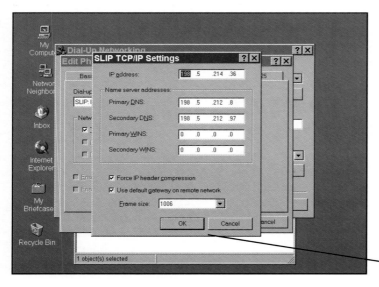

If you have a permanent IP address, it will be listed here. If you are assigned a different one each time you connect, the last one you were assigned will be listed here.

If your ISP or network changes its DNS address or you want to add a secondary DNS, type it in here.

If your ISP uses SLIP and requires a particular frame size, it can be set here.

5. Click OK to save your changes and close the dialog box, **or Cancel** to close without making any changes.

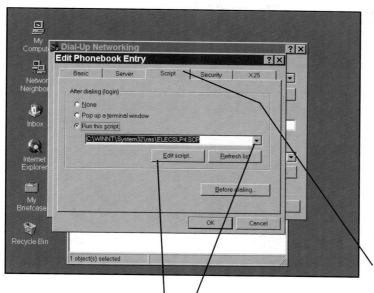

Editing a Script

Scripts can be used to automate your connections by entering your username or password for you or setting up parameters for your COM port or modem. Scripts are used mostly for SLIP connections and generally aren't used for PPP. If the connection to your ISP uses a script, your ISP should provide a copy of it. NT comes with generic scripts that you can edit.

1. Click the **Script tab** to bring it to the front.

On this tab you can choose to run a script or not, or select one from the drop-down list that opens when you click on the ▼. You can edit a script after it's been selected.

2. Click on **Edit script**. The script file will open in Notepad.

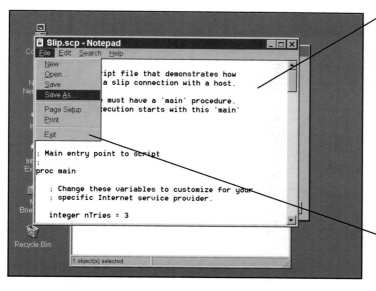

You can use Notepad to read through the generic scripts that come with NT to see if they can be used for your connection, or to modify a script that you received from your network administrator or ISP. If you customize one of NT's generic scripts for your connection, save it with a new name using the Save As command so that the original generic script won't be overwritten.

3. Click on **File** then on **Exit** to close Notepad without making any changes.

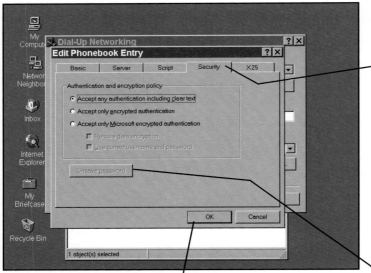

Selecting Levels of Security

1. Click on the **Security tab** to bring it to the front.

Authentication is a security measure used during logon. Make a note of these options and ask your network administrator or ISP if they are used. If you don't know or the connection doesn't use any, select the top choice, "Accept any..."

Notice the Unsave Password button. When you sign on to a system, DUN asks for your username and password and gives you the option of saving your password to make your next connection more convenient. If you have saved the password but want to change it or unsave it later, click on the Unsave Password button on this dialog box.

2. Click on **OK** to save your changes or **Cancel**. The dialog box will close.

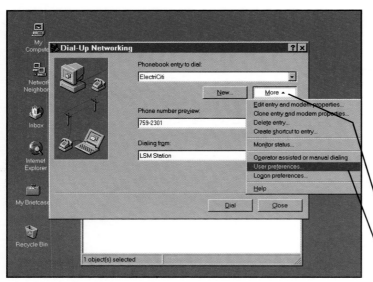

Setting Autodial and Other User Preferences

Autodial automatically starts DUN when you use a program such as Internet Explorer that needs to connect to a dial-up system such as your ISP.

1. Click on **More**. A menu will appear.

2. Click on **User preferences**. The User Preferences dialog box will appear.

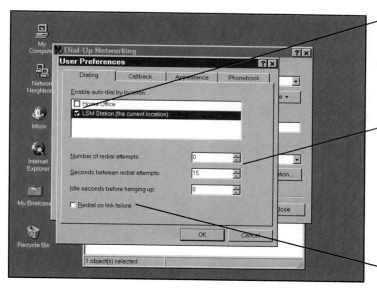

3. Click in the **box** next to a location name to enable autodial for that location. DUN will start automatically when you open a program that requires a dial-up connection.

To have DUN keep trying a difficult connection, set the number of attempts here. If the connection sometimes "hangs" (does nothing) at logon, set an "Idle seconds" number, but remember that some systems take a while to get going.

For DUN to redial if you get disconnected, check here.

If the system you call uses "callback" for security, click on the Callback tab and enable it. If you shut off the New Phonebook Entry Wizard but want it turned back on, click on the Appearance tab and enable it.

4. Click on **OK** to save your changes or **Cancel**.

Creating a Connection Shortcut

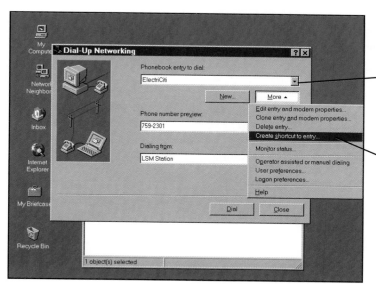

For convenience, you may want to place a shortcut for a connection on your desktop.

1. Select the **connection**.

2. Click on **More**. A menu will appear.

3. Click on **Create shortcut to entry**. A Create Shortcut dialog box (not shown here) will appear.

4. Click OK. The shortcut icon will appear on your desktop (it may be hidden behind an open dialog box at first).

Making a Connection

Start DUN from its icon in the My Computer window, or put a copy of the icon on your Start menu (see Chapter 10). You can also make a shortcut for a particular connection and start it from your desktop (see the previous section). We'll show autodial in the next chapter. If for any reason autodial doesn't function, you can work around it by making your connection first, as shown here, and then starting the program that requires a dial-up connection.

1. Open Dial-Up Networking.

2. Select the **connection** you want to use.

3. Click on **Dial**. A Connect to dialog box will appear.

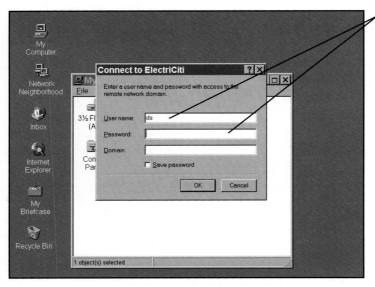

4. Type your **username** and **password**.

5. Click in the **box** next to "Save password" if you want to use this convenient feature. The next time you want to dial this connection, you won't have to go through this dialog box. If you save the password, any one with access to your workstation will be able to use this phonebook entry. You can "unsave" the password later if you want to (see "Selecting Levels of Security," earlier in this chapter).

6. Click on **OK**. DUN will make the connection.

Using the Dial-Up Networking Monitor

When a connection has been made, the Dial-Up Networking Monitor's icon will appear in the taskbar tray. The Monitor is a terminate-and-stay-resident (TSR) program. This is particularly convenient if you connect to and disconnect from your ISP or dial-up network several times during the day.

1. Double-click the **Monitor icon**. The Dial-Up Networking Monitor dialog box will appear.

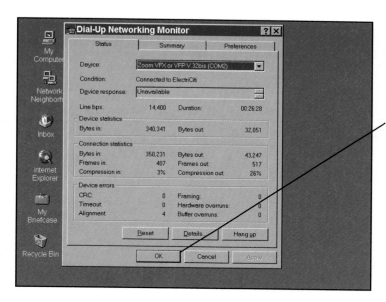

The Dial-Up Networking Monitor dialog box has three tabs that give you information about your connection and let you set Monitor preferences.

2. Click on **OK or Cancel**. The dialog box will close, but you will remain connected.

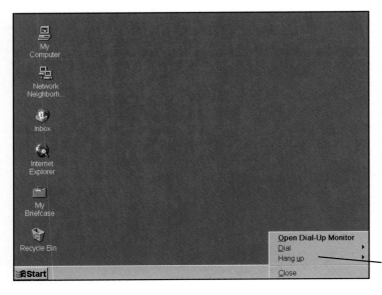

3. Right-click on the **Monitor icon**. A small menu will appear.

If you make several dial-up connections during the day, you may want to leave the Monitor running for convenience. You can use this menu to select a connection to dial and to hang it up when you're done. The other menu choices open the dialog box shown in the previous screen, or close the Monitor.

4. Move the **mouse pointer** over Hang up. The list of active connections will appear.

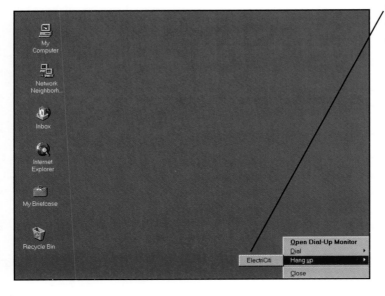

5. Click the **connection** you want to hang up. A message will appear.

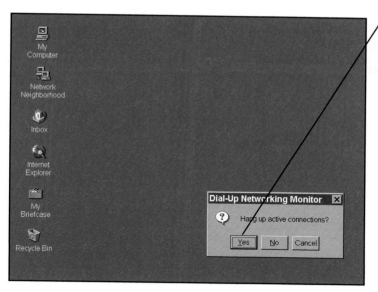

6. Click Yes to hang up the connection. Your modem will hang up, but the Dial-Up Networking Monitor will still be running.

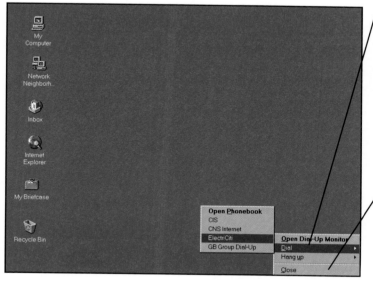

7. The next time you want to connect, **right-click** on the **Dial-Up Networking Monitor icon** and **move** the **mouse pointer** over **Dial**. A menu listing phonebook entries will appear.

8. Click on the **phonebook entry** you want to dial. DUN will make the connection.

9. To turn the Monitor off, or to hang up your connection and turn the Monitor off, **click** on **Close**.

Surfing With Internet Explorer

Internet Explorer is Microsoft's World Wide Web browser. In addition to Internet Web pages, Explorer can be used to display HTML (Hypertext Markup Language) and graphics files on your workstation and other computers in your network. Explorer is in a state of constant evolution. Soon after NT 4.0's release, a newer version became available; we'll show you how to find and install it. Before doing that, we'll show you an autodial connection and give you some tips on using Explorer that also apply to the newer version. Please note that the update file for Internet Explorer that we downloaded as an example in this chapter took just over an hour to download using a 14,400 baud modem. Also, Microsoft strongly recommends that you install NT 4.0's Service Pack 1 (see Chapter 33, "Adding Features to NT") before installing the updated version of Internet Explorer. You will need to have completed Chapters 22 ("Setting Up Your Modem"), 23 ("Adding Remote Access Service"), and 24 ("Using Dial-Up Networking") to use Explorer with a dial-up Internet Service Provider, as is shown in our example. In this chapter, you will do the following:

✔ Start Internet Explorer and connect to the World Wide Web
✔ Try out some of the browser's features
✔ Visit Microsoft's WWW site, and download and install a newer version of Explorer

Starting Internet Explorer

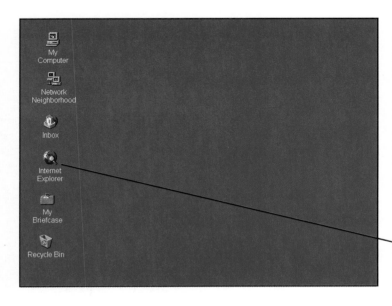

Explorer's icon is placed on your desktop during NT's installation. Because it doesn't work like other icons and shortcuts, we recommend that you don't delete it. If you do and later want to use Explorer, you'll have to reinstall the program. If you must remove the icon from your desktop, use the Tweak program that we'll tell you about in Chapter 33, "Adding Features to NT."

1. Double-click the **Internet Explorer icon**. The Internet Explorer window will appear.

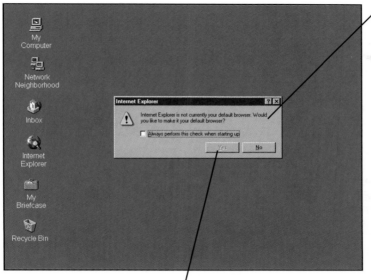

When you start Internet Explorer, you may receive the message, "Internet Explorer is not currently your default browser..." as shown here. This is because Windows associates certain file types with certain programs. For example, if you double-click a text file (one with the .txt extension) in Windows NT Explorer, the Notepad program opens to display it. The message means that no browser program has been associated with the types of files that browsers display.

You will see this message each time you open Explorer unless you either click on Yes, or you click in the square next to "Always perform this check when starting up" to remove the ✔. Some browsers cleverly make themselves the default during installation. If you add another browser later, you may see the message again the next time you use Internet Explorer.

2. Click on **Yes** if you want Explorer to be your default browser; otherwise, **click** on **No**.

Initially, Explorer displays this generic page. It was copied to your computer's hard disk during NT's installation. Though this page isn't located on the World Wide Web, it's very similar to what you'll find there. You can designate a different page that will be displayed when Explorer starts, but you must have the page showing in Explorer to do this. We'll show you how later in the chapter.

3. Scroll down the **page** to see the rest of it.

Web pages are files that are written in HTML (Hypertext Markup Language). They use *hyperlinks* to connect you to other Web pages and Internet resources. These links can take the form of icons, graphics, or text that's underlined or in a distinctive color to make it stand out.

When you click on a link, the browser sends a message over the Internet to the computer that has the Web page or other resource that the link represents. The other computer then sends a copy of the page to your computer, where it's displayed in Internet Explorer.

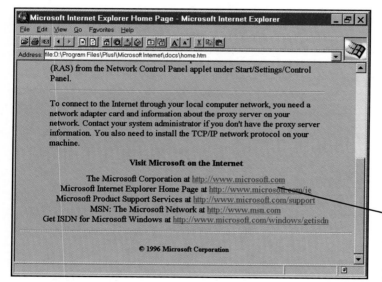

If you want to see what HTML looks like, click on View in the menu bar, then click on Source. Notepad will open and display the HTML file for this page. (Click on the ⊠ in the upper-right corner of Notepad's window to close it.)

At the bottom of the page are several links, in the form of underlined text.

4. Click on a **link**. Internet Explorer will start looking for the linked page.

If your Internet connection is through your company's network, your systems administrator will handle the NT setup that's needed to make the connection work, and you can skip the next section ("Autodialing"). If you connect through your workstation's modem and a dial-up Internet Service Provider, read on.

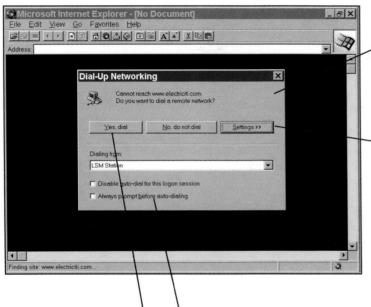

Autodialing

If autodial is enabled, this message box will appear. If not, you will receive an error message (Note 1 or 2 on the next page).

1. Quickly click on **Settings**, or Dial-Up Networking (DUN) will automatically select "No, do not dial" and the message box will disappear. Ordinarily, you would just click on "Yes, dial," but we want to show you something. If the lower half of the message box disappears, click on the Settings button again to get it back.

We recommend selecting "Always prompt before auto-dialing" if you use more than one connection. This lets you choose which connection to dial. Otherwise, autodial will automatically redial the last successful connection.

2. Click on **Yes, dial**. If this is the first time you've used DUN or if you selected "Always prompt before auto-dialing," the DUN dialog box will appear. Otherwise, DUN will just dial, and various messages will appear as the connection is made.

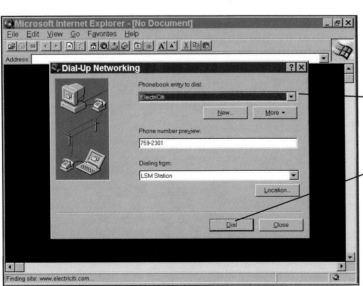

3. Click on the ▼ next to the **Phonebook entry to dial** box if needed to find and click on the entry you want to use.

4. Click on **Dial**. If this is the first time you've used DUN, or if you do not save your password (see step 5), a dialog box for the connection will appear. Otherwise, various messages will appear as DUN makes the connection.

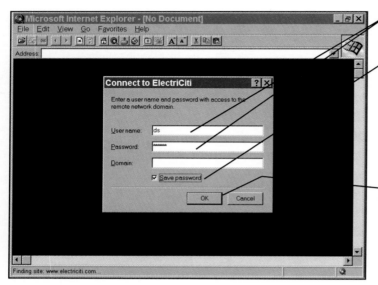

5. Type in your **user name** and **password**.

6. Click on **Save password** if you want to use this convenience feature and don't have to worry about security (others with access to your workstation can use this connection if it's selected).

7. Click on **OK**. Various messages will appear as the connection is made.

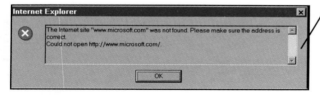

Note 1: If you do not use autodial or it does not function correctly, you may receive an error message similar to the one shown here. If this happens, use Dial-Up Networking to make your Internet connection (see "Making a Connection" in Chapter 24), then use Internet Explorer.

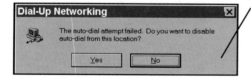

Note 2: If autodial is working correctly, but the connection is not made, you will receive the error message shown here. Click on No. (Yes disables autodial.) If autodial is accidentally disabled, see "Setting Autodial and Other User Preferences" in Chapter 24 to re-enable it.

This section detailed the final steps for automating autodial. After a successful connection is made, DUN will "remember" it and autodial the connection the next time you need it. Messages in NT newsgroups (see Chapter 35, "Finding Out More About NT") have reported difficulties in getting autodial to work correctly, so if you have problems, you're not alone.

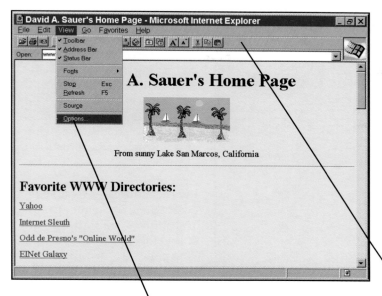

Setting the Start Page

You can set the page that displays when you first start Explorer. If you followed along in the previous sections, you'll see Microsoft's home page instead of this one. We've already set the page shown here our Start Page. You have to go to the page you want to use for a Start Page to set it.

Internet Explorer has toolbar buttons to use for navigating the Web, printing or saving Web pages that you find, and so on. Rest the mouse pointer over a button to see a little tag showing its function.

1. Click on **View** in the menu bar. The View menu will appear.

2. Click on **Options**. The Options dialog box will appear.

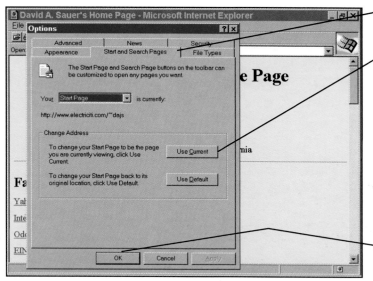

3. Click on the **Start and Search Pages** tab to bring it to the front.

After you're at the page you want to use as your start page, you can click on "Use Current" to select it. "Use Default" selects the generic page shown earlier in this chapter.

The other tabs contain more options that you can set. Use the [?] button (see Chapter 8, "Using Help") to explore them.

4. Click on **OK** to save your choices and close the dialog box.

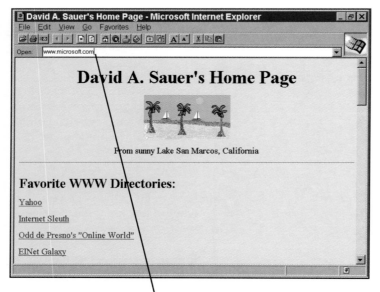

Browsing

You can go to other Web pages by clicking on a link, as mentioned earlier in the chapter. You also can go to another page or site by entering an address (also called an URL, for "Universal Resource Locator") in the Open box and pressing Enter.

Internet addresses seem to be everywhere in the media today. The address can start with any of several prefixes: *http://* for a Web page, *ftp://* for an archive site where you can download files, *gopher://* for a text-only information source, or *file://* for a file located on your computer or another workstation in your network. You don't have to include the prefix when you type an address in the Open box.

1. If you're not already at Microsoft's home page, **type www.microsoft.com** in the **Open box** and **press** the **Enter** key on your keyboard. Microsoft's home page will appear.

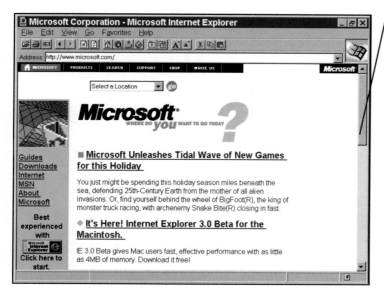

In nearly all cases, the Web page that Explorer retrieves for you won't fit in the screen. Use standard scrollbar techniques to view the whole page.

As you move your mouse pointer around the screen, it will occasionally turn into a hand. When this happens, the pointer is over a link. The address of the link will appear in the Status bar at the bottom of the Explorer window.

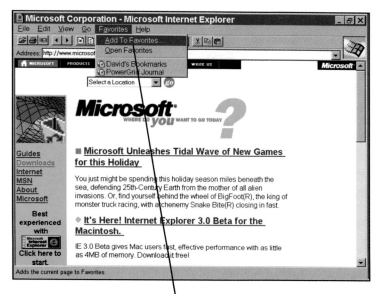

Saving Favorites

When you find a page you know you'll want to see again, you can save it in your Favorites folder. This applies to pages or files located on your computer or other computers in your network, as well as to those on the Web.

1. Make sure you are viewing the page you want to save.

2. Click on **Favorites** in the menu bar. The Favorites menu will appear. A couple of favorites that we added in advance show up in the lower part of the menu in this example.

3. Click on **Add to Favorites**. The Add To Favorites dialog box will appear.

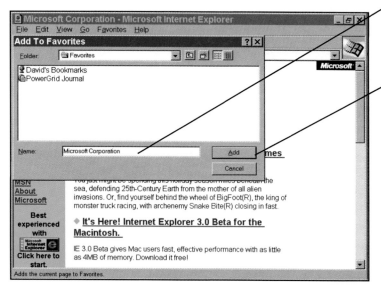

You can change the favorite item's name if you want to by clicking in the name box and typing the name you want.

4. Click on **Add**. The item will be added to your Favorites folder.

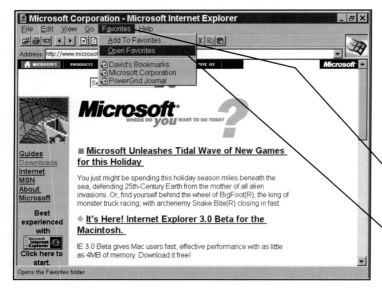

Organizing Favorites

The Favorites folder works just like any other folder. You can create additional folders within it to organize your favorite Web pages.

1. Click on **Favorites** in the menu bar. The Favorites menu will appear.

2. Click on **Open Favorites**. The Favorites window will appear. If you followed along in the last section, there will be at least one icon in the folder, for Microsoft Corporation. There are three in the example shown here.

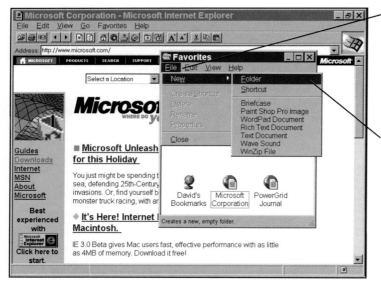

3. Click on **File** in the Favorites menu bar. The File menu will appear.

4. Move the **mouse pointer** over New. The New menu will appear.

5. Click on **Folder**. A new folder will appear. The new folder can be named and Web page icons can be dragged-and-dropped into it.

6. Click on the ☒ in the upper-right corner of the Favorites window to close it.

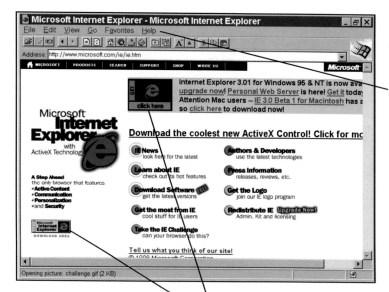

Finding Internet Explorer Updates

To see what version of Explorer you have, click on Help in the menu bar, then on "About Internet Explorer" in the Help menu. A dialog box with Explorer's version number in it will appear. It's easy to find updated versions of Explorer for downloading.

1. Type www.microsoft.com/ie/ (no spaces) in the Open box and press Enter. The Internet Explorer Web page will appear.

2. Click on an **icon or hypertext link** that indicates it leads to the download area. There are at least two on this page.

Note: Web pages change all the time, especially at busy, commercial sites like Microsoft's. The pages you see may not be exactly the same as the ones shown here.

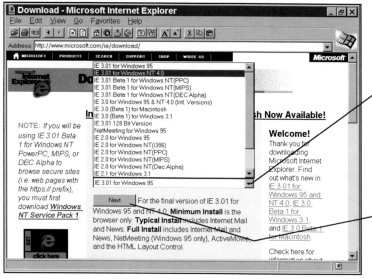

At the download page, select the updated version of Internet Explorer that you want to download from the list box.

3. Click on the ▼ to open the list, and **scroll** up or down until you see the latest version for Windows NT 4.0.

4. Click on the **version** you want. The list will close.

5. Click on **Next**. Another Web page will appear.

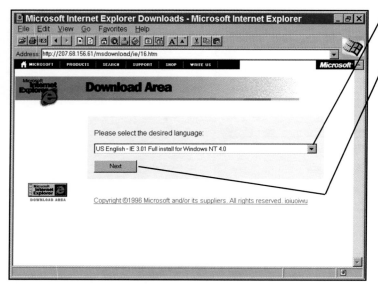

6. Select the **language** you want just as you selected the version.

7. Click on **Next**. Another Web page will appear.

Before we proceed, we want to remind you that it takes about an hour to download this file using a 14,400 baud modem. If you don't want to spend that much time on this exercise, skip to step 12 and just read through the next few pages to see how it's done.

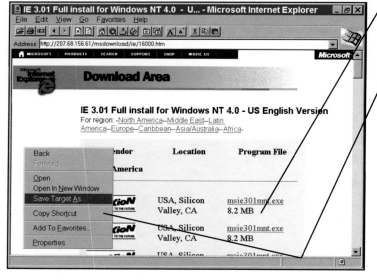

8a. Right-click on the blue, underlined text **link** for one of the download sites. A menu will appear.

9a. Click on **Save Target As**. The Save As dialog box will appear.

OR

8b. Click on the blue, underlined text **link** for one of the download sites. The Confirm File Open dialog box will appear.

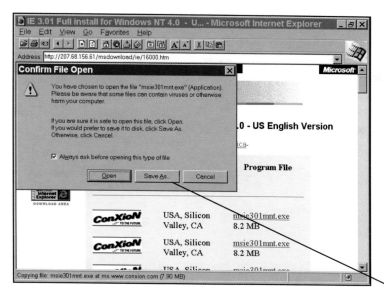

Explorer brings up this dialog box whenever you select a file that it isn't certain how to handle, such as this executable (.exe) file. You could click on Open to download and automatically run the file, but saving it to your hard drive and running it later gives you more control over the process. Also, some setup files that you may download are written to erase themselves after setup. If this happened, you wouldn't be able to save a copy of the setup file for backup purposes.

9b. Click on **Save As**. The Save As dialog box will appear.

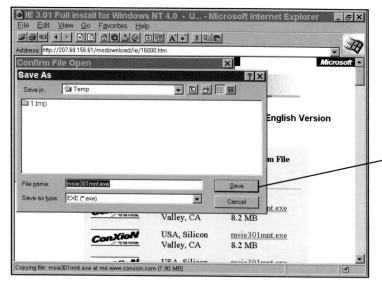

10. Select a **folder** (directory) for saving the downloaded file. In this example, we selected one that we named Temp. Make a note of the name of the file and where you save it so that you can find it for installation in the next section.

11. Click on **Save**. A message box will appear that shows you the download's progress.

12. Close Explorer and use the Dial-Up Networking Monitor to **hang up the connection** after the download is completed.

Installing the Explorer Update

Note: Microsoft recommends that you install the NT 4.0 Service Pack 1 before upgrading Explorer. See Chapter 33, "Adding Features to NT," for more on the Service Pack.

The new version of Explorer will copy any preferences you have set up in the old version.

1. Click on **Run** in the Start menu. The Run dialog box will appear.

2. Type in the **path** to the update file that you downloaded, or click on the Browse button to locate it.

3. Click on **OK**. Explorer setup will begin and the License Agreement (not shown here) will appear.

4. Read the **License Agreement**. If you agree with the terms, continue; if not, click No and installation will stop.

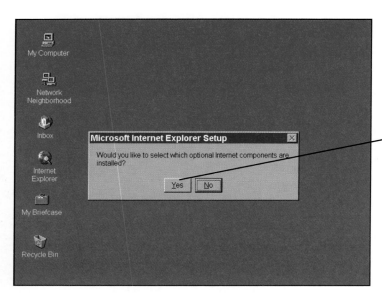

5. Click on the **Yes** button under the agreement to proceed with installation. A message will appear and show that files are being extracted. After a few moments, another message will appear.

6. Click on **Yes**. The Optional Components dialog box will appear.

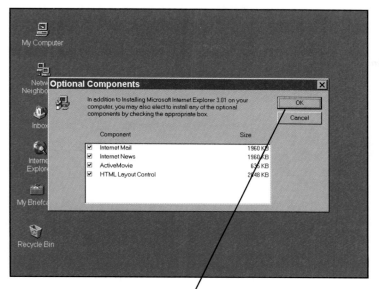

This dialog box lets you pick which components will be installed. Select the ones you want to install by clicking in the square next to them.

✔ Internet Mail is like a miniature version of Windows Messaging (see Chapter 26, "Using Windows Messaging") for Internet e-mail.

✔ Internet News is a program for reading and participating in USENET newsgroups.

✔ ActiveMovie lets Explorer display video formats such as AVI, MPEG, and QuickTime.

✔ HTML Layout Control is a tool for Web developers that provides precise control over object layout in Web pages.

More information on these features is available on the Internet Explorer Web pages.

7. Click on **OK**. A message box will appear showing the progress of the setup. After the setup is finished, you will have to reboot your workstation for the new settings to take effect.

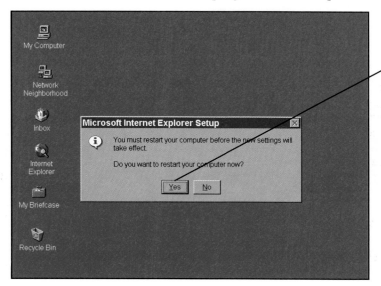

8. Click on **Yes**. Your workstation will reboot, and the new version of Internet Explorer will be ready to use. The new version of Explorer can open many files other than HTML Web pages, including ActiveX files created using Microsoft Office programs, without opening the program that was used to make them. In effect, it lets you "browse" your own computer as well as the Web.

CHAPTER 26

Using Windows Messaging

Windows Messaging is an e-mail program for use on your company network or the Internet. You can use it to connect to the Internet first thing in the morning and download your e-mail messages. Later, as your schedule permits, you can read and reply to the messages, then have Messaging deliver your outgoing mail. To set up Windows Messaging, you should have completed modem, Remote Access Service and Dial-Up Networking installation unless your Internet access is through a company network. If Messaging has not been installed on your workstation, you'll need the Windows NT installation CD or disks. In this chapter, you will do the following:

✔ Set up Windows Messaging
✔ Send an e-mail message
✔ Read and reply to an incoming message
✔ Set up your Messaging address book

Opening Windows Messaging

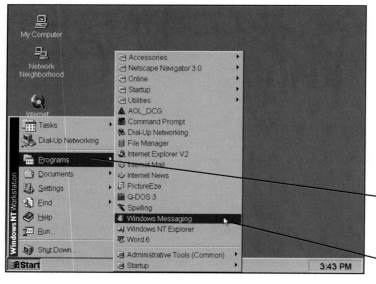

There are two quick ways to open Messaging.

1a. Double-click the **Inbox icon** on your desktop.

OR

1b. Click the **Start button** on your taskbar. The Start menu will appear.

2b. Move the **mouse pointer** over Programs. The Programs menu will appear.

3b. Click on **Windows Messaging**.

If neither the Inbox icon nor the Windows Messaging menu choice are present, see Chapter 33, "Adding Features to NT," for information on adding Windows NT components.

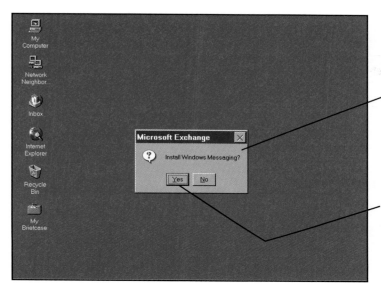

If Messaging has been installed on your workstation, you can skip to the next section, "Configuring Messaging."

If Messaging was not installed when NT was loaded into your workstation, you will receive this message. You will need the NT installation CD or disks to install Messaging.

4. Click on **Yes**. Another message, asking you to insert the installation CD, will appear.

Note 1: This installation method installs both Messaging components: *Internet Mail*, which gives you access to Internet e-mail; and *Microsoft Mail*, the network e-mail system that is covered in Chapter 34. If you don't want to add Microsoft Mail, click on No and close any subsequent dialog boxes, then see Chapter 33 for information on adding only Messaging and Internet Mail to NT.

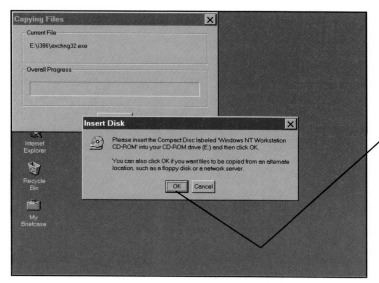

Note 2: To override the CD "autorun" feature, hold down the Shift key on your keyboard when you insert the installation CD. This will keep the CD's menu from appearing and slowing things down.

5. Insert the installation **CD** and **click** on **OK**. NT will copy the files it needs for all of messaging's components to your workstation. Then proceed to the next section, "Configuring Messaging."

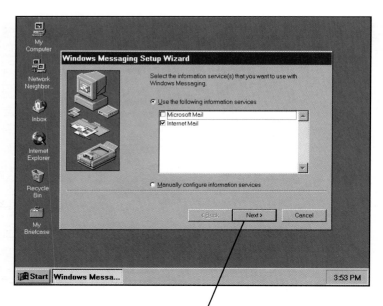

Configuring Messaging

If Messaging was set up for you by your systems administrator, the Inbox window will appear and you can skip to the next section ("Sending E-Mail"). If not, a setup wizard guides you through the configuration process. In our example, we will configure Messaging for Internet mail through a dial-up Internet Service Provider (ISP). If your Internet connection is through a company network, ask your systems administrator to set up the connection.

1. Click in the **square** next to Microsoft Mail to remove the ✔ in it (we'll cover setting it up for network mail separately in Chapter 34).

2. Click on **Next**. Another Windows Messaging Setup Wizard dialog box will appear.

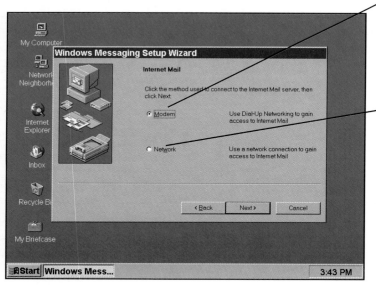

3a. If you connect to the Internet through your computer's modem, **click** on **Modem** to select it.

OR

3b. If you connect through your company's network, **click** on **Network**.

4. Click on **Next**. Another Setup Wizard dialog box will appear.

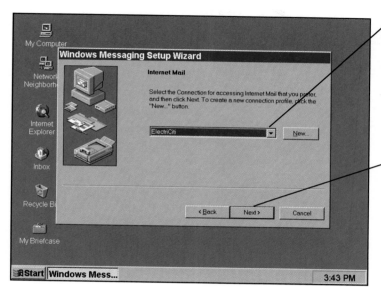

5. Click on the ▼ if needed to open the list of connections. These are the dial-up connections set up in Chapter 24, "Using Dial-Up Networking."

6. Click on a **connection** to select it.

7. Click on **Next**. Another Setup Wizard dialog box will appear.

8. Click on **Specify the name** or on **Specify the address**. Your ISP or systems administrator will provide you with this information. A name will be similar to the example shown here; an address will be a number such as 200.200.200.200.

9. Type the **name** or **address** of your ISP's mail server.

Note: You may need to change this information later if you change your ISP or your ISP changes their address. If that's the case, open the Control Panel window and double-click the Mail icon. A dialog box where you can make the changes will appear.

10. Click on **Next**. Another Setup Wizard dialog box will appear.

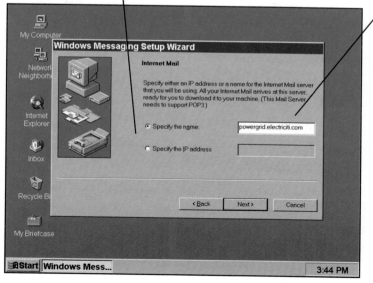

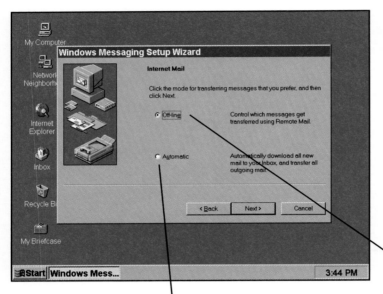

Messaging can automatically retrieve all incoming e-mail and deliver all of your outgoing messages each time you connect to your Internet mail server, or you can set it so that you have to specify which messages are to be sent and received each time. The "Automatic" setting is more convenient, but you may want the added control over what's sent and received by selecting the "Off-line" setting.

11a. Click Off-line to select incoming and outgoing messages individually.

OR

11b. Click Automatic for Messaging to automatically retrieve all incoming and send all outgoing messages each time you connect to your mail server.

12. Click on **Next**. Another Setup Wizard dialog box will appear.

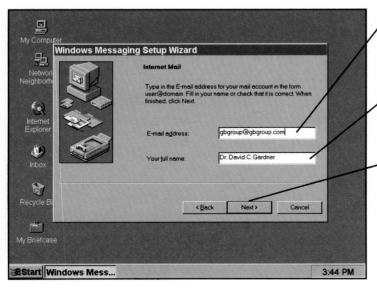

13. Type your **e-mail address**. Your ISP or network administrator will provide this information if you don't already have it.

14. Type your **real name** to identify yourself in your outgoing messages.

15. Click on **Next**. Another Setup Wizard dialog box will appear.

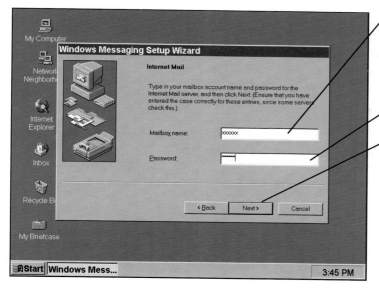

16. Type in your **mailbox name**. Usually this is the same as your user name or account name with your ISP or company network.

17. Type in your **password**.

18. Click on **Next**. Another Setup Wizard dialog box will appear.

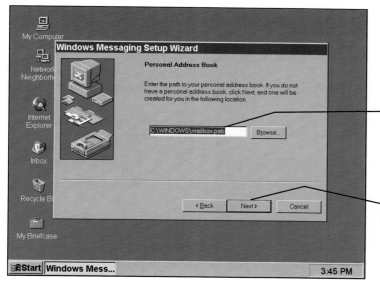

19a. Go to step 20 to accept the default path to the Windows Messaging address book.

OR

19b. Type the **path** to your address book if you have one set up already for another program, or **click** on **Browse** and locate it.

20. Click on **Next**. Another Setup Wizard dialog box will appear.

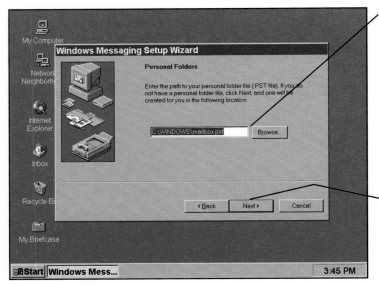

21a. Type in the **path** to your personal folder file if you have already set one up for another program, or **click** on **Browse** to locate it.

OR

21b. Do nothing to accept the default path to the Windows Messaging personal folder file.

22. Click on **Next**. Another Setup Wizard dialog box will appear.

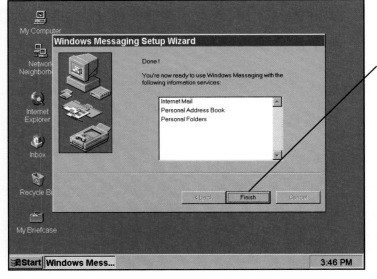

Congratulations! You're ready to start using Windows Messaging.

23. Click on **Finish**. The Inbox Windows Messaging window will appear.

Note: The Inbox is user-specific. If you set it up under one logon name, you won't find it if you log onto your workstation using a different name. Also, if more than one person uses your workstation, each one will have to go through this process to set up his or her own Inbox.

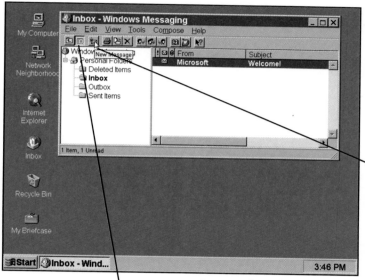

Sending E-Mail

The Inbox window shows a list of folders for your e-mail on the left and a list of messages in your inbox on the right. A welcome message will be listed by default.

1. Click on the **new message icon** in the toolbar. A Windows Messaging window will appear. Whatever subject you type in for your letter will appear in the title bar.

Note: When the Inbox window opens, the list of folders in the left side of it may not be showing. If that is the case, click on the folder list icon in the toolbar to see the list of folders.

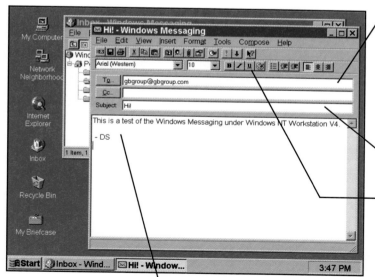

2. Click in the **To box** and **type in** the **e-mail address** of the person to whom you're sending the message.

3. If you want to send a copy to someone else, **click** in the **Cc box** and **type in** the **address**.

4. Click in the **subject box** and **type in** a **subject**.

Messaging works like a word processor, allowing you to specify fonts, colors, and formatting for your message text by using these buttons in the toolbar. However, text colors and formats won't show unless the recipient's e-mail system supports this feature. To see what a toolbar button does, rest the mouse pointer over it for a moment and a label will appear.

5. Click in the **message area** and **type** your **message**.

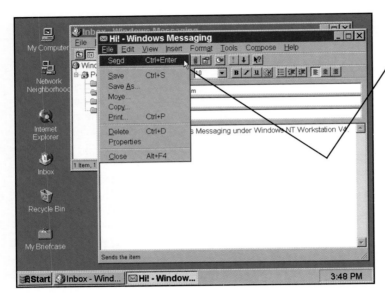

6. Click on **File** in the menu bar. The File menu will appear.

7. Click on **Send**. The message window will disappear and will be saved to your Outbox folder. It won't actually be sent out over the Internet until you connect to the Internet.

8. Click on the **Outbox folder** to highlight it. Any messages waiting to go out will appear in the list on the right.

The message waiting to go out is shown here.

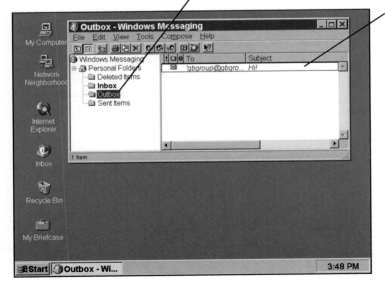

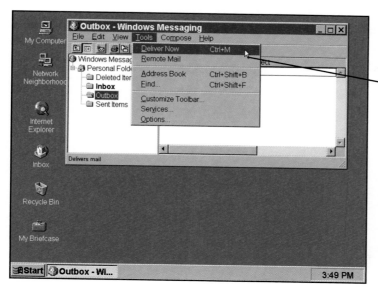

9. Click on **Tools** in the menu bar. The Tools menu will appear.

10. Click on **Deliver Now**.

If your Internet connection is through an ISP and you have set up Remote Access Service and DUN (see Chapters 23, "Adding Remote Access Service," and 24, "Using Dial-Up Networking"), your computer will begin to connect to your ISP. If you haven't used the connection before, you'll be prompted to go through the sign-on process (see "Autodialing" in Chapter 25).

If everything's been set up correctly, DUN will autodial your connection. If autodial fails to perform as expected, make your Internet connection first (see "Making a Connection" in Chapter 24), then repeat steps 9 and 10.

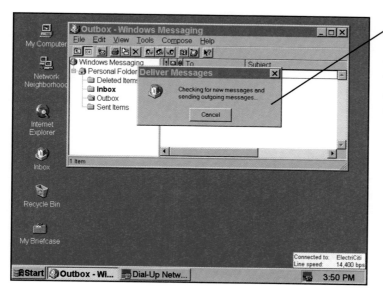

Various message boxes will appear on your screen during the connection process, and while Messaging downloads any incoming e-mail and delivers the outgoing message.

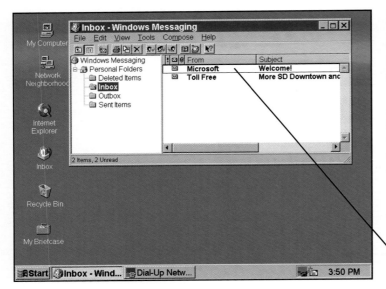

Reading and Replying to E-Mail

After Messaging has retrieved new mail and delivered your outgoing messages, it automatically disconnects from your ISP or company's network Internet connection. Your new messages are listed in the right side of the window.

1. Double-click a **message** to read it. A Windows Messaging window will appear with the message in it.

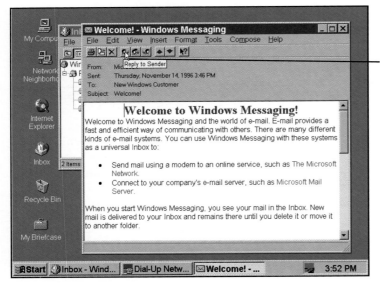

2. Scroll through the **message** to see all of it.

3. Click on the **Reply button** in the toolbar. By default, Messaging is set up to include the entire original message in your reply. (We'll show you where you can change this later.)

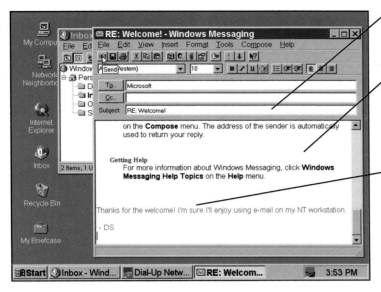

The original subject is listed, preceded by "RE:" in the subject box.

The original message is copied here. You can, of course, drag the cursor over it to highlight it and then press the Delete key on your keyboard to delete it.

4. Click in the **message area** and **type** your **reply**. By default, the text is set to display in blue. This can also be changed.

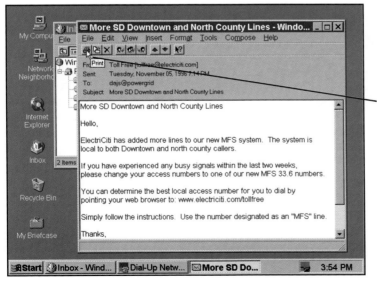

Printing an E-Mail Message

Messages are easily printed.

Click on the **Print button** in the toolbar. The message will be printed.

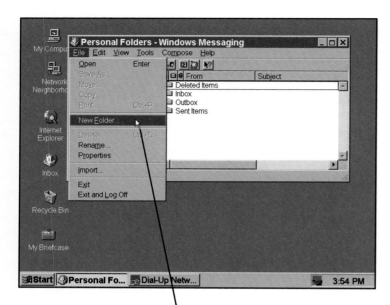

Organizing Your E-Mail

Messaging's built-in filing system works just like NT's overall file management system. You can create as many folders for organizing your e-mail as you want. These folders and your e-mail will be on your computer's hard disk.

1. Click on **Personal Folders** in the folder list to highlight it. If you want to create a folder within another folder, highlight that folder.

2. Click on **File** in the menu bar. The File menu will appear.

3. Click on **New Folder**. A New Folder dialog box will appear.

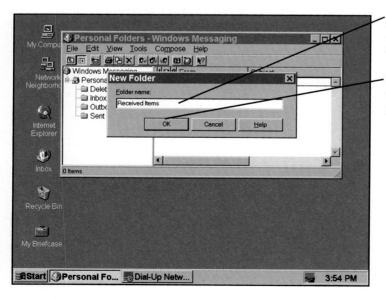

4. Type a **name** for the folder. For this example, we named the new folder "Received Items."

5. Click on **OK**. The new folder will appear in the left side of the Inbox window.

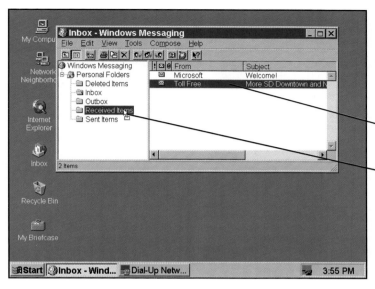

Messages can be dragged and dropped into folders, and folders can be dragged and dropped into other folders to organize your filing system the way you want it.

6. Click on the **message** you want to move to highlight it.

7. Press and hold the **mouse button** as you **drag** the **pointer** to the folder where you want the message to be filed. The pointer changes to include an envelope.

8. To delete a message, **click** on it to highlight it and **press** the **Delete key** on your keyboard. The message will be moved to your Deleted Items folder. The folder will be "emptied" and the message really deleted when you close Messaging.

Customizing Windows Messaging

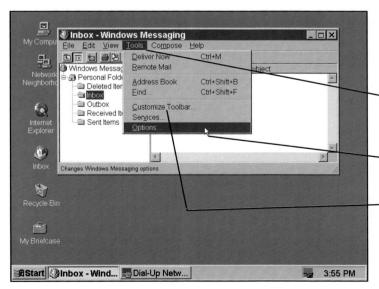

Many of Messaging's features can be customized to make it look or work the way you want it to.

1. Click on **Tools** in the menu bar. The Tools menu will appear.

2. Click on **Options**. The Options dialog box will appear.

Notice the "Customize Toolbar" menu choice. You can use this to add or delete toolbar buttons and to streamline such tasks as adding a new folder and delivering mail.

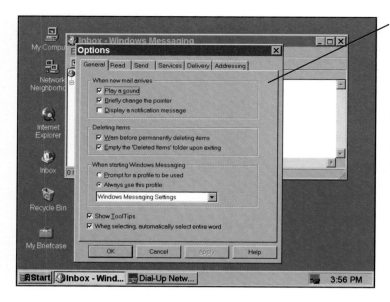

General Options include having Messaging play a sound when new mail arrives. This is useful if you're permanently connected to a network e-mail system and you have Messaging running all the time.

3. Click on an **option** to place a check mark in the square next to it to select it.

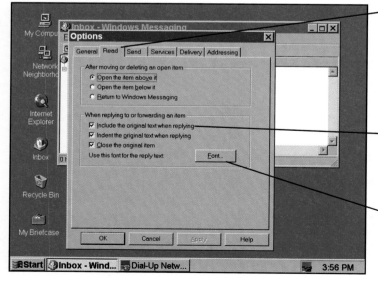

4. Click on the **Read** tab to bring it to the front.

Here's where you tell Messaging whether to include the full text of a message in your reply to it.

5. Click on **Include the original...** to remove the check mark if you want to remove this option.

6. To specify a typeface or color for reply text, **click** on the **Font button**.

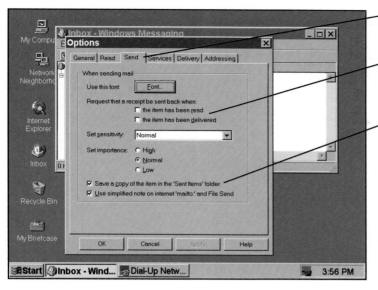

7. Click on the **Send Tab** to bring it to the front.

On this tab, you can ask to be notified when your messages are delivered.

You also can have Messaging save a copy of each outgoing message.

The other tabs deal with such things as what address book to use, where messages are stored, and so on. Generally, they don't require any attention.

Setting Up Your Address Book

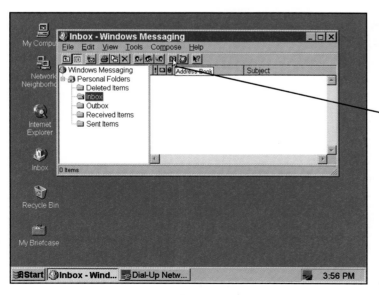

Messaging's address book stores names and e-mail addresses for you so you don't have to type them in when sending messages.

1. Click on the **Address Book button** in the toolbar. The Address Book window will appear.

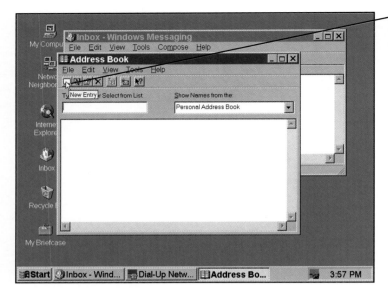

2. Click on the **New Entry button**. The New Entry dialog box will appear.

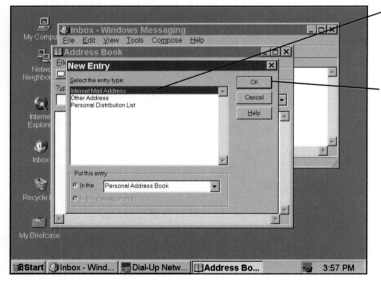

3. Click on the **type of address** you want to add. In this example we selected Internet Mail Address.

4. Click on **OK**. The New Internet Mail Address Properties dialog box will appear.

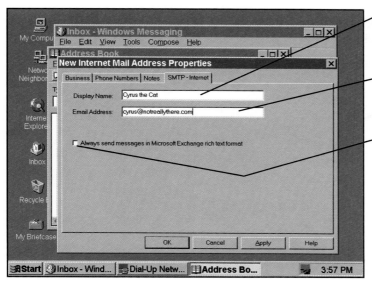

5. Click in the **Display Name box** and **type in** the **personal name** for the entry.

6. Click in the **Email Address box** and **type in** the person's **Internet e-mail address**.

7. If the person's e-mail system supports text formatting and you want to use it, **click here** to place a check mark in the square.

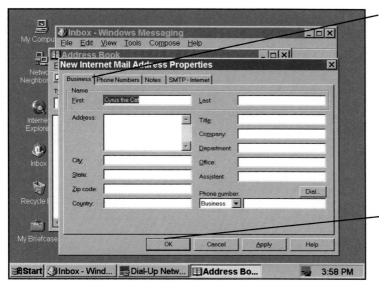

8. Click on the **Business tab** to bring it to the front.

Like personal information programs, Messaging's address book lets you store much more than just the person's e-mail address.

9. Click in a **box** and **type in** the appropriate **information** to make use of this feature.

10. Click on **OK** to save the new entry and close the dialog box. The new entry will appear in the Address Book window.

To use the address book for sending e-mail, highlight an entry and click on the New Message button in the Address Book toolbar (it's a little envelope with a star next to it). The Windows Messaging window will appear with the recipient's name and e-mail address filled in.

CHAPTER
27

Connecting to Your Office by Phone

With a few changes to the settings on your office workstation, you can use your home or laptop computer to connect to it over phone lines. Additional software is generally required to run programs such as word processors or spreadsheets from a remote location. But NT's Dial-Up Networking will let you use programs such as Microsoft Mail and Peer Web Services on the network you dial into, and do file management such as copying or deleting files. The example in this chapter dials into a Windows network using a stand-alone computer running NT Workstation 4.0 with Remote Access Service (RAS) and Dial-Up Networking (DUN) installed. The NT workstation we are dialing in to has a modem that can receive calls, and also has RAS and DUN installed. If you're on a company network, consult with your network administrator beforehand. You need to be logged on as Administrator or a member of the Administrators user group to make these changes, and you need to know the network's protocol and your modem's phone number. In this chapter, you will do the following:

✔ Configure your office workstation to function as a dial-up server
✔ Set up your home computer to interact with your company's network
✔ Explore your office workstation from a remote location

Configuring the Dial-Up Server

Before you can dial into your office workstation, you have to change its Network settings so that it will function as a dial-up server. This will not alter its normal operation as a workstation.

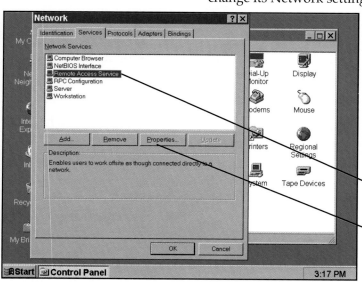

1. Open the **Control Panel window**.

2. Double-click the **Network icon**. The Network dialog box will appear.

3. Click on **Remote Access Service** to highlight it.

4. Click on **Properties**. The Remote Access Setup dialog box will appear.

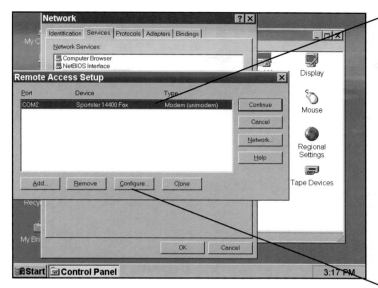

5. Your modem will be listed here and highlighted. If you have more than one modem installed, click on the one you'll be using to receive calls to highlight it.

Setting Protocols and Access

1. Click on **Configure** in the Remote Access Setup dialog box. The Configure Port Usage dialog box will appear.

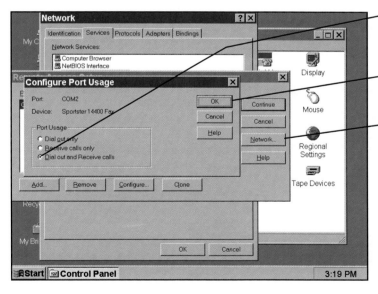

2. Click on **Dial out and Receive calls** to place a dot in the circle next to it.

3. Click on **OK**. The dialog box will close.

4. Click on the **Network** button in the Remote Access Setup dialog box. The Network Configuration dialog box will appear.

Next, tell your computer what protocol to use when functioning as a server. This should be the same protocol used by your network. Generally, Windows networks use NetBEUI and Novell networks use IPX. If you are connecting two stand-alone workstations, select NetBEUI.

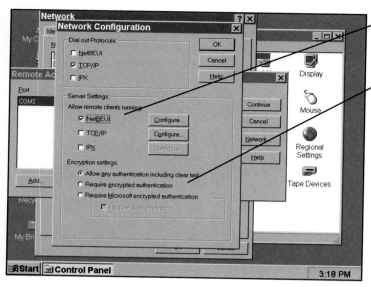

5. Click on the appropriate **protocol** for your network to place a ✔ in the box next to it.

6. Click on whatever type of logon **encryption** security you want to use for authentication (user name and password) to place a ✔ in the box next to it. Make a note of this setting; you will have to set up the computer you use to dial in to use the same type.

7. Click on the **Configure** button next to the protocol you selected. In our example it is NetBEUI. The RAS Server Configuration dialog box will appear. In this dialog box you give the caller access either to your workstation only, or to the entire network. Check with your systems administrator to see what level of access is appropriate.

8. Click on the **type of access** you want to allow. In this example we selected Entire network.

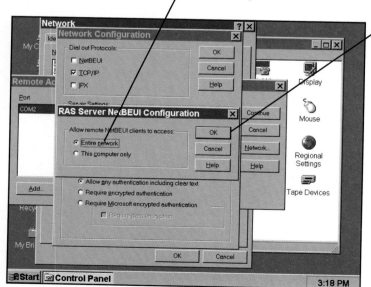

9. Click on **OK**. The dialog box will close. If you selected more than one protocol, a Configuration dialog box for the next protocol will appear. Make your configuration settings for the other protocol and click on OK. The dialog box will close.

10. Click on the **OK** button in the Network Configuration dialog box. The dialog box will close.

11. Click on the **Continue** button in the Remote Access Setup dialog box. The dialog box will close.

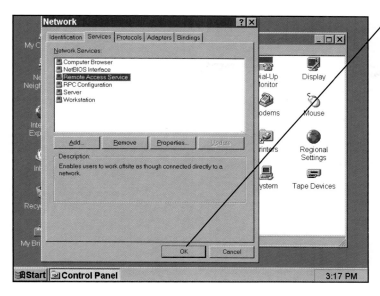

12. Click on **Close**. It will take NT a few moments to check the *bindings*, which are the connections between services, protocols, and adapters in your Network setup. When it's completed, a dialog box (not shown here) will ask if you want to restart your computer now.

13. Click on **Yes** and restart your workstation so that all changes will take effect.

Adding a Dial-Up User to Your Workstation

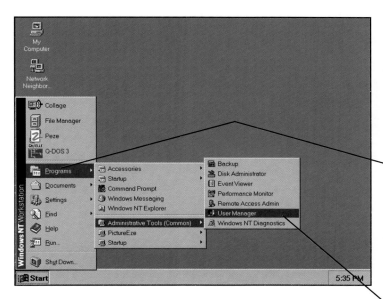

Next, you have to deal with one of NT's security features. You have to be a user with dial-up permission to be able to log on to the workstation.

1. Click on the **Start button**. The Start menu will appear.

2. Move the **mouse pointer** over Programs. The Programs menu will appear.

3. Move the **mouse pointer** over Administrative Tools (Common). Another menu will appear.

4. Click on **User Manager**. The User Manager window will appear.

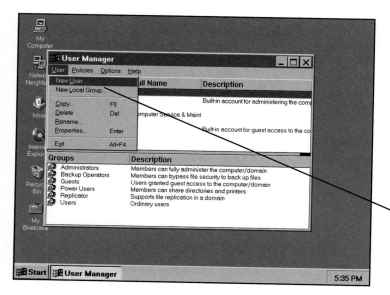

You can either create a new, separate user name for dialing in, or change the properties of your current listing. The New User dialog box and the User Properties dialog box for a current user look the same. By reading the steps for a new user, you'll see what changes need to be made to a current user's properties.

5a. To create a new user, **click** on **User** in the menu bar to open the User menu, then **click** on **New User**. The New User dialog box will appear.

OR

5b. To add dial-up permission to a current user, **double-click** the **name of a user** in the list in the upper part of the dialog box. The User Properties dialog box will appear.

Note: If you are only adding dial-in permission to a current user's properties, do not perform steps 6 through 13, just read them. See Chapter 29, "Controlling Access to Workstations," for more about user properties.

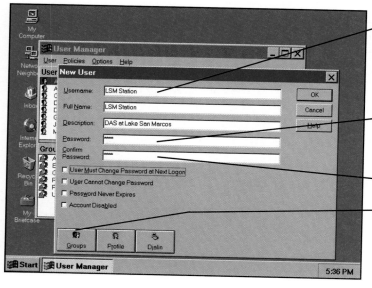

6. Type a **name** for the dial-in user.

7. Type the **Full Name** and **Description** if desired.

8. Type a **password** and make a note of it. You'll need it to dial in.

9. Repeat the **password**.

10. Click on **Groups**. The Group Memberships dialog box will appear.

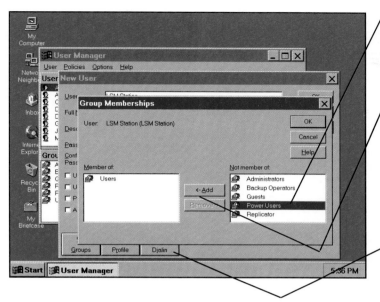

11. Click on the **user group** you want the new user in to highlight it. In this example it's Power Users. (See Chapter 29 for more on user groups.)

12. Click on **Add**.

13. Click on **OK**. The Group Memberships dialog box will close.

Now you're ready to set the dial-up permission.

14. Click on the **Dialin** button in the New User (or User Properties) dialog box. The Dialin Information dialog box will appear.

15. Click on **Grant dialin permission to user** to place a ✔ in the box next to it.

You can set a callback security option in this dialog box. Callback tells the workstation to hang up and call you back after you dial in. If you check "Set By Caller," the workstation will prompt you for a phone number at which to call you when you dial in. This is useful if you'll be on the road. If you check "Preset To," type in the phone number where the workstation can reach you when it calls you back.

16. Click on **OK** in the Dialin Information and New User (or User Properties) dialog boxes.

17. Click on the ⊠ in the corner of the title bar to close the User Manager window.

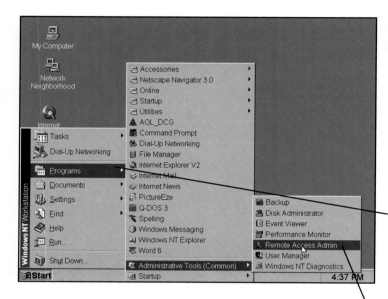

Starting Remote Access Service

The next step is to start the Remote Access Service on the host workstation.

1. Click on the **Start button** on the taskbar. The Start menu will appear.

2. Move the **mouse pointer** over Programs. The Programs menu will appear.

3. Move the **mouse pointer** over Administrative Tools (Common). Another menu will appear.

4. Click on **Remote Access Admin**. The Remote Access Admin window will appear.

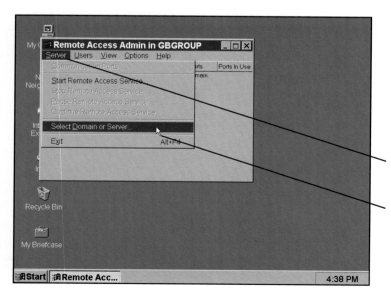

Selecting the Server

On the host workstation, you have to tell the program which computer you want to use for the dial-up server.

1. Click on **Server**. The Server menu will appear.

2. Click on **Select Domain or Server**. The Select Domain dialog box will appear.

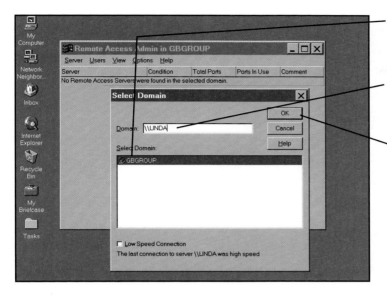

3. If necessary, **click** on the **domain** where the workstation resides to highlight it.

4. Type two backslashes (\ \) and the **name** of the **workstation** in the Domain box.

5. Click on **OK**. The dialog box will close.

Starting the Service

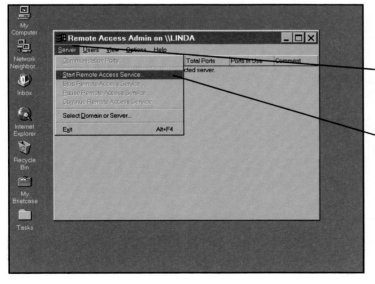

After selecting the server, you have to start the service on the host workstation.

1. Click on **Server** in the menu bar. The Server menu will appear.

2. Click on **Start Remote Access Service**. The Start Remote Access Service dialog box will appear.

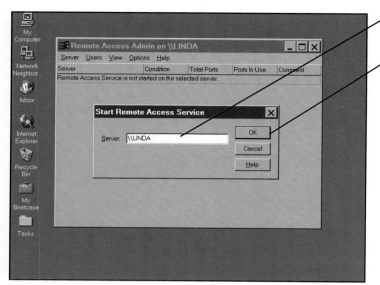

The server's name will appear in the box.

3. Click on **OK**.

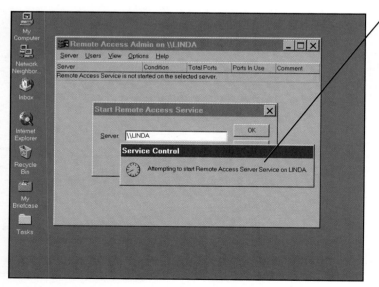

This message will appear for a few moments while the service starts up. Once it's all set, the message and the Start Remote Access Service dialog box will disappear.

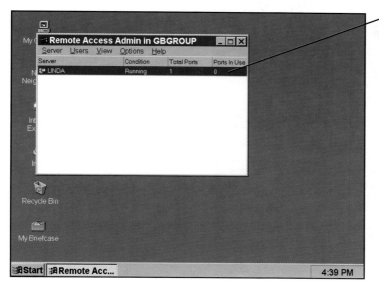

The Remote Access Admin window will indicate that the service is running. The host workstation is now ready to be dialed in to and can continue to be used as a regular workstation. You may either minimize or close the Remote Access Admin window by clicking on the ▬ or ⊠ button in its upper-right corner. Remote Access Service will continue to run in either case.

Securing Your Office Workstation

The workstation has to be turned on and Remote Access Service running for your dial-up connection to work.

To secure your workstation, you can log off or lock it. Once turned on, the Remote Access Service will continue to run in either case. If you log off, the network connections to other workstations will be shut down. If there are problems getting them connected during your usual logons, you may experience even more problems trying to establish them over the slow dial-up connection. Also, if you log off, others with access to the workstation can still log on, but they can also turn off Remote Access Service or the workstation.

Note 1: Remote Access Service can be set to start automatically when your workstation is turned on. The same caution about network connections mentioned before would apply in this case. This uses valuable memory, so only do this when you're going to be away.

Note 2: You can turn off the monitor to save electricity, but do not shut down the workstation or turn it off unless you have special dial-up equipment that starts your workstation for you when you call in, or someone to turn it on for you.

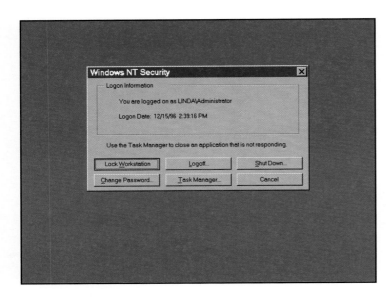

1. Press Ctrl+Alt+Del to bring up the Windows NT Security dialog box shown here. For dialing in, you have several options:

❖ Click on Lock Workstation to secure the workstation and leave it running.

❖ Click on Logoff and leave the workstation running. The network connections will be shut down, and others with access can still log on.

❖ Simply leave the workstation running if it's secure.

❖ Have a coworker start the workstation (see below).

❖ Install special dial-up equipment that will automatically turn the workstation on when you call in (see below).

Starting RAS Automatically

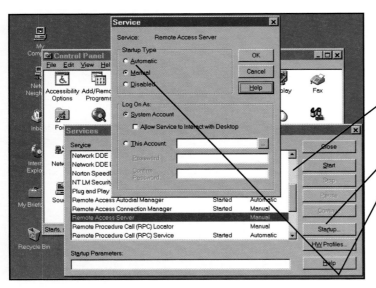

1. Open the **Control Panel** on the workstation.

2. Double-click on the **Services icon**.

3. Scroll down until you see Remote Access Server and click on it.

4. Click on **Startup**.

5. Click on **Automatic**.

6. Close the **dialog boxes**.

The Remote Access Service will start automatically when your workstation boots up.

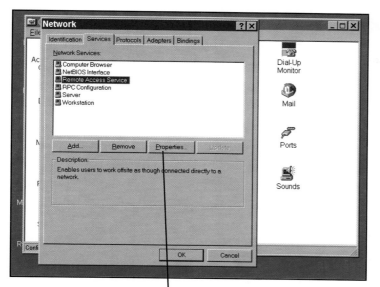

Dialing In

We now move from the office workstation that will be dialed in to to the home computer that will be calling. In our example, the home computer is a stand-alone workstation running Windows NT Workstation 4.0. Remote Access Service and Dial-Up Networking have already been installed on it. (We were also able to dial in to the NT workstation from a Windows 95 computer using its version of dial-up networking.)

1. Open the **Control Panel** on the workstation.

2. Double-click the **Network icon**. The Network dialog box will appear.

3. Click on **Remote Access Service** to highlight it.

4. Click on **Properties**. The Remote Access Setup dialog box will appear.

5. Click on your **modem's name,** if needed, to highlight it.

6. Click on **Network**. The Network Configuration dialog box will appear.

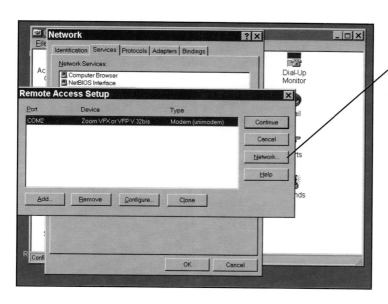

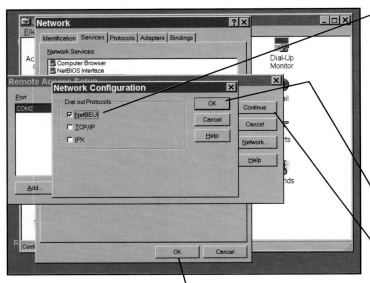

7. Click on the **network protocol**(s) used on the workstation you will be calling to place a ✔ in the box next to it. If you haven't already installed the protocol(s), you'll be prompted for the NT installation CD and walked through installation. (See "Selecting Network Protocols" in Chapter 23.)

8. Click on **OK**. The dialog box will disappear.

9. Click on **Continue** in the Remote Access Setup dialog box. The dialog box will close.

10. Click on **OK** in the Network dialog box. The dialog box will close.

Making a Phonebook Entry for Dial-Up

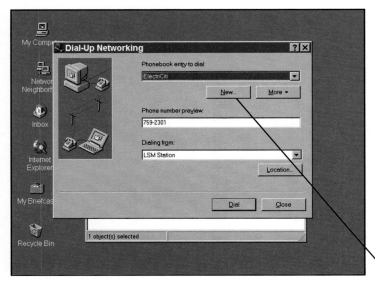

Now we need to set up a phonebook entry for the office workstation's telephone number. In this example, we use the New Phonebook Entry Wizard.

1. Double-click on the **My Computer icon**. The My Computer window will appear.

2. Double-click on the **Dial-Up Networking icon**. The Dial-Up Networking dialog box will appear.

3. Click on **New**. The New Phonebook Entry Wizard will open.

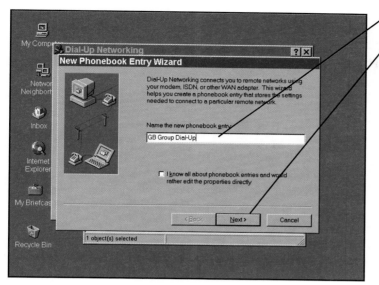

4. Type a **name** for the entry.

5. Click on **Next**. Another New Phonebook Entry Wizard dialog box will appear.

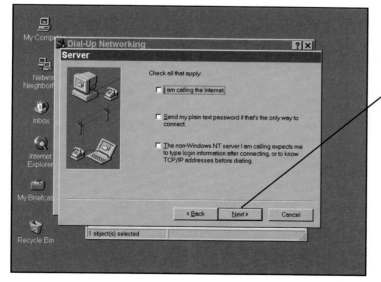

Because none of these options apply when dialing from one NT workstation to another, you don't select one.

6. Click on **Next**. Another New Phonebook Entry Wizard dialog box will appear.

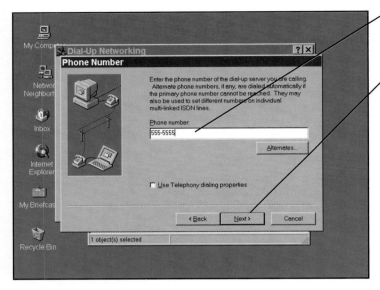

7. Type the **phone number** for the modem in the workstation you will be calling.

8. Click on **Next**. Another New Phonebook Entry Wizard dialog box will appear.

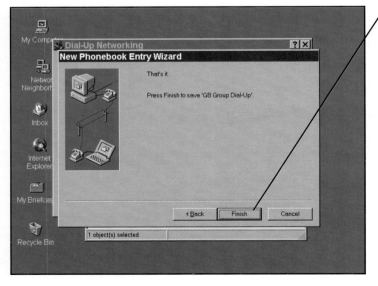

9. Click on **Finish**. The Wizard will go away and the new entry will be listed in the Dial-Up Networking dialog box. Even though the Wizard was helpful, you still have to check the settings for the entry. See the next section, "Editing the Phonebook Entry," for how to do this.

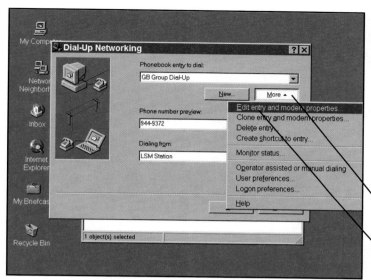

Editing the Phone-book Entry

You have to make sure that your setup at this end matches the one you made on the workstation you're calling. The entry you just made should appear in the Phonebook entry to dial box.

1. Click on the **More button**. A menu will appear.

2. Click on **Edit entry and modem properties**. The Edit Phonebook Entry dialog box will appear.

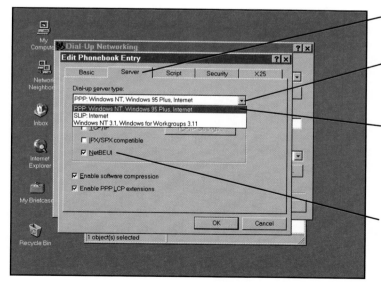

3. Click on the **Server tab** to bring it to the front.

4. Click on the ▼ next to the Dial-up server type box. A list will appear.

5. Click on the server type you're calling. In our case it's **PPP: Windows NT, Windows 95 Plus, Internet**. The list will close.

6. Click on the **network protocol** you will be using. In our example it's NetBEUI.

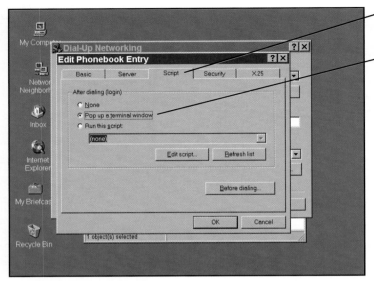

7. Click on the **Script tab** to bring it to the front.

If your network requires that you enter commands when you connect, select "Pop up a terminal window" on this tab so that you can type in the commands after you make the connection. Alternatively, you can use a script to enter the commands, and select it on this tab, as shown in the section titled "Modifying Phonebook Entries and Settings" in Chapter 24.

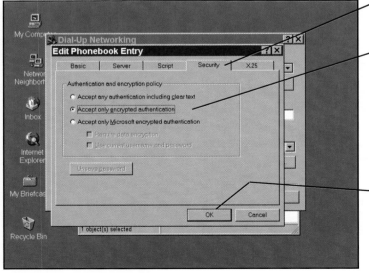

8. Click on the **Security tab** to bring it to the front.

9. Select the same **encryption setting** that was selected for the server in step 6 under "Setting Protocols and Access," earlier in this chapter.

The settings on the other tabs should not need any changes.

10. Click on **OK**. The Edit Phonebook Entry dialog box will close.

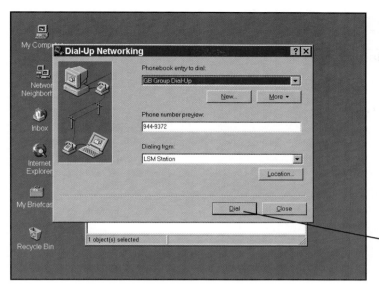

Placing the Call

1. Double-click on the **My Computer icon**. The My Computer window will appear.

2. Double-click on the **Dial-Up Networking icon**. The Dial-Up Networking dialog box will appear.

3. Select the **entry** for dialing in to your workstation.

4. Click on **Dial**. The Connect dialog box will appear.

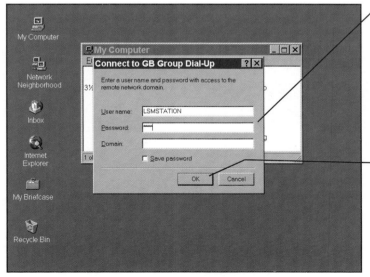

5. Type the **user name** and **password** that you set up with dial-in permission in the section titled "Adding a Dial-Up User to Your Workstation" earlier in this chapter. DUN will enter these for you automatically during the connection process.

6. Click on **OK**. DUN will make the call.

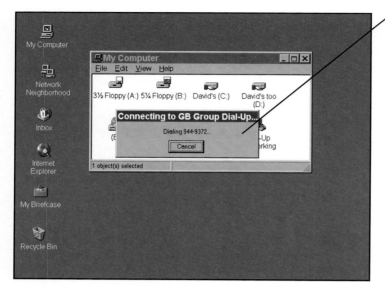

This message appears while DUN on your remote machine negotiates with the machine you are dialing in to. After the connection has been made, the message goes away. See the section titled "Using the Dial-Up Networking Monitor," at the end of Chapter 24, if you want to check on the connection.

Using the Connection

After you're connected, you can use the Network Neighborhood icon or Windows NT Explorer for file management basics such as copying, renaming, or deleting.

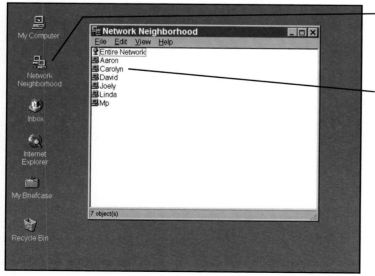

1. Double-click on the **Network Neighborhood icon**. The Network Neighborhood window will appear.

The other machines on the network you dialed in to will be shown here. If you have access to them, you can double-click their icons to reach their files.

2. Click on the ⊠ in the corner of the title bar to close the window.

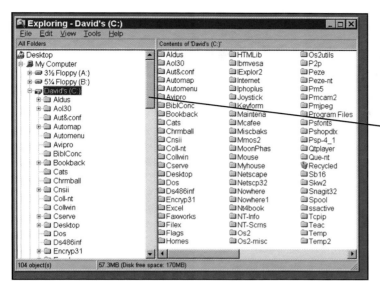

With Windows NT Explorer, the access to the other workstations is different.

3. Open Windows NT Explorer.

4. Scroll down the **list** of folders on your computer.

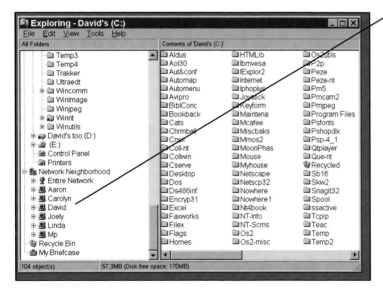

The computers on the network you dialed in to are shown at the bottom of the list under Network Neighborhood. You can double-click on their icons to reach their files.

Files can be copied or moved using drag-and-drop. For convenience, you can open two copies of Windows NT Explorer on your desktop to drag-and-drop files between computers.

Networked programs such as Microsoft Mail also work over the dial-up connection. Be patient using dial-up networking. Even with fast modems on both machines, it will work much more slowly than you're used to.

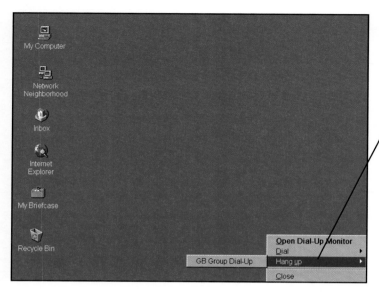

Disconnecting

1. Right-click on the **Dial-Up Networking Monitor icon** (not shown here) in the tray of your taskbar. A menu will appear.

2. Move the **mouse pointer** over Hang up. The list of open connections will appear.

3. Click on the **connection** you want to close. A message box will appear.

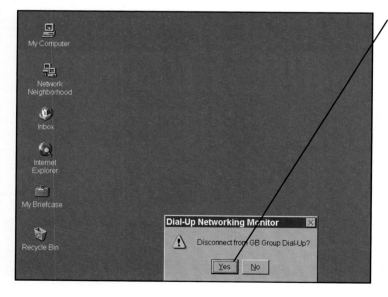

4. Click on **Yes**. The connection will be hung up.

Note: The Dial-Up Networking Monitor will still be active after you hang up the connection. See the end of Chapter 24, "Using Dial-Up Networking," for more on the Monitor.

Chatting with Another Workstation

Chat is an "accessory" program that comes with NT Workstation. It lets you and others type messages back and forth between your workstation and other workstations on your network or a network that you dial into (see Chapter 24, "Using Dial-Up Networking"). When someone calls your workstation using Chat, your workstation makes a "beep" sound, similar to the noise it makes when there's an error, to tell you there's an incoming call. If your workstation has a sound card, you can change the standard incoming call sound to something more pleasant or distinctive. We found that we could use Chat between workstations running NT 4.0, Windows 95, and Windows 3.11. However, the 3.11 machines could only answer calls, not initiate them. In this chapter, you will do the following:

✔ Use Chat to talk with someone at another workstation
✔ Set a sound to announce an incoming call

Starting Chat

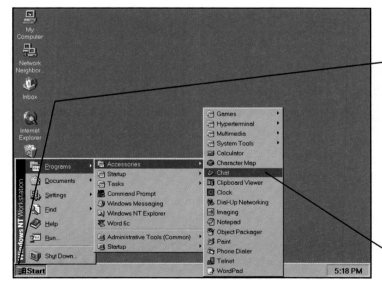

Chat is listed on your Accessories menu.

1. Click on the **Start button** on your taskbar. The Start menu will appear.

2. Move the **mouse pointer** over Programs. The Programs menu will appear.

3. Move the **mouse pointer** over Accessories. The Accessories menu will appear.

4. Click on **Chat**. The Chat window will appear. A message will appear briefly telling you that NetDDE services are being started.

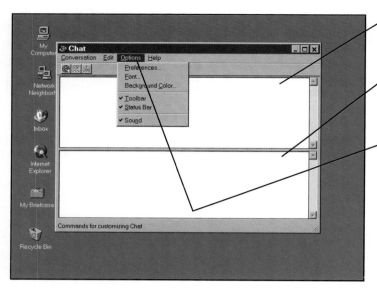

The upper part of the window will display the message you type.

The lower part will display the reply from the workstation you call.

You can make changes to Chat's appearance by clicking on the Options menu. The Preferences choice lets you choose a side-by-side split in the window instead of the upper-lower split. The Font choice lets you set the typeface and size of the type, and Background Color lets you select a color other than white for the background.

Calling Another Workstation

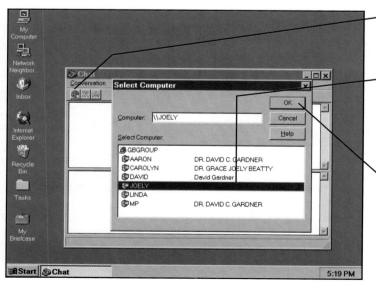

1. Click on the **Dial button** in the toolbar. The Select Computer dialog box will appear.

2. Click on the **name** of the workstation you are calling to highlight it. The name will appear in the Computer box in the upper part of the dialog box.

3. Click on the **OK button**. The dialog box will disappear.

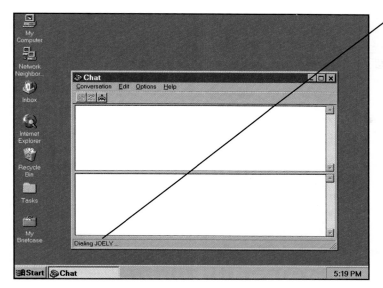

The message, "Dialing" and the name of the computer you are calling will appear in the Status bar at the bottom of your Chat window.

At the same time, the computer you are calling will start "beeping" to tell the person working at it that there is an incoming call.

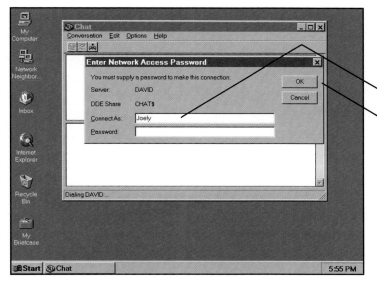

If a password is required for you to gain access to the workstation you are calling, this dialog box will appear.

4. Type the **password**.

5. Click on **OK**.

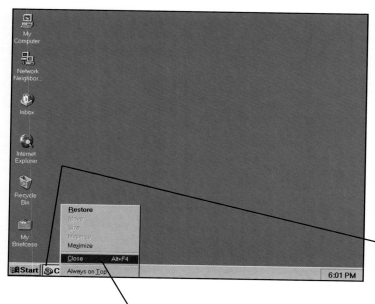

Declining or Accepting an Incoming Call

When a Chat call is coming in, your workstation will beep and you'll see the Chat icon and the name of the workstation that's calling in your taskbar. There are bound to be times, though, when you won't be able to take the call.

1a. If you *do not* want to accept the call, **right-click** on the **Chat icon** in your taskbar. A menu will appear.

2a. Click on **Close**. The menu and icon will disappear, and the workstation that is calling will receive the message, "The other computer did not respond." This is the same message that Chat sends if your workstation isn't turned on, if there's a network problem preventing communication, or if you simply don't answer. Just like with a telephone call, the connection must be made and the other person has to open Chat before you can start to talk.

OR

1b. If you *do* want to accept the call, **click** on the **Chat icon** in your taskbar. The Chat window will appear.

2b. Click on the **Answer button** in the toolbar.

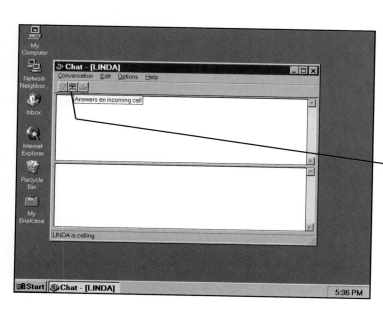

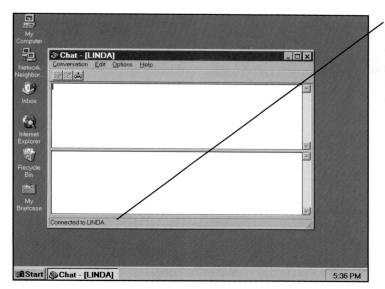

After the connection is made, the message in the Chat window's status bar on both machines will change to "Connected to" and the name of the other workstation.

Chatting

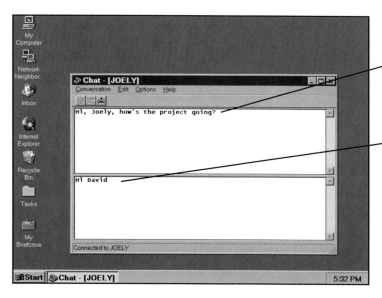

The cursor will be blinking in the upper part of the window.

1. Type your **message**. As you type, your message will appear in the lower half of the other workstation's Chat window.

As the person at the other workstation types, his or her reply appears in the lower half of your window.

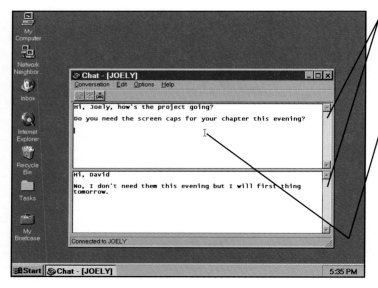

Both persons' input will continue to fill the halves of the window, then scroll up. You can use the scroll bars to see the parts or the messages that have scrolled out of view.

The mouse pointer turns into an I-beam when moved over either half of the window. You can select (highlight) text in either half just as you would in a word processor—double-click it or drag the I-beam pointer over it. You cannot print or save the messages directly. However, the Edit menu on the menu bar lets you copy or cut and paste selected text to a word processor or Notebook file.

Hanging Up

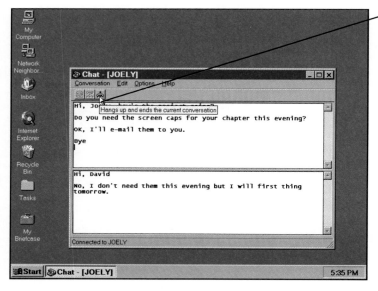

1. Click on the **Hang up** button in the toolbar when you've finished chatting. Either party in the chat can end the call in this way. The message in the Status bar at the bottom of both workstation's Chat windows will change to "Hung up."

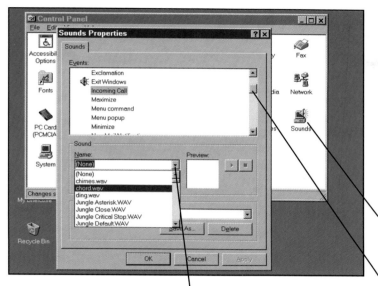

Changing the Incoming Call Sound

If your workstation has a sound card, you can customize the incoming call sound.

1. Open the **Control Panel window**.

2. Double-click the **Sounds icon**. The Sounds Properties dialog box will appear.

3. Scroll down until you see Incoming Call.

4. Click on the ▼ to open the list of available sounds.

5. Scroll up or down the list to see all of the sounds that are available. Some sounds shown here may not be on your machine. See Chapter 33, "Adding Features to NT," for installing additional sounds.

6. Click on a **sound** to select it. The list will close.

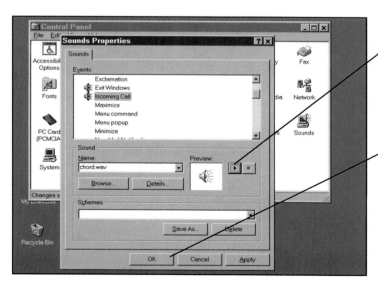

7. Click on the **Preview button**. The sound will play.

8. Repeat steps 4 through 7 until you are satisfied with your choice.

9. Click on **OK**. The sound you selected will play whenever a Chat call comes in.

You can use these steps to customize other sounds as well. Also, sets of sounds can be named in the Schemes box and saved just like color schemes (see Chapter 4).

Setting Up Workstations in a Peer-to-Peer Network

Most small offices or home offices are set up as peer-to-peer networks. In this type of network, every machine has the ability to connect to all other machines and to share files, folders, drives, and printers. Another major advantage of a network is that you can restrict access to certain machines, folders, and files so that only authorized people can use them. For example, you probably don't want everyone in your network to have access to accounting and payroll data.

The following chapters are designed to be used by SOHO (small office/home office) owners who want to set up their network with workstations in an NT peer-to-peer configuration. Although these chapters will give you the basics to get your peer-to peer office network up and running, they in no way cover the many permutations of Windows NT. If you want to set up a more sophisticated system, we urge you to consult a technical expert, preferably a licensed NT engineer.

PART

I

PART

II

PART

III

PART

IV

PART

V

PART

VI

PART

VII

Controlling Access to Workstations

When NT 4.0 is set up as a peer-to-peer network, each computer can talk to, or connect with, every other computer. However, NT makes it easy to limit access to your critical data, such as accounting and payroll, to specific people. The assumption in this chapter is that you are the owner or a key player in a small business and, therefore, have complete access to every machine.

There are several ways you can control access to critical data:

❖ **Deny a User Total Access to a Workstation**. You can determine not to let a user access a specific machine. In this case, you simply do not add the user's name to the specific machine. Without a user's name being added to a specific machine, a user cannot log on to that machine. Period.

❖ **Control Access to a Workstation with Passwords**. You can grant access to a specific machine by entering the user's name and assigning a password to that user. Only a user whose name has been added to the machine with a password can access the workstation.

❖ **Control the User's Level of Access.** When you assign a password to a user for a specific machine, you can at the same time grant a designated level of access privileges by also assigning them to an appropriate user group . For example, you can give a key employee a password for a specific machine and also grant them "administrator" group status. This means that by using their password to log on, they have full access to that machine. This does not mean that they have access at the same level to other machines unless you set up each machine the same way, one at a time.

❖ **Control the Sharing Status of Drives or Folders**. You can grant access to a specific folder on a workstation drive but not allow access to the other folders on that drive. Or, if the workstation has more than one hard drive, you can allow access to one but not the other. For example, you could grant access to the D drive on the workstation (no critical data) but to only one folder on the C drive.

❖ **Control User Access to Specific Files**. You can assign passwords to specific documents (e.g., a word processing or spreadsheet document). See Chapter 12, "Using Files over the Network."

In this chapter, you will do the following:

✔ Assign a password to a user for a specific workstation
✔ Assign a level of access to a user for a specific workstation
✔ Limit access to one folder on a specific workstation to all users

Adding a User to a Workstation

For anyone to have access to this NT Workstation, he or she can be assigned a password and a level of access. The assignment of users and passwords is done in the administrator mode.

1. Log on as the **Administrator**.

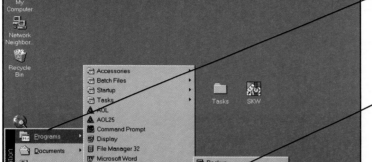

2. Click on the **Start button**. A pop-up menu will appear.

3. Move the **mouse pointer** to Programs. Another menu will appear.

4. Slide the **mouse pointer** onto Administrative Tools (Common). A third menu will appear.

5. Click on **User Manager**. The User Manager dialog box will appear.

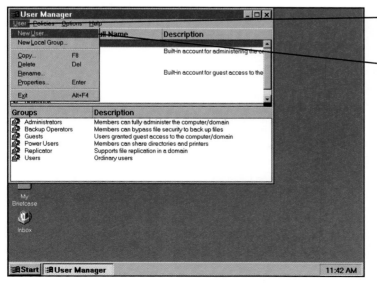

6. Click on **User** in the menu bar. A menu will appear

7. Click on **New User**. The New User Properties dialog box will appear.

Assigning a Password to a User

1. Type the **new user's name, press** the **Tab key**, and then **type** the user's **full name**.

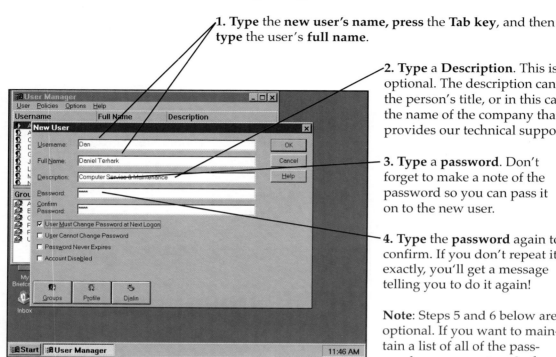

2. Type a **Description**. This is optional. The description can be the person's title, or in this case, the name of the company that provides our technical support.

3. Type a **password**. Don't forget to make a note of the password so you can pass it on to the new user.

4. Type the **password** again to confirm. If you don't repeat it exactly, you'll get a message telling you to do it again!

Note: Steps 5 and 6 below are optional. If you want to maintain a list of all of the passwords on your network, then you do not want the individual users to change the password you assigned to them.

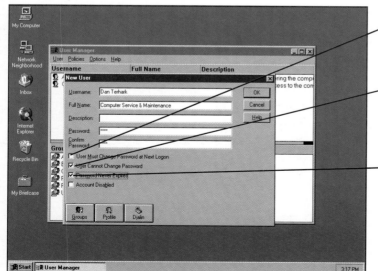

5. Click on **User Must Change Password** at **Next Logon** to **remove** the ✔.

6. Click on **User Cannot Change Password** to put a ✔ in the box. *If you do this step, you must do step 7 below.*

7. Click on **Password Never Expires** to put a ✔ in the box. If you don't do this, the password will expire in 45 days, and you'll have to do this all over again.

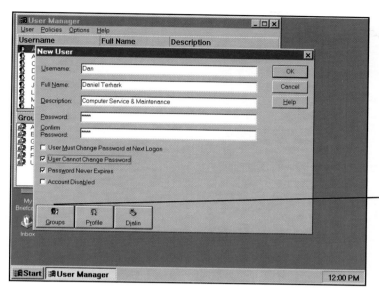

Assigning a User to a Group Membership

You can assign an individual to a particular status (group of users) who have varying degrees of access to this machine.

1. Click on **Groups.** The Groups Membership dialog box will appear. It is shown at the top of the next page.

Note: Check out the Group Membership Options shown on this information only screen before you go on to steps 2 and 3 on the next page.

In many small companies, with peer-to-peer networks, most employees share their folders and files (with some exceptions; i.e., the files on the bookkeepers machine). Therefore, in this section, we chose "Power Users" membership. This means that this person will have top-level access to the files and folders on this machine. If you want the user to have the same access to other machines, you will have to repeat these steps for each machine.

The choice of group membership for a particular individual is a management decision and is always based on security precautions.

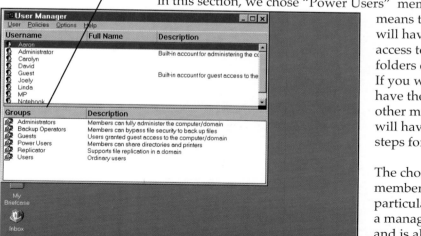

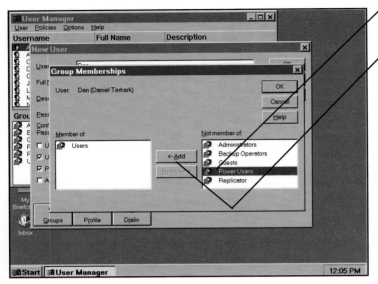

2. Click on **Power Users** to highlight it.

3. Click on **Add**. PowerUsers will move to the Member of box.

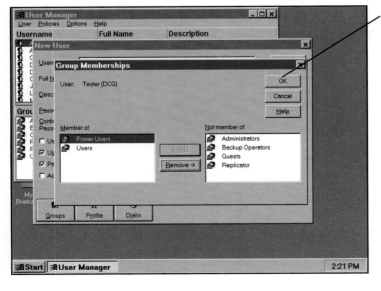

4. Click on **OK**. You'll go back to the New User dialog box.

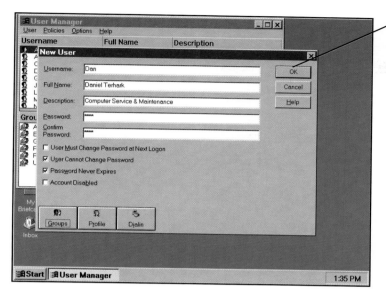

5. Click on **OK**. The User Manager dialog box will appear.

Notice that the new user you just added is now on the list.

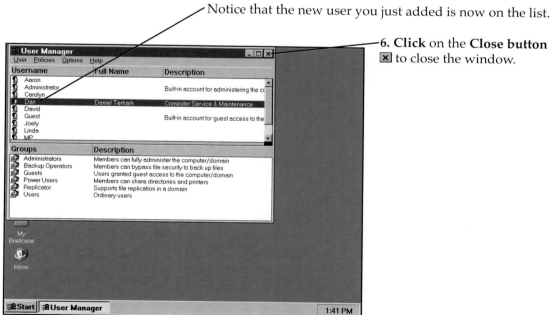

6. Click on the **Close button** ☒ to close the window.

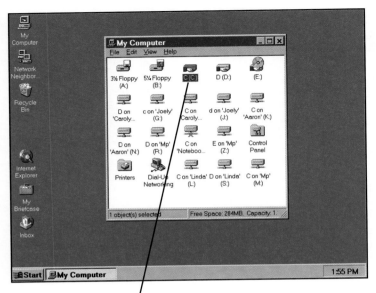

Limiting Access to a Workstation

Upon installation, a workstation is set to allow its folders and files to be shared by the users to whom you have assigned passwords. However, you can limit access to a specific folder on a drive or a specific drive by marking them "Not Shared." In the specific folder case, users who have been assigned passwords can access only the folder you set up to be shared rather than being able to access all of the folders on the machine. In this section, you will set the machine to allow access only to one specific folder. Next, you will see how to set up the workstation to prevent access to password holders to a specific drive.

1. **Double click** on **My Computer** to open its window.

2. **Double-click** on the **C drive (C:) icon** to open the C drive window.

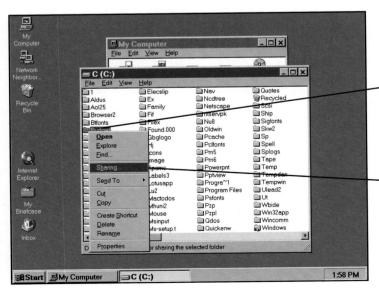

Limiting Access to One Folder

1. **Right-click** on the **folder** you are willing to let other users view. In this example, it is the Budget folder. A menu will appear.

2. **Click** on **Sharing**. The Properties dialog box for that folder will appear.

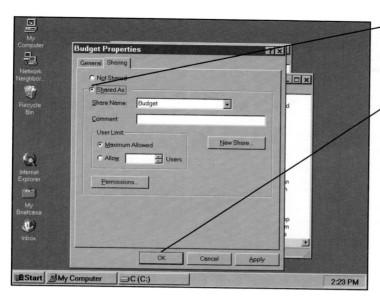

3. **Click** on **Shared As** to put a dot in the circle. The name of the folder will appear in the Share Name box.

4. **Click** on **OK** to close the dialog box. Users with password authorization can access only the Budget folder on this drive.

5. **Click** on the **Close button** ☒ to close the C window. *If you plan to follow along, do not close the My Computer window.*

Limiting Total Access to a Drive on a Workstation

With just a few clicks, you can limit access (stop sharing) to a drive on this machine. When you do that, other workstations, even though they are connected to the machine by cable and password, cannot access the drive when you turn off the sharing option.

1. **Right-click** on the **C drive icon.** A menu will appear.

2. **Click** on **Sharing.** The Properties dialog box will appear.

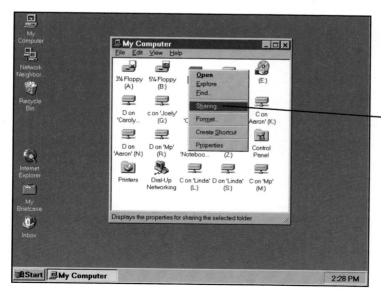

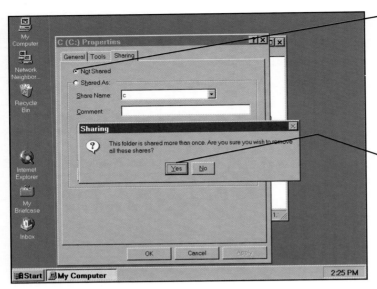

3. Click on **Not Shared** to **place a dot** in the **circle**. A Sharing message box will appear as shown here. If you have not yet mapped the drives on the system, the message box will not appear. In that case, go on to step 5 below.

4. Click on **Yes** if you are certain that you no longer want to share this drive with other machines.

—**5. Click** on **Apply**.

6. Click on **OK**. The dialog box will close.

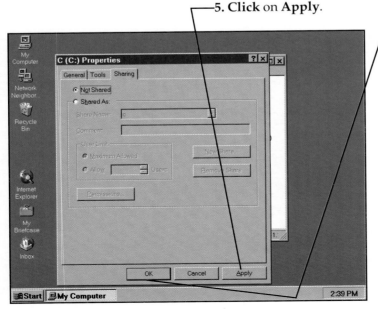

Installing Printers

Installing a printer on your workstation couldn't be easier, and, believe it or not, installing a network printer (a printer located on another machine in your Workgroup) is just as easy. The assumption in this chapter is that you are the owner or a key player in a small business and, therefore, have complete access to every machine on the network. In this chapter, you will:

✔ Install a local printer on your computer
✔ Install a shared network printer

Installing a Local Printer on a Workstation

NT 4.0's Printer Wizard will quickly walk you through the printer installation process.

1. Click on the **Start button** on the taskbar. A pop-up menu will appear.

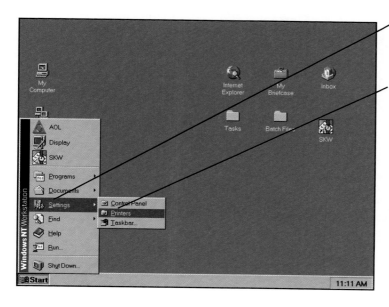

2. Move the **mouse pointer** to **Settings**. Another menu will appear.

3. Click on **Printers**. The Printers dialog box will appear.

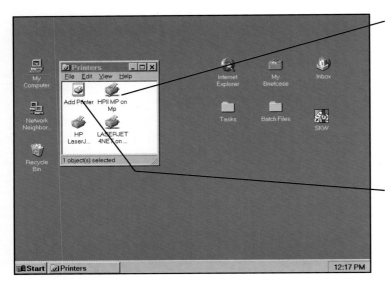

Notice the HPII icon in this window. The printer name plus location (HPII MP on Mp) indicates that this is a Network printer. In this example, the HPII is the only printer available for this workstation. Later in this chapter, you will learn how to add a second network computer.

4. Double-click on the **Add Printer icon**. The Add Printer Wizard dialog box will appear.

5. Click on **My Computer** to **put** a **dot** in the **circle**, if there isn't one there already.

Note: See the section entitled, "Installing a Network Printer" later in this chapter if you want to install a network printer.

6. Click on **Next**. Another Wizard dialog box will appear.

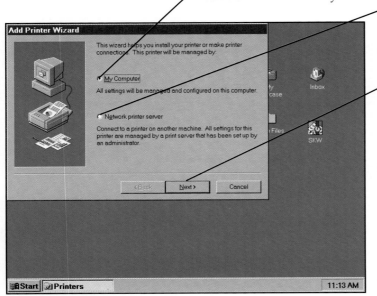

Notice that LPT1 is highlighted. Typically, LPT1 is the port setting for most printers on most computers. If you have any questions about ports, refer to the manual that came with your computer.

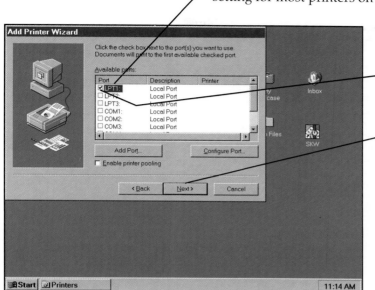

7. If LPT1 is the correct port, **click** on the **box** to the **left** of **LPT1** to place a ✔ in it.

8. Click on **Next**. Another dialog box will appear.

Selecting the Printer

1. Click on the ▼ and scroll down the list until you find the name of your printer's manufacturer.

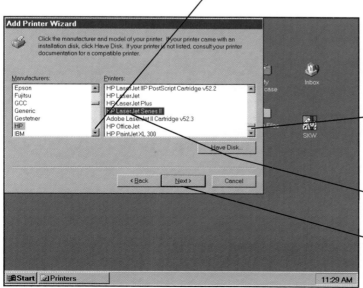

2. Click on the manufacturer's **name** to highlight it. In this example, it is HP.

3. Click on the ▼ to scroll down the list of printer models until you find your printer's name (model).

4. Click on the **name** of the **model** to highlight it.

5. Click on **Next**. Another dialog box will appear.

Selecting Printer Driver Options

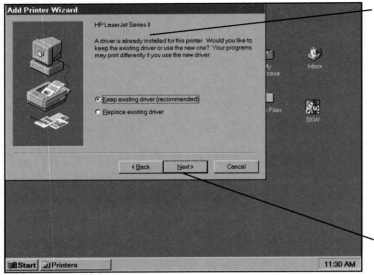

Notice that, in this example, the driver for the HP LaserJet is already installed (available on your hard drive). Therefore, we do not need to replace the existing driver (the second option in this dialog box).

If the driver you need for your printer is not installed on your machine, a message will appear prompting you to insert the appropriate CD or floppy into the CD-ROM or floppy drive.

1. Click on **Next**. Another dialog box will appear with a suggested name for this printer.

Setting the Local Printer's Status

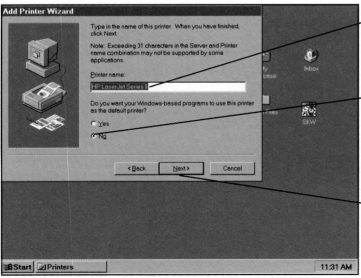

1. Type a new **name** for the printer if you want to give it a more personalized label (e.g., Joely's LaserJet II).

2. Click on **No** to **put** a **dot** in the **circle** if you do not want this printer to be the default (standard) printer at your workstation. Otherwise, **click** on **Yes**.

3. Click on **Next**. Another Wizard dialog box will appear.

Sharing or Not Sharing a Local Printer

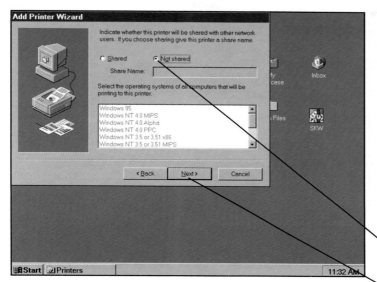

If you do not want to share your printer with another workstation, choose the "Not shared" option in this window. The printer will not be available to anyone else in your workgroup because the printer icon will not appear on the list of network printers. See the section later in this chapter entitled, "Installing a Network Printer" for help with network printer installation.

1. Click on **Not shared** to **put** a **dot** in the **circle**.

2. Click on **Next**. Another dialog box will appear.

3. Click on **Yes (recommended)** to **put** a **dot** in the **circle** if one isn't there already. This will allow you to perform a test of your printer at the end of the installation process. In this case, we clicked on **No** because we know our printer works OK.

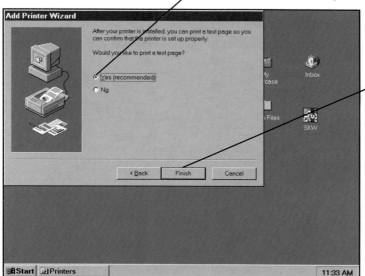

4. Click on **Finish**. The Printers dialog box will appear.

Note: If you clicked on **Yes** in step 3 above, the printer will print a sample page. You will then be asked if it printed. If it didn't, you will be guided through steps to correct the problem (not shown here).

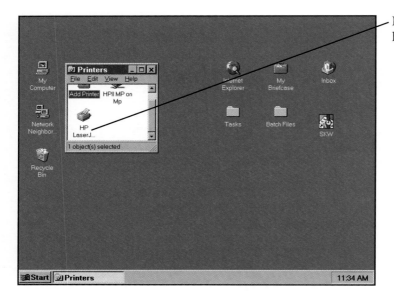

Notice the new icon for the local printer you just installed.

Installing a Network Printer

NT's wizard makes the process of installing (having access to) a printer located on another workstation painless. One caution, however: If you are prompted to install a new printer driver later in this section, you will need to have the NT 4.0 CD-ROM available to complete the task.

1. Repeat steps 1-4 on the first two pages of this chapter to open the Add Printer Wizard.

2. Click on **Network printer server** to **put** a **dot** in the **circle**.

3. Click on **Next**. The Connect to Printer dialog box will appear.

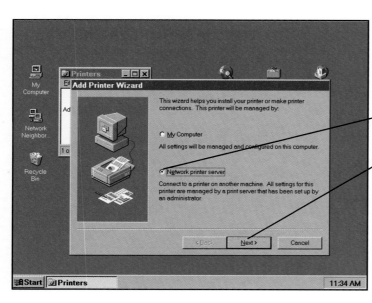

Selecting a Network Printer

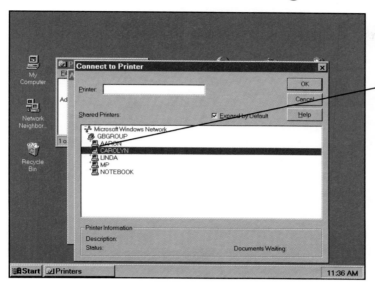

In this section, you will select the network printer that you want to install.

1. Double-click on the **workstation** where the network (shared) printer is located. (In this example, each workstation has been named for its occupant.) The name of the shared printer(s) for this drive will appear under the Driver icon.

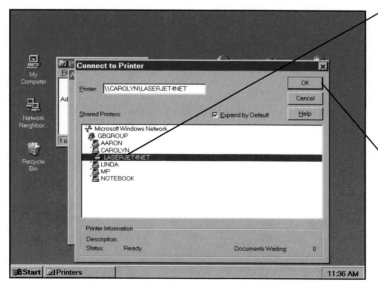

Notice that there is only one shared printer available at this workstation.

Note: If more than one printer appears on your list, make sure you highlight the printer that you want to install.

2. Click on **OK**. The Connect to Printer dialog box will appear.

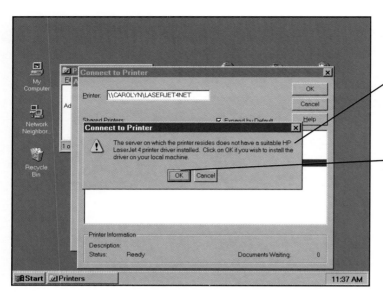

Installing a Printer Driver

Notice that this message confirms that we need to install a printer driver for the Network printer.

1. Click on **OK** to proceed with the printer driver installation. The Add Printer Wizard dialog box will appear.

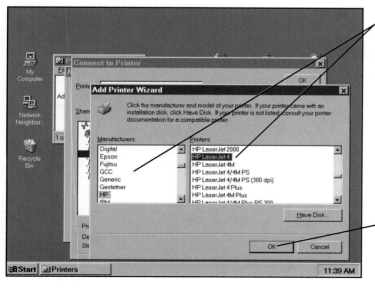

2. Repeat steps 1-4 in the section, "Selecting Your Printer" earlier in this chapter to select the correct manufacturer and printer model.

3. Click on **OK**. The Files Needed dialog box will appear.

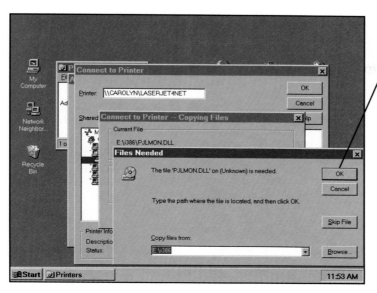

4. Insert your **NT 4.0 CD-ROM disk** into your CD-ROM drive to complete the installation.

5. Click on **OK**. The Connect to Printer -- Copying Files dialog box will appear.

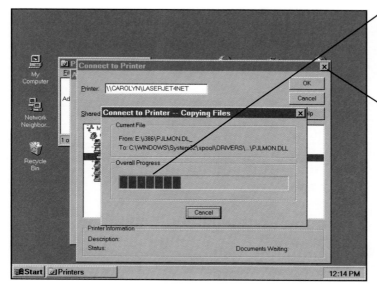

You can watch the process of the installation, as files are being copied. When the copying process is complete, the message box will so indicate.

6. Click on the **Close button** ☒ to close this window.

Setting the Network Printer's Status

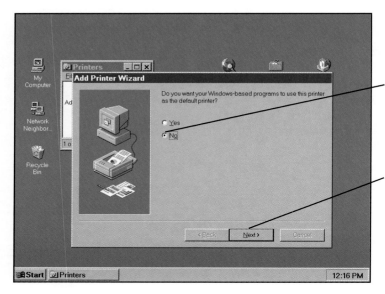

1. Click on **No** to **put** a **dot** in the **circle** if you do not want to use the new printer as your standard (default) printer. Otherwise, **click** on **Yes**.

2. Click on **Next**.

3. Click on **Finish**. The Printers dialog box will appear.

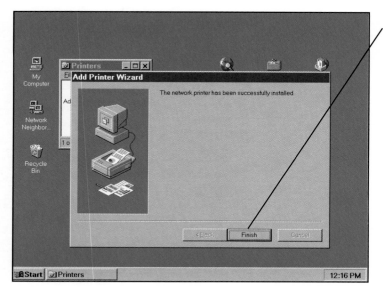

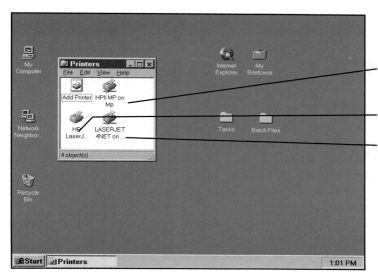

Notice the printers now available at this workstation:

❖ A previously installed shared printer

❖ A local printer you installed

❖ Another network printer that you just installed

Mapping Network Drives

Small businesses are often set up as peer-to-peer networks, where each computer has the ability to connect to other computers *to which it has access*. (See Chapter 29, "Controlling Access to Workstations.") Before you can actually connect to another workstation in your workgroup, you must map a route to the network drive. Creating a map is no more difficult than opening up the list of available drives in your network and assigning a letter to each drive to which you want to connect. The assumption in this chapter is that you are the owner or a key player in a small business and, therefore, have complete access to every machine on the network. In this chapter, you will do the following:

✔ Map a network drive
✔ Assign an identifying letter to a network drive

Mapping a Network Drive

When you map a drive, you create a connection between your machine and the specific drive (e.g., C: or D:) on the machine with which you want to connect. In this section, you will begin the mapping process by opening the list of available network drives in your workgroup.

1. Double-click on **Network Neigborhood** to open the Network Neighborhood window as shown here.

This example shows the names of the computers on our network.

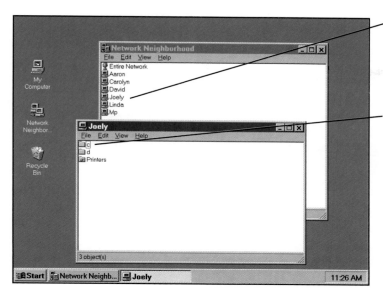

2. Double-click on the computer to which you want to connect. In this example, it's **Joely**. The window for that specific computer will open.

3. Right-click on the drive to which you want to connect (in this example, C). A menu will appear as shown in the screen below.

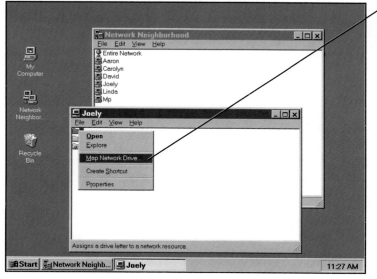

4. Click on **Map Network Drive**. The Map Network Drive dialog box will appear.

Assigning a Network Drive Letter

When you map a connection to a drive on another machine, you are, in effect, telling your machine that it has another drive. If, for example, you have a C: drive and a D: drive, and your CD-ROM drive is E:, then this new connection has to be given a letter other than C, D, or E because those letters are already taken.

In this example, you will assign a letter to the C: drive on the Joely machine.

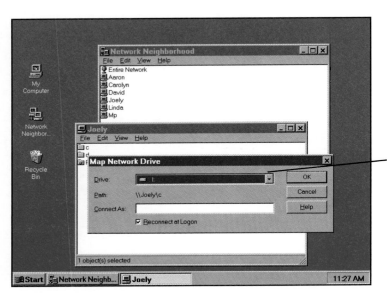

1. Click on the ▼. A list of available drive letters will appear.

2. Click on the **letter** that you want to assign to the other machine's C: drive. In this case, we assigned the letter "G" to Joely's C: drive. G: is now the local network drive letter on your machine that identifies the C: drive on the Joely machine.

Note: Each machine in your network can assign "G" to Joely's C: drive, or it can assign a different letter to her C: drive. The letter chosen has no effect on the connection. It's simply a label.

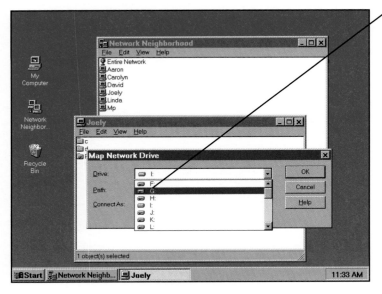

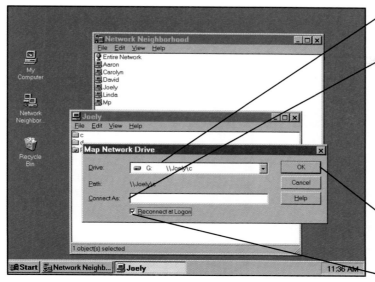

Notice that Drive G: is identified as Joely\c.

Note: Connect As is used when you want to connect to another machine using a different user name and password. In that case, you would type the different user name here and then would be prompted to enter a password in order to make the connection.

3. Click on **OK**. The window showing the C: drive of the Joely machine will appear.

Notice that Reconnect at Logon is automatically checked (✔).

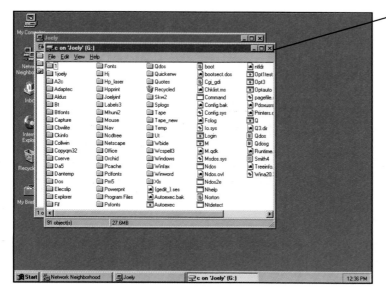

4. Click on the **Close button** ⊠ to close the window.

Connecting Other Drives in Your Network

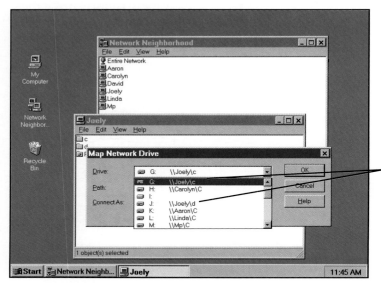

You must map each drive to which you want to connect from this machine.

1. Repeat the steps in the previous section to assign letters to the other drives and machines on your network to which you want to connect.

As you map drives, you create a list in the Map Network Drive dialog box. Notice in this example that you are connected to both the C: and D: drives on the Joely machine and that each drive has a separate letter (local network drive) on your machine.

Installing Peer Web Services

NT's Peer Web Services lets you set up a full-featured Web site. It can be set up on a workstation in any type of NT network. Though intended for low-volume use, you can connect your Web site to the Internet so that people outside your corporate network can tap into its resources. And it's an excellent choice for running an intranet that provides information services restricted to the people who are on your company or organization's network. Peer Web Services can be set up on one workstation for centralized control of the company's intranet, or on several if many departments will be contributing to it. In any of these uses, it includes all of the administrative and security features you'll need.

The workstation running Peer Web Services and any that will make use of it need to have the TCP/IP protocol installed (we'll cover this in this chapter just in case). Because it's a network service, you'll need to be logged on as Administrator or a member of the Administrators group to install Peer Web Services, and you'll need the NT Workstation installation CD. The service includes an online, hypertext guide that you can consult before installation (see the last page of this chapter). In this chapter, you will do the following:

✔ Install Peer Web Services on a workstation
✔ Explore Peer Web Services' features
✔ Use Internet Explorer to bring up a Web page on your intranet
✔ Locate the Peer Web Services Installation and Planning Guide

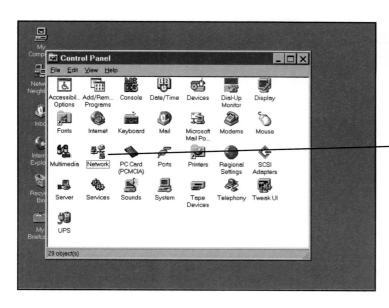

Starting Installation

1. Open the **Control Panel** window.

2. Double-click the **Network icon**. The Network dialog box will appear.

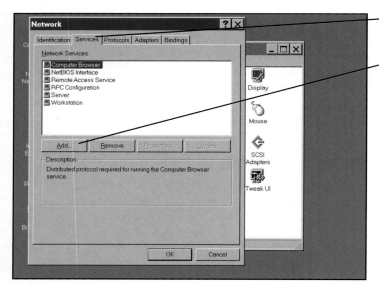

3. Click on the **Services tab** to bring it to the front.

4. Click on **Add**. The Select Network Service dialog box will appear.

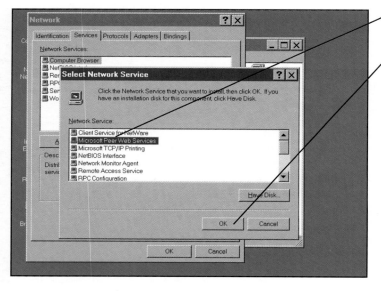

5. Click on **Microsoft Peer Web Services** to highlight it.

6. Click on **OK**. A dialog box prompting you for the NT installation CD will appear.

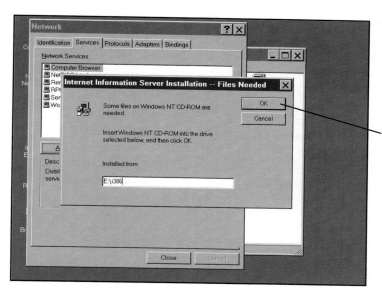

7. Hold down the **Shift key** on your keyboard as you **insert** the **CD** into your CD drive. This prevents the autorun feature from bringing up the CD's menu.

8. Click on **OK**. The Microsoft Peer Web Services Setup dialog box will appear.

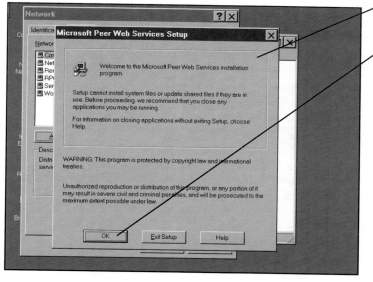

9. Read the **information** in the dialog box.

10. Click on **OK**. The contents of the dialog box will change.

Selecting Components

The upper-left side of the dialog box (shown on the next page) lists the components you can install and how much space they'll take up on your hard disk. If you click on one, you'll see a description of it on the right. In most cases, you won't need FTP or Gopher Service. Consider the hard disk space you have available, and remember that you'll need more for the Web pages, etc. that you will be making available. Here's a little about each component, why you would or would not want to install them, and (in parenthesis) how much hard disk space each requires:

❖ **Internet Service Manager** - You must have this administrative component to manage the Web site. (1,200K)

❖ **World Wide Web Service** - Sets up a Web server on which you "publish" Web pages (see Chapter 25, "Surfing with Internet Explorer," for more on Web pages). Publishing consists of providing storage space for the pages on your hard disk, and access to them through this service. This, and the Internet Service Manager, are all you need for the most basic setup of Peer Web Services. (340K)

❖ **WWW Service Samples** - These are sample Web pages and graphics files that can be very helpful to you. (450K)

❖ **Internet Service Manager (HTML)** - This is an HTML interface for the Internet Service Manager that lets you manage the Web site using your browser. It can be installed in addition to the regular Internet Service Manager, but not in place of it. (230K)

❖ **Gopher Service** - This is a system that leads to information through layers of menus. It is entirely text-based (it does not contain any graphics) and was developed before the graphics-based World Wide Web for providing information over the Internet. Someone using your gopher would, for example, first encounter a welcome menu that listed the major categories of information available. When they chose a category, it would lead to another, more detailed menu. Eventually, the menu choices would be for individual text documents that they could read or print from their browser, or files that they could download. While still common on the Internet, most gophers are being replaced by Web pages. (260K)

❖ **FTP (File Transfer Protocol) Service** - An FTP site is an archive that stores files so that others can download them from the site. For example, most computer and software companies maintain FTP sites where samples of their products or support files are stored. The sites can be reached on the Internet and the files on them downloaded using FTP software or Web browsers. If you don't anticipate a need for such an archive, there's no need to install it. (230K)

❖ **ODBC (Open Database Connectivity) Drivers** - These are drivers (program files) needed to link your Web site to databases. You may, for example, want to set up a Web page that links your sales staff to a database of information about your products, or one that links your customers to a database of information on the orders they've placed. In a corporate intranet, you may want to link your staff to a database on benefits. The ODBC drivers take up very little additional space and give you the option of using databases with your site in the future, even if you have no plans to do so now. (less than 1K)

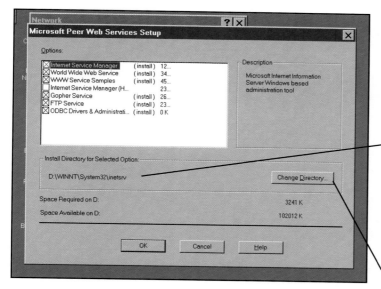

1. To select a component, **click** in the **square** next to it to place an × in it.

2. To deselect a component, **click** in the **square** next to it to remove the ×.

The directory on your hard disk where the files will be stored is shown here. (If you want to use the directory shown, skip steps 3 through 7.) It's easy to choose another directory, if you prefer.

3. To designate another directory, **click** on **Change Directory**. The Select Directory dialog box will appear.

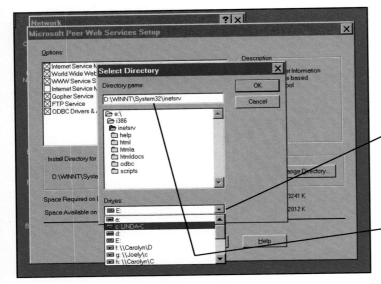

The machine we used for this example has NT installed on the D: drive. We want the Peer Web Services files on the C: drive. When we opened this dialog box, the E: (CD) drive was selected!

4. Click on the ▼ to open the drive list.

5. Click on the **drive** you want to use.

6. Type a **name** for the directory in the Directory name box. The default name, and the one we typed, is "inetserv."

7. Click on **OK**. The dialog box will close.

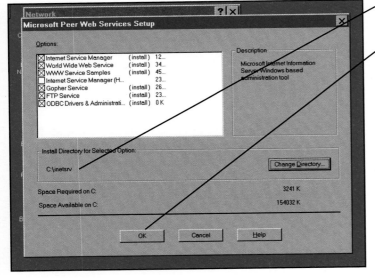

The drive and directory selected will appear here.

8. Click on **OK**. A message will appear.

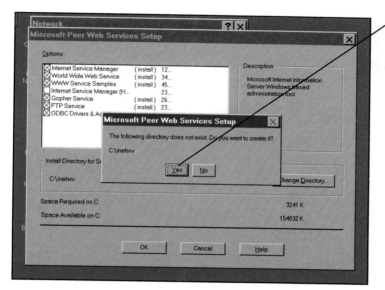

9. Click on **Yes**. The Publishing Directories dialog box will appear.

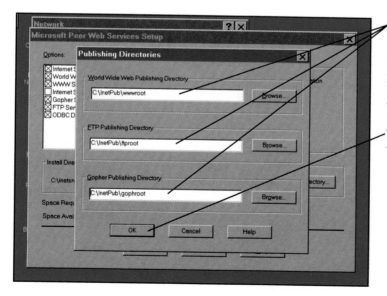

These are the directories where your Web page, FTP, or gopher files will be stored. To change any of them, click on the Browse button next to it and designate your choice.

10. Click on **OK**. A message will appear.

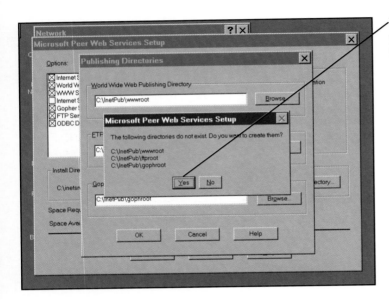

11. Click on **Yes**. The install program will begin to copy files to your computer.

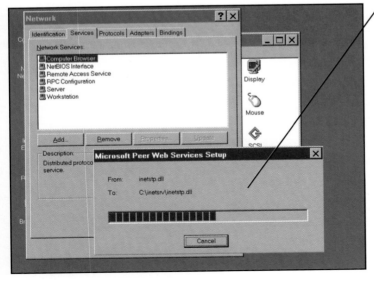

Message boxes such as this one will appear and show the progress of various stages of the setup. If you're installing all of the components, this takes about fifteen minutes, so be patient.

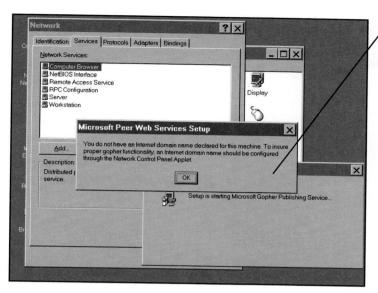

You may see a warning message such as this one, telling you that some action needs to be taken after setup is complete. If so, make a note of what it says, and attend to it following setup. For more information, Chapter 11 in the online guide to Peer Web Services (shown at the end of this chapter) tells you about troubleshooting and error messages.

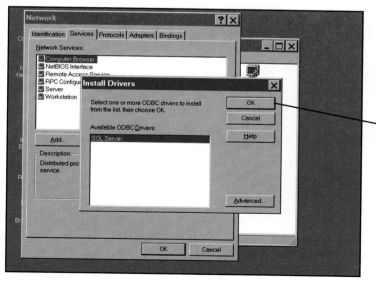

Eventually, a dialog box for the ODBC driver installation will appear. There will be only one set of drivers listed in the box for you to choose, and it will already be highlighted.

12. Click on **OK**. Setup will continue.

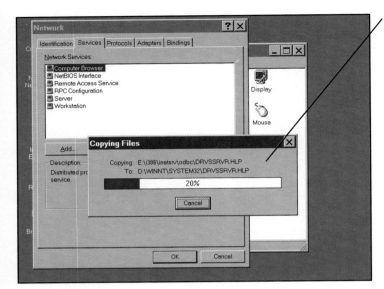

More messages will come and go, showing the progress of the installation.

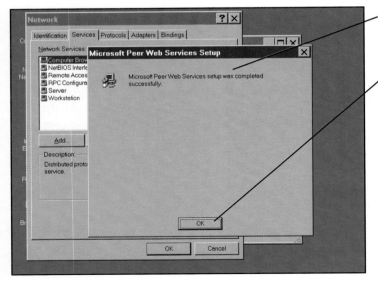

When installation is finally complete, you'll see this message.

13. Click on **OK**. The message will disappear.

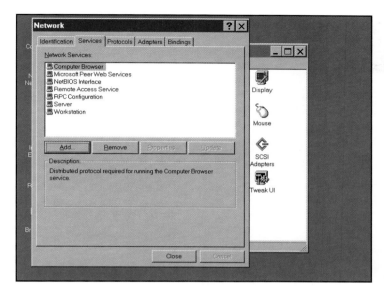

Before you close the dialog box and Control Panel, check to make sure that the TCP/IP network protocol is installed.

14. Click on the **Protocols tab** (not shown here) to bring it to the front.

If TCP/IP is not listed on the Protocols tab, click on Add. The Select Network Protocols dialog box will appear. Select TCP/IP, click on the OK button, and follow the directions on your screen. (See "Configuring TCP/IP" in Chapter 23.) You will have to restart your workstation when you're done.

Managing Your Web Site

The Internet Service Manager is used to configure and maintain your Web site.

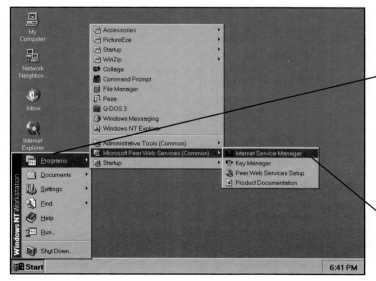

1. Click on the **Start** button on your taskbar. The Start menu will appear.

2. Move the **mouse pointer** over Programs. The Programs menu will appear.

3. Move the **mouse pointer** over Microsoft Peer Web Services (Common). Another menu will appear.

4. Click on **Internet Service Manager**. The Microsoft Internet Service Manager window will appear.

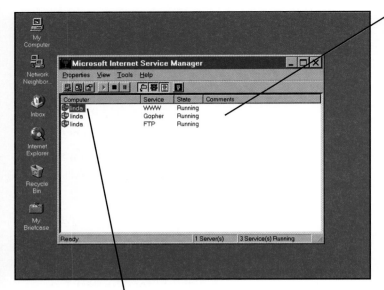

The service components (Web, FTP, etc.) that are installed and the computer(s) they are installed on are listed here.

You use the toolbar buttons and menu choices to (among other things) choose the computers and services on your network to display in this window; to start, stop or pause a service; and to open the Key Manager.

The Key Manager is used for setting up SSL (Secure Sockets Layer), a method for encrypting data that passes to and from your site. This is a security measure used mainly for commercial transactions. For more on SSL, see Chapter 5 of the online guide to Peer Web Services (discussed at the end of this chapter)

You also can check on or change service configurations from here.

5. Click on a **computer/service** to highlight it.

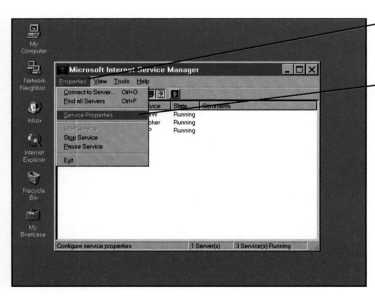

6. Click on **Properties** in the menu bar. The Properties menu will appear.

7. Click on **Service Properties**. The Service Properties dialog box will appear.

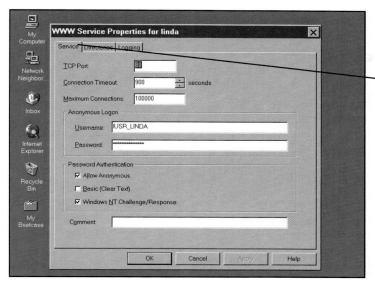

The Service Properties dialog box has three tabs. It's virtually the same for each service.

On the Service tab you can set connection parameters, designate user names and passwords for anonymous login, and set authentication. When you installed Peer Web Services, it added the user name shown here and a randomly generated password to your workstation's list of "Guest" users. When someone requests a Web page, etc., they are automatically logged on using this name and password. Anonymous login basically means that anyone who has access to your workstation can see the pages on the Web site. Generally, you shouldn't have to change any of these settings. For more on these settings, consult Chapters 3 and 5 of the online guide to Peer Web Services (discussed at the end of this chapter) or click the Help button.

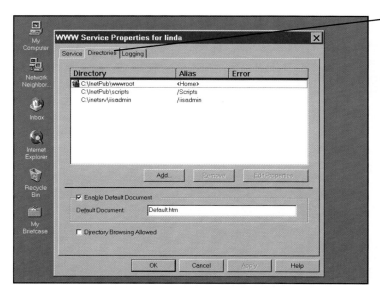

8. Click on the **Directories tab** to bring it to the front.

This tab lets you designate or create new directories on your hard disk for the services' files. You can also set a default Web page that displays if a particular one isn't requested, and set up hypertext browsing for your site. For more on these settings, see Chapter 6 of the online guide to Peer Web Services (discussed at the end of this chapter) or click the Help button.

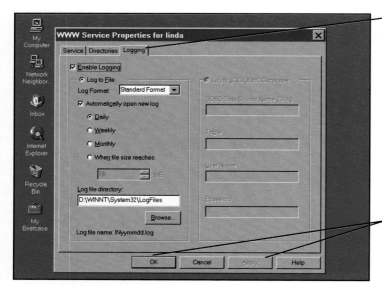

9. Click on the **Logging tab** to bring it to the front.

This tab is used to set up files that keep a log, or record, of the use your site receives. This is useful to determine whether and how it's being put to use. For more on logging, see Chapter 7 of the online guide to Peer Web Services or click on the Help button.

10. If you make changes to any of the settings, **click** on **Apply** to continue using the dialog box, **or click** on **OK** to save the changes and close it.

You can also click on Cancel or the ⊠ in the upper-right corner to close the dialog box without making any changes.

Making Web Files Available

During installation, Peer Web Services creates "root" directories for each component service that you install to hold the

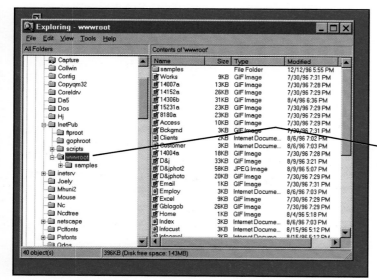

files you make available at your site. Subdirectories and other directories can be set up using the Internet Service Manager, shown in the previous section. For a very basic service, you can simply copy the files to the root directory of the service.

For this example, we used NT Explorer to copy some files from our Internet Web site to the *wwwroot* directory of our test workstation. From there, others with network access to the workstation can easily get at them using their browsers.

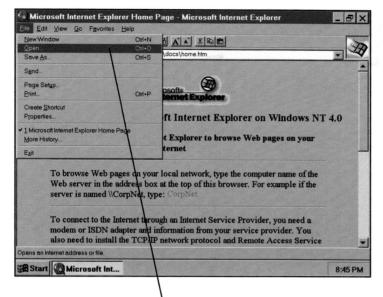

Checking Out Your Site

You can, of course, use the browser on your workstation to see if Web pages are displaying properly. But to be sure they're getting out over the network, you'll need to use another workstation.

1. Open Internet Explorer or whatever browser is installed on the alternate workstation.

You can use standard browser techniques to reach the site.

2a. Click on **File** in the menu bar and then **click** on **Open**. A dialog box will appear into which you can type the path and file name you want. Click on OK and the file will be displayed.

OR

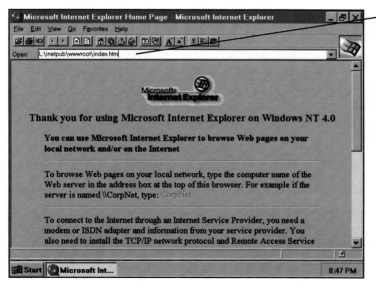

2b. Type the **path and file name** into the Open box and **press Enter**. In our example, the file is named "index.htm" and is located on the L: drive (the networked C: drive on our test workstation). The file will be displayed.

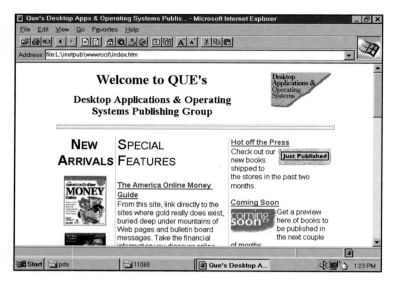

Use standard browser procedures to check all of the pages at your site. See Chapter 25, "Surfing with Internet Explorer," for more on using Internet Explorer.

Consulting the Online Guide to Peer Web Services

Peer Web Services includes an excellent online guide. It provides in-depth information and advice on using the service to create a full-featured site.

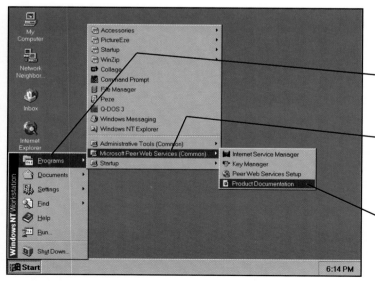

1. Click on the **Start** button on your taskbar. The Start menu will appear.

2. Move the **mouse pointer** over Programs. The Programs menu will appear.

3. Move the **mouse pointer** over Microsoft Peer Web Services (Common). Another menu will appear.

4. Click on **Product Documentation**. Internet Explorer will open and the Peer Web Services Installation and Planning Guide will appear.

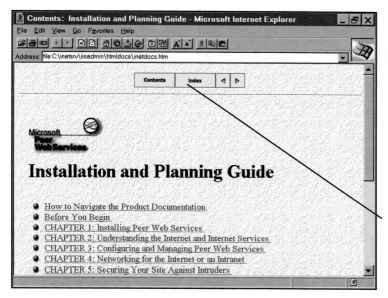

The online guide uses hyperlinks (the blue, underlined text) to index and interconnect its various parts.

5. Click on a **chapter title**. The opening page of the chapter will appear. Text in the chapter will also contain cross-referencing links to subjects that are covered in other chapters of the guide.

You'll see these four buttons throughout the guide. The Contents button returns you to the first page of the guide, shown in this example. The Index button takes you to an alphabetical list of hyperlinks. The ◄ and ▶ buttons lead to the previous and next pages.

Checking the Online Guide Before Installation

The online guide is copied to your computer when you install Peer Web Service. You can also consult it using the NT installation CD before installing the service:

1. Hold down the **Shift key** on your keyboard **while you insert** the **NT installation CD** into your CD drive. This keeps the autorun feature from bringing up the CD's menu.

2. Open Internet Explorer.

3. In Internet Explorer's Open box, **type** (for example, if your CD drive is drive E:)

> **file:E:\i386\inetsrv\htmldocs\inetdocs.htm**

and **press Enter**. The page shown above will appear, and you can browse through the guide as previously explained.

Enhancing NT

The standard Windows NT Workstation 4.0 installation will probably give you everything you need for your day-to-day computer use, but we don't know of any computer user who is content to leave things alone. Everyone has ideas about how they'd improve their hardware and software, or things that their operating system should include but doesn't.

In the case of NT, you have many options. Several chapters in Part I show you how to customize NT to suit your personal tastes and work habits. The chapters in Part VI will tell you about updates to the operating system, how to add NT accessories that weren't installed on your workstation, Internet sources for programs that enhance NT, and how to add and use Microsoft Mail.

CHAPTER
33

Adding Features to NT

Software either improves or is forgotten, left by the wayside. As good as NT 4.0 is, you can be certain that eventually there will be a newer, better version. But before a full update appears, Microsoft will release *Service Packs* that upgrade or make fixes to the operating system. As of this writing, the first Service Pack had already appeared. In addition to showing you how to find and install the Service Packs, we'll show you some add-on programs and a unique piece of software that "tweaks" NT 4.0's user interface. We'll also show you how to add accessories that may have been left out during NT's standard installation, and a couple of "undocumented" NT programs, carry-overs from older versions of Windows that aren't publicized. In this chapter, you will do the following:

✔ Add Accessories and other programs
✔ Download and install the Service Pack
✔ Install Tweak UI and see how you can use it to customize NT's user interface
✔ Find some add-on programs that help you work with NT

Adding NT Accessories

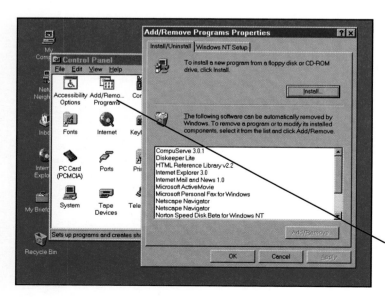

Many people choose a setup procedure for NT 4.0 that does not include all of the Accessories and other programs that could be installed. It's easy to see what programs were installed on your workstation and add any that were left out. (You'll need the NT installation CD to add programs.)

1. Open the **Control Panel window**.

2. Double-click on the **Add/ Remove Programs icon**. The Add/Remove Programs Properties dialog box will appear.

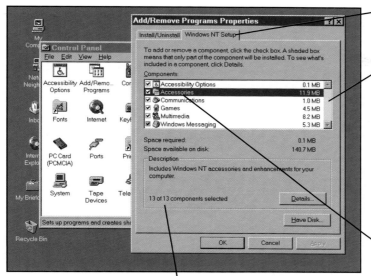

3. Click on the **Windows NT Setup tab** to bring it to the front.

Groups of programs that were added during installation are listed here. If only some programs in a group were added, the box with a ✔ next to it will be gray. Groups in which no programs were added won't have a check mark. Scroll through the list to see all of the categories.

4. Click on **Accessories** to highlight it.

The number of programs in the highlighted category that were installed is given here. In this case, we had installed all of the Accessories, so it says "13 of 13 components selected."

5. Click on the **Details button**. The Accessories dialog box will appear.

Installing Programs

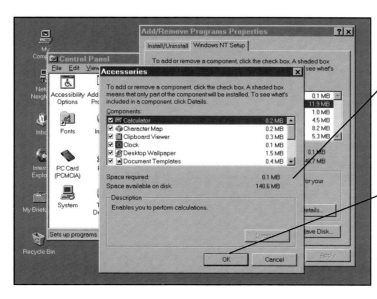

1. Click in the **box** next to a program that you want to select to place a ✔ in it.

The hard disk space needed to add the program, the amount of disk space available, and a description of the program are shown in the lower part of the dialog box.

2a. Click on **OK** when you are finished making selections.

OR

2b. Click on **Cancel** to close the dialog box without making any changes.

3. Repeat this process to select any programs you want to add from the other groups.

4. Click on **OK** in the Add/Remove Programs Properties dialog box. You will be prompted for the NT 4 Workstation installation CD.

5. Hold down the **Shift key** on your keyboard while you insert the CD into your CD drive. This keeps the CD autorun feature from starting the CD's built-in menu.

6. Follow the **prompts** that appear on your screen to complete the installation.

7. Reboot your **workstation** when you're done. It's a good idea to reboot after making any changes to your system whether you are prompted to do so or not.

"Un-Hiding" Program Manager, or What to Do if You Absolutely, Positively Can't Stand the Windows 95 Interface

The people at Microsoft spent many years and millions of dollars developing and refining the "Windows 95 interface." The hope was that it would be considered such an improvement that no one would want to use anything else, even the old tried-and-true Windows 3.x interface. However, if you are among the unconvinced and want your Windows 3.x back, a version of it is still available in a somewhat modified form, hidden within NT 4.0.

Windows 3.x can be approximated by using two NT 4.0 programs: the Program Manager and File Manager. Installing an icon for File Manager is covered in "Adding a Shortcut Icon Directly to the Folder" in Chapter 9. The version of File Manager in NT 4.0 is 32-bit, supports long file names, and runs faster than the original.

NT 4.0's Program Manager doesn't look exactly like the one in Windows 3.x, but it works in the same way.

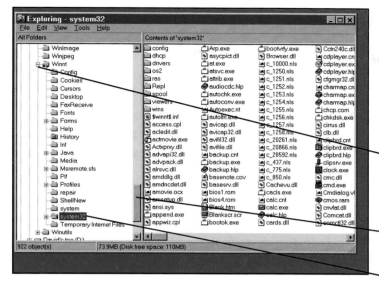

1. Open Windows NT Explorer.

2. Scroll down the **Folders list** until you see the folder that contains the NT operating system; it will be named either Windows or Winnt.

3. Click on the **+** next to the Windows or Winnt folder to show the list of subfolders that are in it.

4. Scroll down until you see the subfolder named system32.

5. Click on **system32** to highlight it. The list of files in the folder will appear on the right.

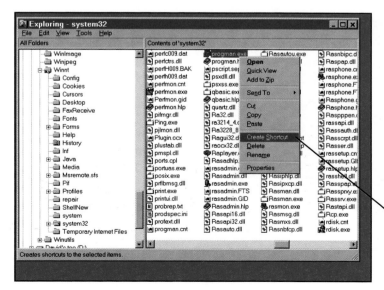

Making a Shortcut

Here are the steps to bring Program Manager back. First, make a shortcut to the program.

1. Scroll horizontally until you see progman.exe.

2. Right-click on **progman.exe**. A menu will appear.

3. Click on **Create Shortcut**. A new file named "shortcut to progman.exe" will appear at the end of the file list.

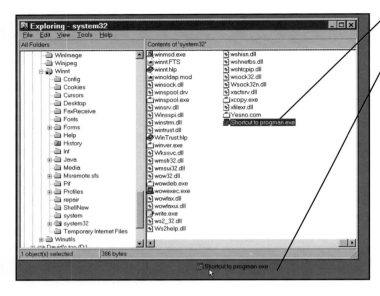

4. Move your **mouse pointer** over the new shortcut.

5. Press and **hold** the **mouse button** as you drag the shortcut to the desktop.

6. Release the **mouse button**. The shortcut will now be on your desktop.

7. Click on the ☒ in the upper-right corner of the Explorer window to close it.

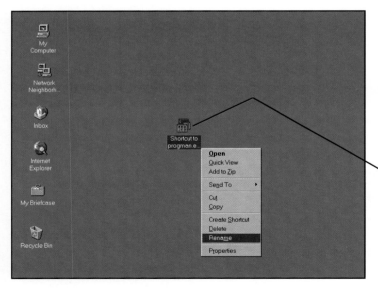

You can rename the shortcut icon to something more recognizable.

8. Right-click on the **shortcut icon**. A menu will appear.

9. Click on **Rename** if you want to rename it.

10. To see what the NT Program Manager looks like, **double-click** on the **icon**. The Program Manager window will appear.

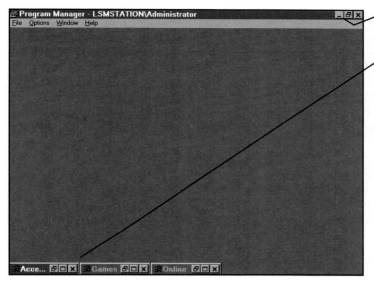

11. Click on the ▣ button to maximize the window.

Unlike the little file folder icons in Windows 3.x, program groups show up as little rectangles along the lower edge. If you upgraded over Windows 3.x, your program groups and icons will be present. Otherwise, you'll have to create groups and program icons just as you would using Windows 3.x's Program Manager.

12. To create a new group, **click** on **File** in the menu bar. The File menu will appear.

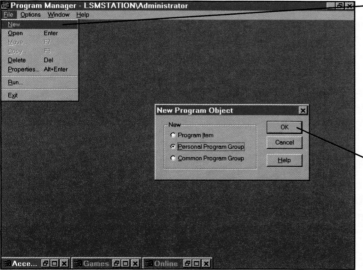
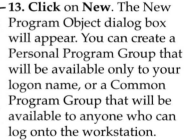

13. Click on **New**. The New Program Object dialog box will appear. You can create a Personal Program Group that will be available only to your logon name, or a Common Program Group that will be available to anyone who can log onto the workstation.

14. Click on **OK**. Another dialog box will appear, in which you can name the program group and click on OK to create it.

With the new program group open, you can click on File and New to create program icons, just as in Windows 3.x. The shortcut icon for Program Manager can be moved to your startup file (see Chapter 11, "Using the Automatic Startup Feature") to open it automatically every time you start your workstation. See Chapter 10, "Customizing the Start Menu," for information on placing the shortcut on the Start menu, if that's where you'd like to have it.

Locating and Installing the Windows NT Service Packs

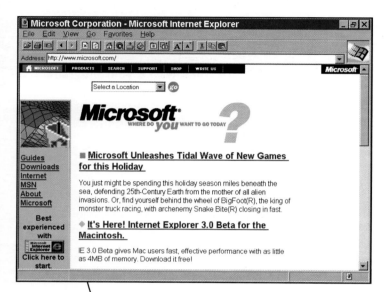

Service packs are made by Microsoft to fix problems that come to light or improve the performance of NT between revisions of the entire operating system.

To see whether a service pack has been installed on your workstation, watch your workstation's monitor carefully during startup. When the "blue screen" appears, a note at the top of the screen will indicate whether a service pack is present and what its number is. Make a note of it if one has been installed.

New service packs contain all the fixes that were in previous ones. If, for example, Service Pack 3 is installed on your workstation and number 5 is available, you don't have to install Service Pack 4 before installing the newer Service Pack 5.

Service packs are stored at Microsoft's Web site, where you can easily locate and download them.

1. Open Internet Explorer and **go to** the **Microsoft home page**, as shown in Chapter 25, "Surfing with Internet Explorer."

2. Click on the **Downloads link**. The Downloads page will appear.

Note: Web pages change all the time. Microsoft's home page may not look the same as this one when you see it.

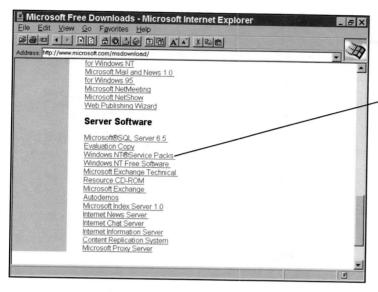

3. **Scroll down** the **Downloads page** until you see Windows NT Service Packs under the Server Software heading.

4. **Click** on **Windows NT Service Packs**. The Windows NT Service Packs page will appear.

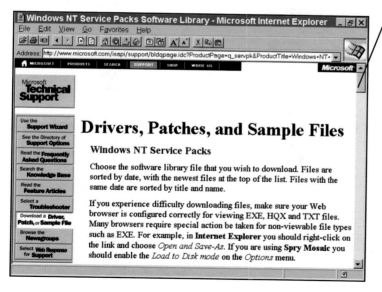

5. **Read** what they have to say **about the Service Packs**, then **scroll down** the **page** until you see the one you need.

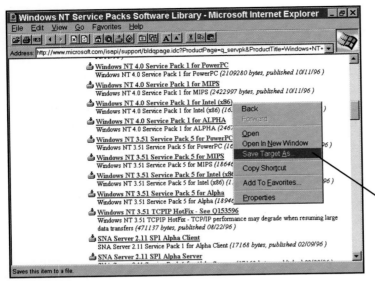

There are separate service packs for each type of processor that NT is compatible with. Most PCs have Intel or Intel-like processors. Check your computer owner's manual if you aren't sure which you have.

6. Right-click on the **service pack** that you want to download. A menu will appear.

7. Click on **Save Target As**. The Save As dialog box will appear.

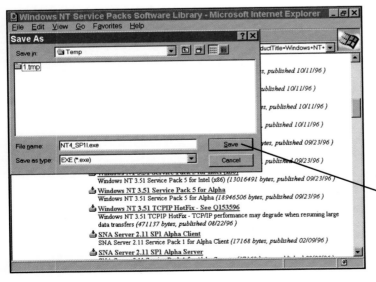

You can use standard navigation techniques to go to whatever directory you want the file save in. In this example, it's the Temp directory. Make a note of the directory you saved the file in. You'll need to know it later when you install the service pack. The file's name will appear in the File name box.

8. Click on **Save**. The download will start. When downloading is completed, close Explorer and, if needed, hang up the connection to your ISP.

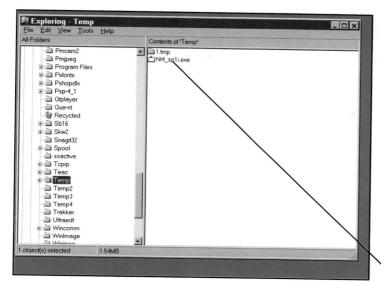

Installing the Service Pack

The service pack is what's called a "self-extracting archive" file. That is, it's an executable file containing several compressed files that automatically expand when the file is run.

1. Open Windows NT Explorer and **go to** the **directory** where you saved the service pack.

2. Double-click on the **service pack file**.

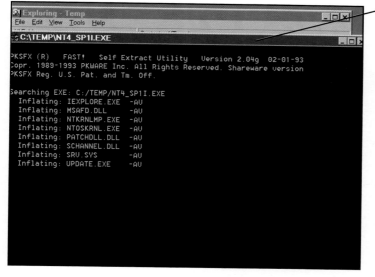

A window like this one will open and you will see file names appearing in it as the compressed files are expanded. When all the files have been extracted, the window will close.

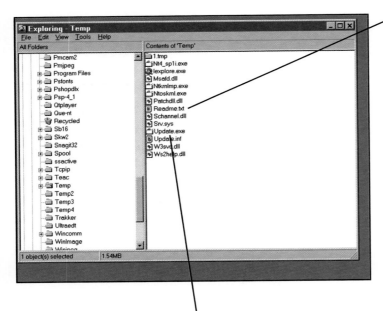

Among the files will be one named Readme.txt that contains information on the service pack and its installation. If you double-click on this file, Notepad will open and the file will be displayed. (We've already read it, so we won't show this, but you should read it for important information that could affect your installation.) It says that to install the service pack, you run the program named Update.exe, and that only the service pack files that are appropriate for your workstation's configuration will be installed. It also says that you should close any open programs before running Update.exe.

3. Double-click on **Update.exe**. A Windows NT Setup window will appear.

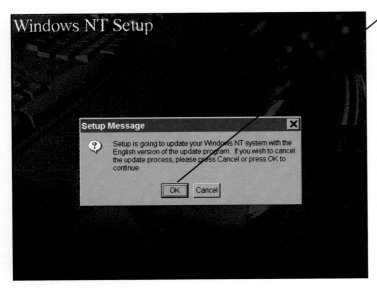

4. Click on **OK**. The setup process will proceed. You'll see various messages as the update files are copied to your computer.

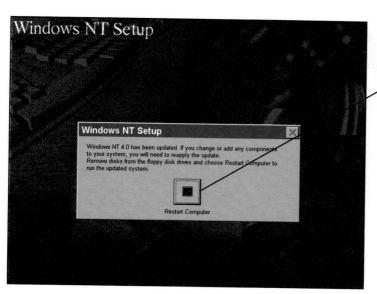

When the update is complete, you'll be prompted to restart your workstation.

5. Click on the **button** above Restart Computer. Your workstation will restart.

Watch for the "blue screen" as it restarts, and notice that the new service pack's number is there.

"Tweaking" NT's User Interface

Soon after the Windows 95 Interface appeared, some people started complaining about aspects of it that they didn't like. A few, for example, didn't like the unfamiliar icons that were installed on their desktops and deleted them without knowing that this causes problems. (The Network Neighborhood icon, along with those for Internet Explorer, My Computer, Inbox and Recycle Bin cannot simply be deleted like ordinary icons without affecting your system.) Others didn't like such features as CDs automatically starting up when inserted into the CD drive.

Apparently someone at Microsoft heard about these issues and created a program called Tweak UI in response to them. Although Tweak was written by the Windows 95 Shell Team, and is labelled a "User interface customization toy," Microsoft wants you to know that they don't guarantee or support it and that you use it at your own risk.

We've been using the Windows 95 version for some time without complications, and have had the NT version running trouble-free on both a standalone workstation and several workstations on a peer-to-peer network. However, we also want you to know that you use it at your own risk, and that we also offer no guarantees or support for it.

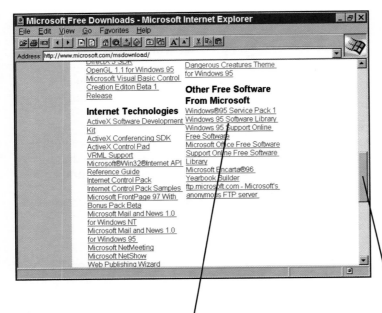

Tweak is available for downloading at Microsoft's Web site.

1. Open Internet Explorer, go to the **Microsoft home page**, and **click** on the **Downloads link** as shown in "Locating and Installing the Windows NT Service Packs," earlier in this chapter. The Downloads page will appear. Because Web pages change constantly, the one you see may not be exactly like the one shown here.

2. Scroll down the **Downloads page** until you see Windows 95 Software Library under the Other Free Software From Microsoft heading.

3. Click on **Windows 95 Software Library**. The Windows 95 Software Library page will appear.

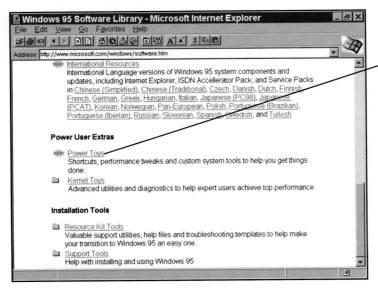

4. Scroll down the **page** until you see Power Toys.

5. Click on the **Power Toys link**. The Power Toys page will appear.

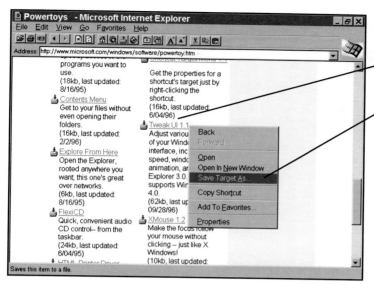

6. Scroll down the **page** until you see Tweak UI.

7. Right-click on the **Tweak UI link**. A menu will appear.

8. Click on **Save Target As** and proceed to download the file as shown in "Locating and Installing the Windows NT Service Packs," earlier in this chapter.

Installing Tweak UI

Tweak is installed as though it were a part of Windows NT Setup.

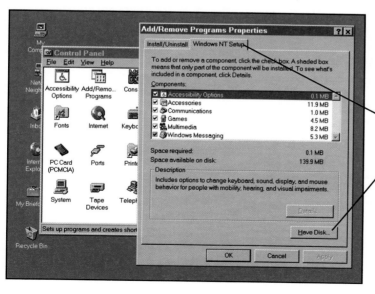

1. Open the **Control Panel window** and double-click on the Add/Remove Programs icon as shown at the beginning of this chapter.

2. Click on the **Windows NT Setup tab** to bring it to the front.

3. Click on **Have Disk**. The Install From Disk dialog box will appear.

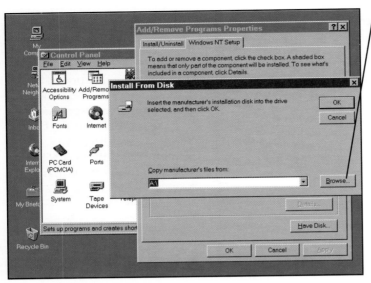

4. Click on **Browse**. (We found that even if we typed the path and file name in the "Copy manufacturer's files from" box, we had to browse to the install file.) A Locate File message box or Locate File dialog box will appear.

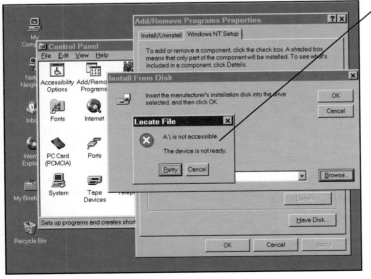

5. If you get this message, **click** on **Retry**. A Locate File dialog box will appear.

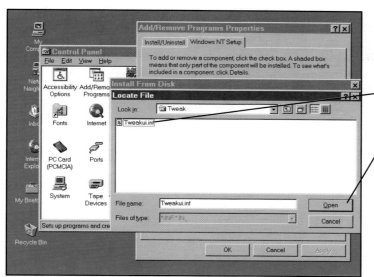

6. Use standard navigation techniques to **go to** the **directory** where you saved the Tweak installation file.

7. Click on the **file**. Its name will appear in the File name box.

8. Click on **Open**. The Locate File dialog box will close. The "Copy manufacturer's files from" box in the Have Disk dialog box will show the file's name.

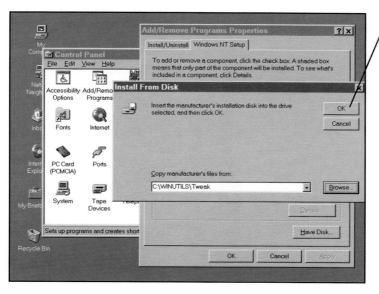

9. Click on **OK**. The Have Disk dialog box will appear.

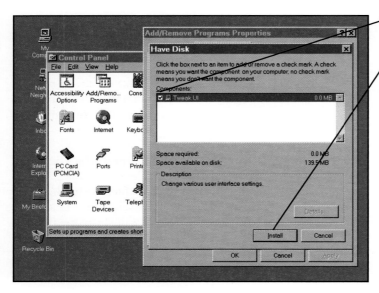

10. Click in the **box** next to Tweak UI to place a ✔ in it.

11. Click on **Install**. You'll see various messages as Tweak is installed. Close the Add/Remove Programs dialog box when it's done. The Tweak UI icon will appear in your Control Panel window.

Using Tweak to Customize NT

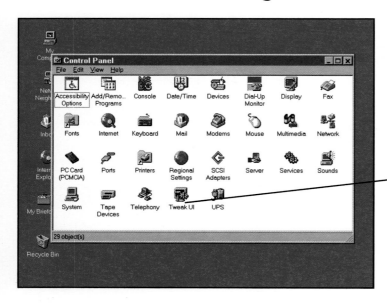

Tweak includes many options. We'll just go over some of them here, and you can decide which ones you want to make use of. You can get more information on Tweak's options by using the 🛈 (Help) button in the title bar of its dialog box (see Chapter 8, "Using Help").

1. Double-click on the **Tweak UI icon**. The Tweak UI dialog box will appear.

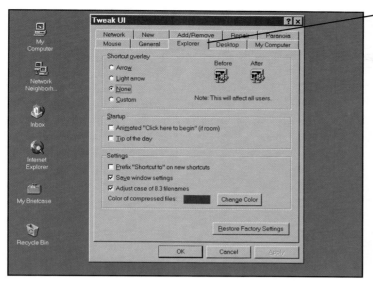

2. Click on the **Explorer tab** to bring it to the front.

The Explorer tab includes settings to remove the little arrows from shortcut icons, remove the "Click here to begin" message from the taskbar, and others.

If you want an option to be in effect, click in the box next to it to *put* a ✔ in it.

If you do not want the option in effect, click in the box to *remove* the ✔.

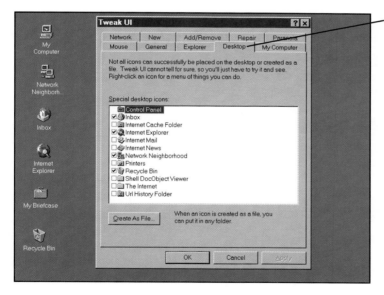

3. Click on the **Desktop tab** to bring it to the front.

This tab is where you can safely remove an unused or unwanted system icon from your desktop, or add one that you'd like to have there.

To remove the icon, click in the box to remove the ✔.

To add the icon, click in the box to put a ✔ in it.

Note: If you choose to remove the Recycle Bin icon, first set its configuration so that deleted files are no longer kept. Otherwise you'll forget all about it and have files taking up space in the "Recycled" folder on your hard disk long after you thought they were gone. To do this, right-click on the Recycle bin icon, then click on Properties. On the Global tab, click in the box next to "Do not move files to the Recycle bin" to put a ✔ in it, and then click on OK.

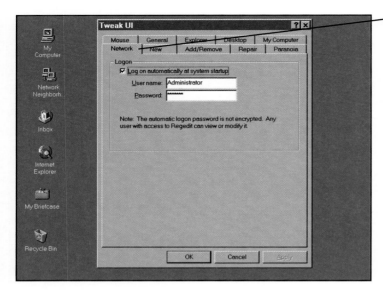

4. Click on the **Network tab** to bring it to the front.

This tab has our favorite Tweak option. Because our workstations are all in secure locations, we considered having to log on each time the workstation is started or rebooted to be a major inconvenience. You can bypass this security feature on the Network tab.

The Paranoia tab (not shown here) includes a setting to turn off the CD autorun feature that some consider annoying.

Finding Add-On Programs for NT

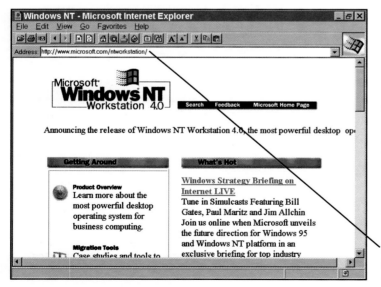

The USENET newsgroups dealing with NT have been a source for both common complaints about NT and excellent solutions to the problems people complain about. We'll list these newsgroups in Chapter 35, "Finding Out More About NT." In this section of this chapter, we'll show you where to find a couple of programs we discovered in the newsgroups.

1. Open Internet Explorer.

2. Type www.microsoft.com/ ntworkstation/ (no spaces) in the Address box and **press Enter**. The NT Workstation page will appear.

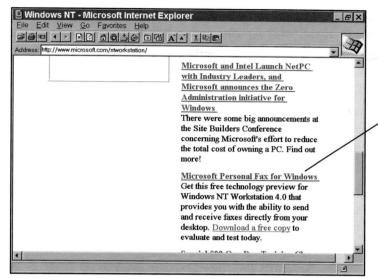

The NT Workstation page may have changed by the time you see it. At some place on the page, however, you're bound to find a link to files you can download to enhance NT.

When we visited the page, we found this link to the test version of Microsoft Fax for Windows NT. (We downloaded and installed it, and it worked fine.) If it isn't available when you visit, you're sure to find other programs that you can use.

Other Web sites you may want to visit to investigate NT add-on programs include:

www.execsoft.com/dklite/
(Diskeeper Lite from Executive Software International, Inc.) and
www.symantec.com/nu/
(Norton Utilities from Symantec Corporation)

These pages lead to downloadable versions of "defrag" programs written for NT version 4.0, or provide information on how to obtain them. When a defrag program wasn't included with NT 4.0 many comments were made in newsgroups. The need for a defrag program is covered in Chapter 21, "Managing Virtual Memory."

www.v3inc.com
(Fax COMponents from V3, Inc.) and
www.blkbox.com/~jonk
(FaxMail Network for Windows NT)

These sites have information on shareware versions of fax programs that were written for NT.

No endorsement of or support for any of the programs listed should be implied. They are listed for your information only.

CHAPTER

34

Installing and Using Microsoft Mail

Microsoft Mail (MS Mail) is a network e-mail system included with Windows NT. It can manage electronic mail between people on your company's network, and also can be configured to handle your Internet e-mail. It integrates with Windows Messaging (see Chapter 26), can be used through Dial-Up Networking (see Chapter 24), and can be scheduled to automatically transfer mail from your Internet Service Provider.

In planning for MS Mail service, you have to select a workstation with about one megabyte of disk space (plus room to store e-mail) to house the "postoffice," and someone to act as postoffice administrator. The postoffice is where the network's e-mail will be delivered and stored, and from which it will be retrieved. The administrator is responsible for setting up and maintaining user accounts. If MS Mail is not already on your workstation, you will need the NT Workstation installation CD to install it. People on the network who want to use the system will also have to install MS Mail on their workstations. In this chapter, you will do the following:

✔ Install Microsoft Mail
✔ Set up a network postoffice on a workstation
✔ Set up user accounts
✔ Configure MS Mail to automatically send and retrieve your e-mail

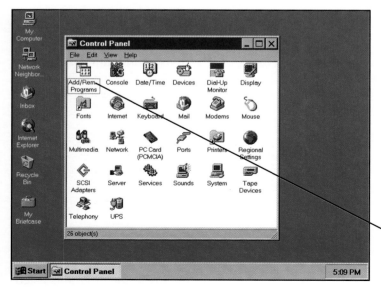

Setting Up

1. Open the **Control Panel window**.

If there is no icon for the MS Mail Postoffice in your Control Panel window, the program is not installed on your workstation. If it's there, you can skip to the next section, "Setting Up the Postoffice."

2. Double-click on the **Add/Remove Programs icon**. The Add/Remove Programs Properties dialog box will appear.

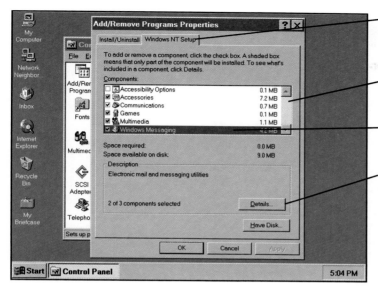

3. Click on the **Windows NT Setup tab** to bring it to the front.

4. Scroll down until you see Windows Messaging.

5. Click on **Windows Messaging** to highlight it.

6. Click on **Details**. The Windows Messaging dialog box will appear.

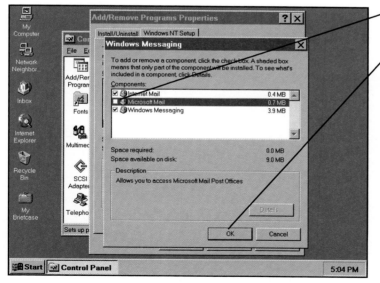

7. Click in the **box** next to Microsoft Mail to put a ✔ in it.

8. Click on **OK**. The Windows Messaging dialog box will close.

9. Click on **OK** in the Add/Remove Programs Properties dialog box. You will be prompted for the NT installation CD.

10. Hold down the **Shift key** while you **insert** the **installation CD** to prevent the CD autorun feature from bringing up the CD's menu.

11. Follow the **directions** on your screen to complete installation.

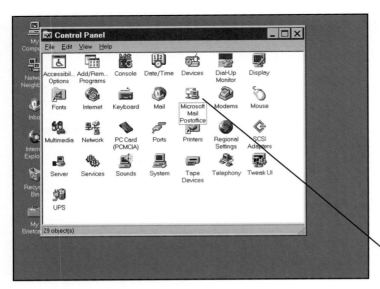

Setting Up the Postoffice

1. Open the **Control Panel window** on the workstation selected to have the postoffice.

The Postoffice icon will be present on any workstation that has MS Mail installed on it, though only one workstation will be set up with the actual postoffice.

2. Double-click on the **Microsoft Mail Postoffice icon.** The Microsoft Workgroup Postoffice Admin dialog box will appear.

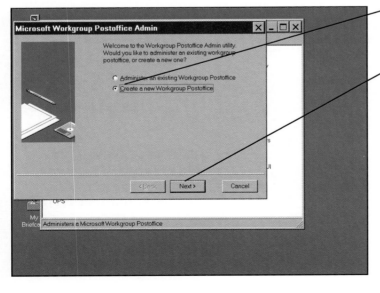

3. Click on **Create a new Workgroup Postoffice** to place a dot in the circle next to it.

4. Click on **Next**. The dialog box will change.

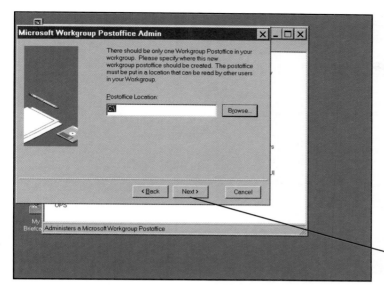

The dialog box now asks you to select a drive where the postoffice files will be set up. The main drive of the workstation where you are located will be listed by default. If you want to put the files on another drive, click the Browse button and locate the drive. As noted in the dialog box, all others who will be using the postoffice must be able to reach the drive over the network or by using Dial-Up Networking.

5. Click on **Next** once you've selected a drive. The dialog box will change again.

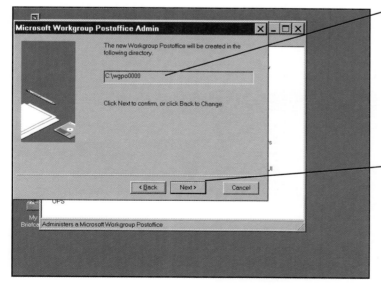

The dialog box shows you the drive it will use and the folder it will create for the postoffice files. Make a note of the name if it is different from the one indicated here. You will need it for the "Sharing the Postoffice Folder" section, later in this chapter.

6. Click on **Next**. The Enter Your Administrator Account Details dialog box will appear.

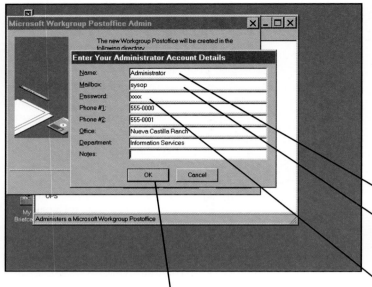

Setting Up the Administrator Account

The dialog box lets you enter data for the Administrator's name, password, mailbox name, etc. All of this can be changed later.

1. Type a **name**.

2. Type a **name** for the mailbox (a user name that will be used for access to the postoffice).

3. Type a **password**.

4. Type the **rest of the data**.

5. Click on **OK**. A message comes up to remind you to share the folder so that others can get to it. See Chapter 29, "Controlling Access to Workstations," for more on sharing and access.

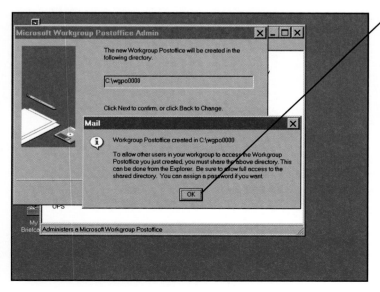

6. Click on **OK**. The message will disappear.

MS Mail will create the postoffice files and the Microsoft Workgroup Postoffice Admin dialog box will close.

7. Close the **Control Panel**.

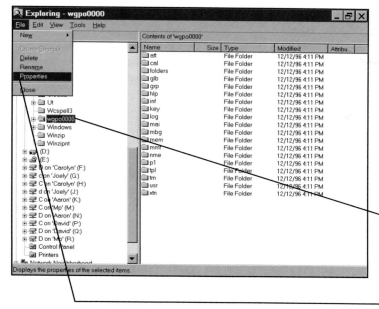

Sharing the Postoffice Folder

1. Open Windows NT Explorer.

2. Navigate to the **wgpo0000 folder** (or whatever it was named when set up on your workstation).

3. Click on the **folder** to highlight it.

4. Click on **File** in the menu bar. The File menu will appear.

5. Click on **Properties**. The folder's Properties dialog box will appear.

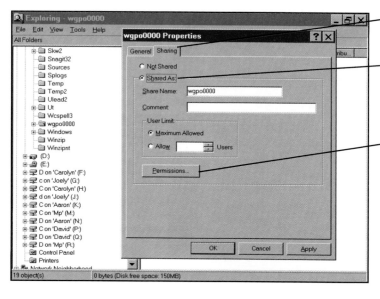

6. Click on the **Sharing tab** to bring it to the front.

7. Click on **Shared As** to place a dot in the circle next to it. The folder's name will appear in the Share Name box.

8. Click on **Permissions**. The Access Through Share Permissions dialog box will appear.

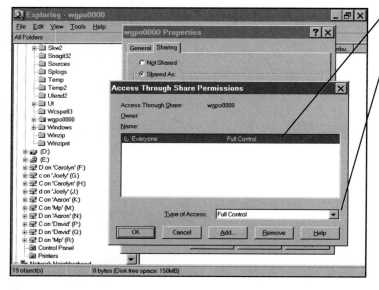

Everyone and Full Control are selected by default.

You can change the access by clicking on the ▼ to open the list of access types and selecting another. Click on the Help button for more on access types, user groups that can be specified, and other security controls that you can set here.

9. Click on **OK**. The dialog box will close.

10. Click on **OK** in the folder's Properties dialog box to close it.

11. Close Windows NT Explorer.

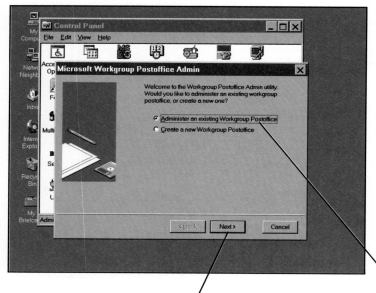

Setting Up and Managing User Accounts

Next, the Administrator has to set up an account for each person who will be using the system.

1. Open the **Control Panel** and **double-click** on the **Microsoft Mail Postoffice icon**. The Microsoft Workgroup Postoffice Admin dialog box will appear.

2. Click on **Administer an existing Workgroup Postoffice,** if needed, to put a dot in the circle next to it.

3. Click on **Next**. The dialog box will change.

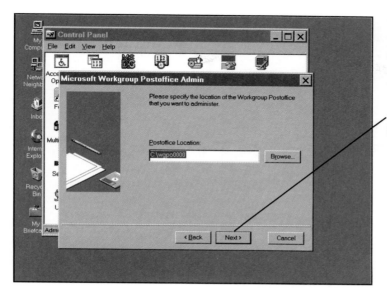

The drive and folder for the postoffice files should be shown in this box. If it is not, click on the Browse button and locate them.

4. Click on **Next**. The dialog box will change again.

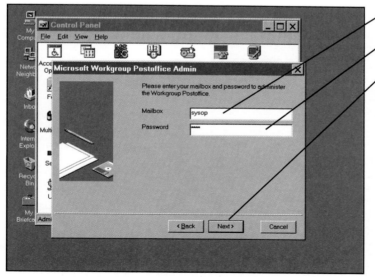

5. Type your **mailbox name**.

6. Type your **password**.

7. Click on **Next**. The Postoffice Manager dialog box will appear.

Adding Users

Now that you have the postoffice and Administrator account set up, it's time to add user accounts for each person who will be using the mail system. User accounts are set up in the same way as the Administrator account. The Administrator assigns each user a mailbox name and password that the user will have to enter for access to the postoffice.

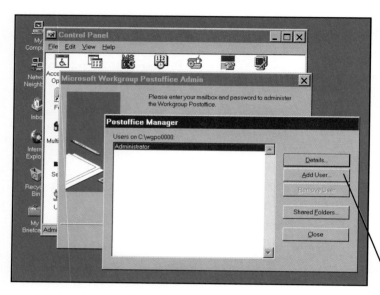

1. Click on **Add User**. The Add User dialog box will appear.

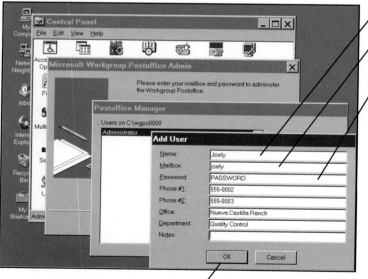

2. Type the **user's name**.

3. Make up a **mailbox name** for the user and **type it** here.

4. Make up a **password** for the user and **type it** here. The user can change it later from his or her workstation.

5. Write down the **user's mailbox name and password** and give it to them. You will also have to tell users which workstation houses the postoffice, and the name of the drive and folder where the postoffice files are kept.

6. Fill in the other **details** as desired.

7. Click on **OK**. The user's mailbox is now ready for use.

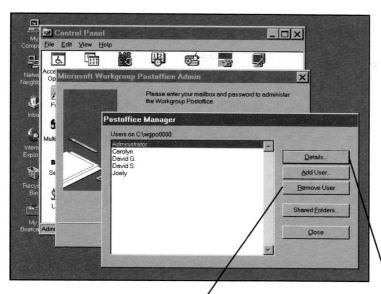

Maintaining the Postoffice

User accounts and shared folders will require some maintenance from time to time. For example, as people move around in or leave the organization, their records may have to be changed or deleted.

1. Click on a **user record** that you want to change to highlight it.

If you click on Details, the user's account information will appear, and any information in it can be edited.

If you click on Remove User, you'll be prompted to confirm that you want to delete the record.

The shared folders used for postoffice files will occasionally require "compressing." As messages are added to the folders, they grow in size. When messages are deleted, empty, wasted space is left where the messages used to be.

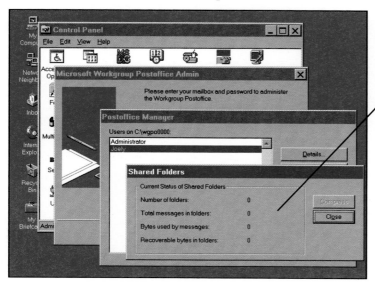

2. Click on the **Shared Folders** button in the Postoffice Manager dialog box. The Shared Folders dialog box will appear.

This dialog box will show how many folders are in use, how much space is taken up by them, and how much space could be recovered by clicking on the Compress button. Because we just set up the postoffice, we obviously don't need to compress our folders right now.

Setting Up MS Mail
on a User's Workstation

After the postoffice is in place, users can start to set up MS Mail on their workstations. See the beginning of this chapter for how to check on whether MS Mail has been installed on the workstation, and how to install it if it has not. If MS Mail has been installed, the user can proceed.

If more than one person uses the workstation, each one will have to set up his or her MS Mail separately. Each person who logs on to the workstation will have his or her own Inbox and Windows Messaging configuration.

1. Open the **Control Panel window**.

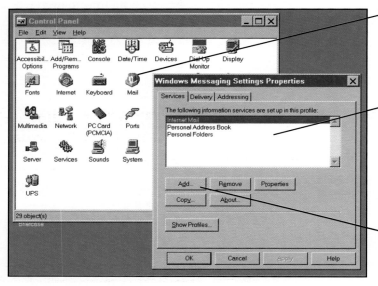

2. Double-click the **Mail icon** (*not* the Microsoft Mail Postoffice icon). The Windows Messaging Settings Properties dialog box will appear.

The services that are currently installed for the workstation user are listed here. If Microsoft Mail is listed, the user can skip to the next section, "Configuring MS Mail on the User's Workstation."

3. Click on **Add**. The Add Service to Profile dialog box will appear.

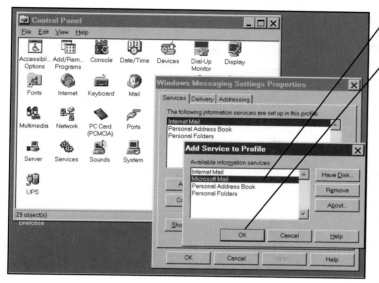

4. Click on **Microsoft Mail** to highlight it.

5. Click on **OK**. MS Mail will be added to the user's Messaging services. The Microsoft Mail dialog box will appear so that the user can configure it for his or her use.

Configuring MS Mail on the User's Workstation

If Microsoft Mail appears in the list of Windows Messaging services (see the Windows Messaging Settings Properties dialog box on the previous page), the Microsoft Mail dialog box can be opened by clicking on Microsoft Mail to highlight it, then clicking on the Properties button.

Each user can set up MS Mail to suit his or her work habits. Considerable customiztion is allowed for such things as regularly scheduled mail delivery. Because the Administrator is also a user, he or she will also have to go through these steps. The first is to tell MS Mail where the postoffice files are located.

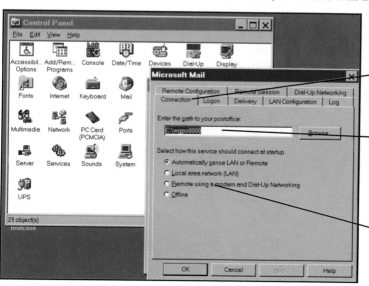

1. Click on the **Connection tab,** if needed, to bring it to the front.

2. Type the **path and folder name** where the postoffice files are located. (You also can click on the Browse button to locate them.)

Note: If using MS Mail by dial-up connection, click on "Remote using a modem" to place a dot in the circle by it.

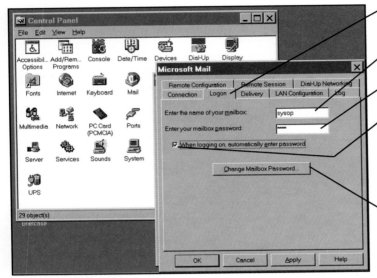

3. **Click** on the **Logon tab** to bring it to the front.

4. **Type** your **mailbox name**.

5. **Type** your **password**.

Note 1: For security, you can uncheck this box. Each time you connect to the postoffice, you will be asked for your password.

Note 2: Click on the Change Mailbox Password button if you want to change your password.

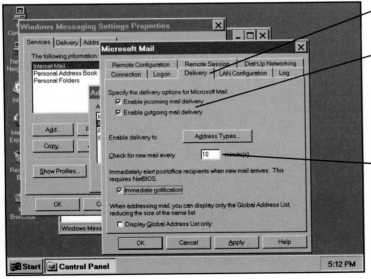

6. **Click** on the **Delivery tab** to bring it to the front.

You will want both of these options checked to enable mail delivery. You can specify certain types of e-mail to block by clicking on the Address Types button.

If you want to automatically send and receive e-mail in the background at regular time intervals, set them here. If you want your workstation to beep when new e-mail is received, check the Immediate Notification box. Settings on the LAN Configuration tab or Remote Configuration tab enable or disable automatic mail delivery.

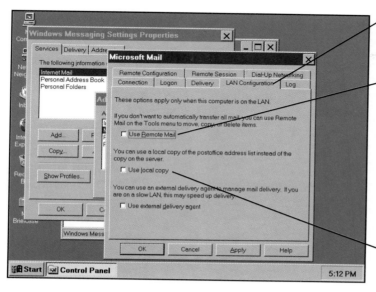

7. Click on the **LAN Configuration tab** to bring it to the front.

Note 1: For automatic mail delivery at the time interval you specified on the Delivery tab, do not put a ✔ here. If you want to control the delivery and receipt of e-mail (from the Inbox - Windows Messaging dialog box—see later in the chapter), click here to place a ✔ next to Use Remote Mail.

Note 2: If you click to place a ✔ by "Use local copy," it could speed up your use of mail. Otherwise, each time you want to address mail to someone on the network, your workstation will have to connect to the postoffice to get the network address list.

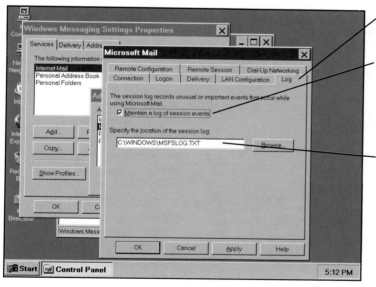

8. Click on the **Log tab** to bring it to the front.

If you want to keep a log of "unusual events" (undelivered mail and other problems) during your e-mail activity, click here to place a ✔.

You can specify the file for the log here.

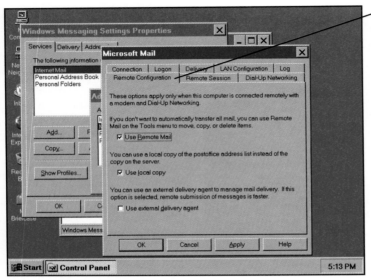

9. Click on the **Remote Connection tab** to bring it to the front.

If you will be using Dial-Up Networking to connect and check your e-mail, use this tab. These are the same settings that appear on the LAN Configuration tab for networked e-mail (see step 7 and the notes that follow it). Also, see step 8 in the next section whether or not you use automatic scheduling.

Scheduling Automatic E-Mail Delivery

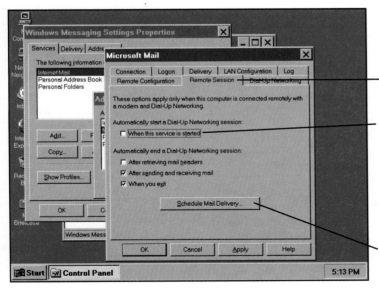

You can set up Messaging to connect to your ISP automatically at specific times to check for e-mail.

1. Click on the **Remote Session tab** to bring it to the front.

If you are using Dial-Up Networking for your e-mail connection and want to check for new mail automatically each time you open the Inbox, click here to place a ✔ in the square.

2. Click on **Schedule Mail Delivery**. The Schedule Remote Mail Delivery dialog box will appear.

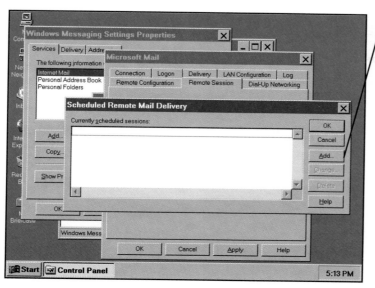

3. Click on **Add** to set up a session schedule. The Add Scheduled Session dialog box will appear.

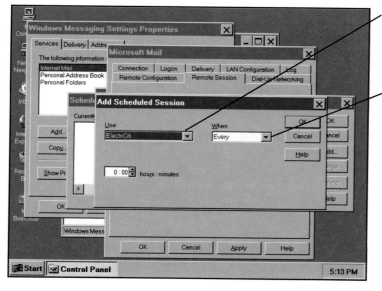

4. Click on the ▼ next to the Use box if needed to select the connection you will use for the scheduled service.

5. Click on the ▼ next to the When box to open the list of frequency options.

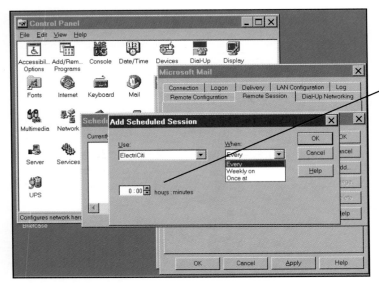

There are three frequency options. The Add Scheduled Session dialog box changes for each one.

If you click on "Every," a box that lets you specify hours and minutes appears. You can click on the tiny up and down arrows to change the time. Dial-Up Networking will automatically make the connection and check for mail at the frequency you set.

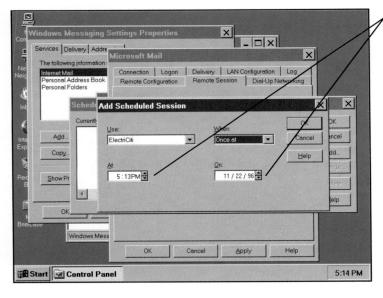

If you click on "Once at," the dialog box lets you set a specific date and time for the automatic check.

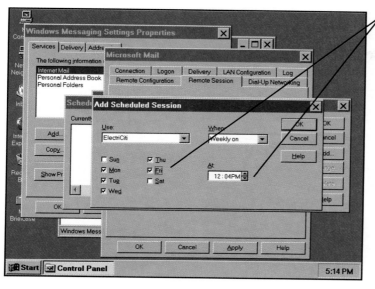

If you click "Weekly on," boxes will appear where you select which days of the week and at what time each day the automatic dial-up and mail check will be performed. For example, you could check the Monday through Friday boxes and set the time to 12:04 p.m. to automatically have your mail sent and received in the middle of each work day.

Note: Mail administrators often suggest setting automatic checks such as this to times just before or just after the hour or half-hour to spread out the workload on mail servers.

6. Click on **OK** once you've set the schedule you want to use (or click on Cancel to close the dialog box without setting a schedule). The dialog box will close.

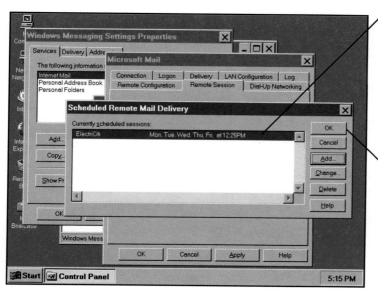

The schedule is now listed in the Scheduled Remote Mail Delivery dialog box. You can click on "Add" to add another schedule, on "Change" to edit the highlighted schedule, or on "Delete" to delete the high-lighted schedule.

7. Click on **OK** to put the schedule to use (or on Cancel to close the dialog box without setting up the schedule). The dialog box will close.

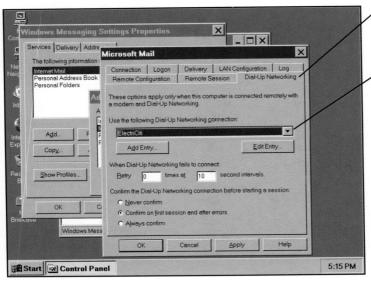

8. Click on the **Dial-Up Networking tab** to bring it to the front.

9. Click on the ▼ next to the "Use the following..." box if needed to select the connection you will use if you use Dial-Up Networking for your e-mail. Make this selection whether or not you use the scheduled delivery option.

10. Click on **OK** when all of your configuration settings are complete. Your setup will be saved, and the Microsoft Mail dialog box will close.

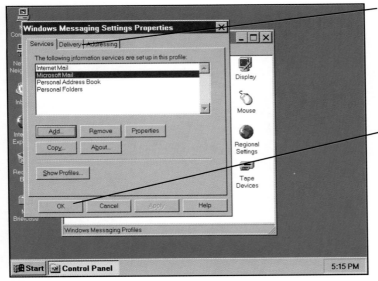

The Delivery and Addressing tabs contain settings that you will probably not need to change. Click on the Help button on each tab for more information on the settings there.

11. Click on **OK**. The Windows Messaging Settings Properties dialog box will close.

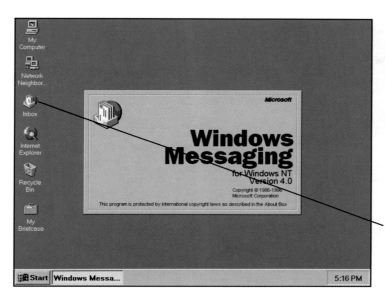

Sending and Receiving Network E-Mail with Microsoft Mail

Many of the things covered in Chapter 26, "Using Windows Messaging," apply to MS Mail.

Double-click on the **Inbox icon** on your desktop. The Inbox - Windows Messaging window will appear.

Getting the MS Mail Postoffice Address List through a Dial-Up Connection

If you use MS Mail over a dial-up connection, you will want to download the postoffice address list for convenience.

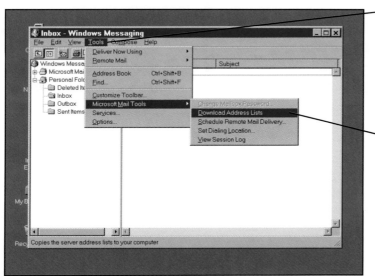

1. Click on **Tools** in the menu bar. The Tools menu will appear.

2. Move the **mouse pointer** over Microsoft Mail Tools. Another menu will appear.

3. Click on **Download Address Lists**. The Connect to Server dialog box will appear.

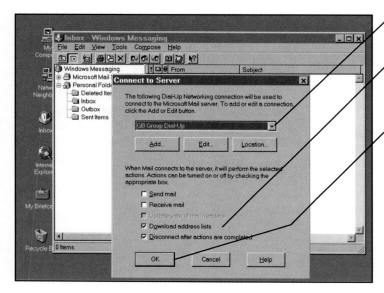

4. Click on the ▼ to select the connection if needed.

"Download address lists" and "Disconnect after actions are completed" will be selected.

5. Click on **OK**. The dial-up connection will be made.

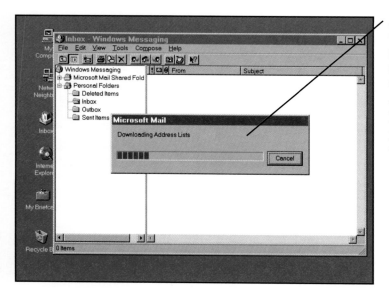

A message box appears while the download takes place. The message changes from Connecting to Microsoft Post Office to Downloading Address Lists. After the download is complete, the message box goes away and the connection is hung up.

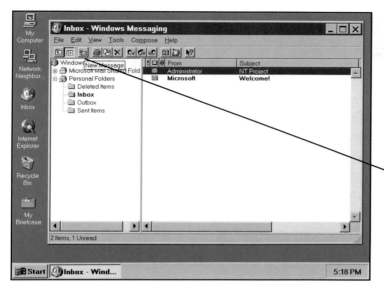

Sending a Message

After you have the network's address list, sending a message is almost identical to doing so as shown in Chapter 26, "Using Windows Messaging."

1. Click on the **New Message button** in the toolbar. The New Message window will appear.

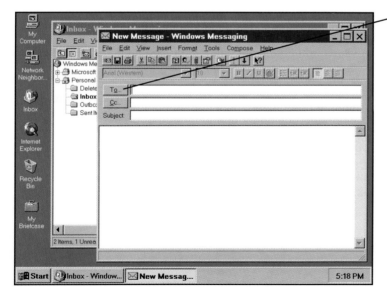

2. Click on the **To button**. The Address Book dialog box will appear.

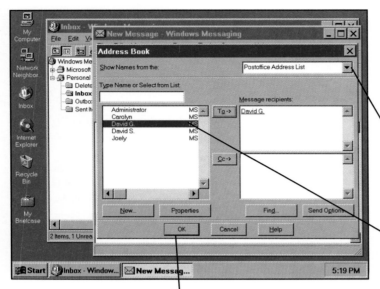

You now have both your personal address book (see Chapter 26) with Internet e-mail addresses in it, and the Postoffice Address List from which to choose.

3. Click on the ▼ next to the "Show Names from the" box to open the list of address sources and select either your personal address book or the postoffice list.

4. With the Postoffice Address List open, **click** on the **name** of the person you want to send mail to to select it.

Note: You can annotate the entry for the selected name by clicking on the Properties button.

5. Click on **To**. The name will appear in the Message Recipients box.

6. Click on **OK**. The Address Book will close and the name you selected will appear in the To line of the New Message window.

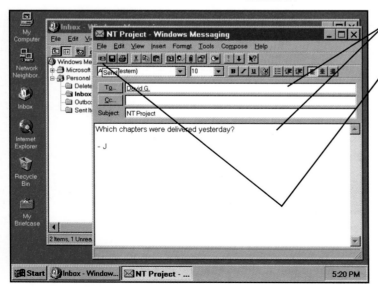

7. Type your **subject and message**.

8. Click on the **Send** button. The message will move to your Outbox folder and the New Message window will close.

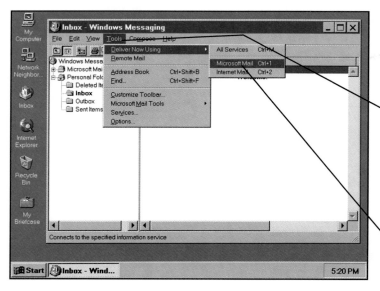

If you didn't set up MS Mail for automatic deliveries, you connect to your network and send and receive e-mail using the Tools menu.

9. Click on **Tools** in the menu bar. The Tools menu will appear.

10. Move the mouse pointer over **Deliver Now Using**. Another menu will appear.

11. Click on **Microsoft Mail**. Your mail will be delivered and any mail waiting for you at the postoffice will be received. If you are using Dial-Up Networking to connect to the postoffice, DUN will make the connection for you.

CHAPTER

35

Finding Out More About NT

There's far more to know about an operating system as complex as NT 4.0 than could ever be covered in just one book. Fortunately, NT itself makes a vast quantity of online information available to you. If you followed the directions in Part IV of this book, "Communicating," and installed the updated version of Internet Explorer and its newsgroup reader, or use any of the many other browsers and news readers available, you'll be able to tap into NT expertise and share others' experience with it. Following are some of the Web pages and newsgroups we've found useful both in working with NT and in writing this book.

Web Pages About Windows NT 4.0

www.conitech.com/windows/winnt.html
Frank Condron's World O'Windows—Windows NT Page (Frank Condron)
An excellent all-around resource for NT. Great source for the latest information on NT, updated drivers, easy-to-use index to Microsoft resources, and links to other NT pages.

techweb.cmp.com/ntsolutions/
CMP's NT Solution Center (CMP Media, Inc.)
Another outstanding source for up-to-date information on NT, drivers, and information on software available for NT.

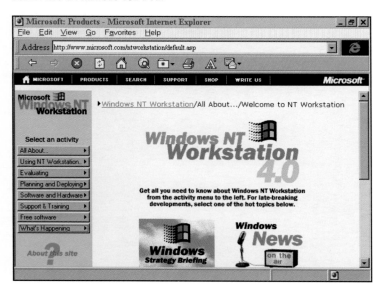

Note: Web pages are notorious for changing all the time. At the time of this writing, all of the addresses shown here worked. If you cannot connect to any of them, use one of the Web directories, such as Yahoo!, to search for NT.

◀ Microsoft Internet Explorer displaying the Windows NT Workstation 4.0 page.

NT Web sites, continued:

www.winsite.com/
The WinSite Archive (WinSite Group, Inc.)
Self-described as the "World's Largest Software Archive for Windows Shareware and Trialware
on the Internet." Browse the archive and you'll probably agree.

www.microsoft.com/ntserver/
Windows NT Server (Microsoft Corporation)
and
www.microsoft.com/ntworkstation/
Windows NT Workstation (Microsoft Corporation)
The official sites for NT. Source for the latest Service Packs and "fixes," online support, and the
ultimate authority, Microsoft's Knowledge Base.

www.indirect.com/www/ceridgac/ntsite.html
MS Windows NT® Sites (PVEP)
A directory in the form of an alphabetical HTML guide to Web sites about NT.

**www.yahoo.com/Computers_and_Internet/Operating_Systems/Microsoft_Windows/
Windows_NT/**
Yahoo! - Windows NT (Yahoo!)
Our favorite Internet directory and a great jumping-off point for investigating NT resources on
the Web.

USENET Newsgroups About Windows NT

Newsgroups are an excellent place to learn about other people's experience with NT and to ask
for help or clarification with NT-related issues. There are thousands of USENET newsgroups on
the Internet. When you first try one out, "lurk" for a while before posting questions and replies.
That is, just read the messages until you get a feel for what's being discussed and the level of
the discussion. Don't cross-post the same message to several newsgroups; limit your comments
to the topic at hand, and don't "flame" (harangue) others. This list is based on the FAQ (Frequently Asked Questions) titled "A Guide to the Windows Newsgroups," posted weekly to
Windows newsgroups by Tom Haapanen.

Windows newsgroups about NT include:

   comp.os.ms-windows.nt.admin.networking
        Network administration and management
   comp.os.ms-windows.nt.admin.misc
        Administration issues other than networking or security

comp.os.ms-windows.nt.admin.security
System and network security issues
comp.os.ms-windows.nt.advocacy
Comparisons and arguments about NT versus other operating systems
comp.os.ms-windows.nt.announce
Announcements and news about NT applications, drivers, events, etc.
comp.os.ms-windows.nt.pre-release
Discussion about unreleased and future versions of NT
comp.os.ms-windows.nt.setup.hardware
Setting up and configuring hardware
comp.os.ms-windows.nt.setup.misc
Setting up and configuring, except hardware issues
comp.os.ms-windows.nt.misc
All other topics except programming and advocacy

Software that's specifically for Windows NT:

comp.os.ms-windows.nt.software.backoffice
Microsoft BackOffice
comp.os.ms-windows.nt.software.services
System services software for Windows NT, including daemons, servers, and background processes; not general desktop software

Software compatibility issues for NT:

comp.os.ms-windows.nt.software.compatibility
Running Win16 and MS-DOS applications under NT

Networking with Windows 3.x, 95 and NT:

comp.os.ms-windows.networking.ras
Remote Access Services (RAS) dial-up networking
comp.os.ms-windows.networking.tcp-ip
TCP/IP-based networking for Windows, including NFS and apps
comp.os.ms-windows.networking.windows
Windows native networking: WFWG, NT, NTAS, and LAN Manager
comp.os.ms-windows.networking.misc
All other networks, such as Netware, Banyan Vines, and LANtastic

Software that's available; covers Windows 3.x, 95, and NT:

comp.os.ms-windows.apps.comm
> Communications and fax applications

comp.os.ms-windows.apps.financial
> Financial applications

comp.os.ms-windows.apps.word-proc
> Word processing and desktop publishing

comp.os.ms-windows.apps.misc
> Miscellaneous software

Winsock-based TCP/IP software for Windows 3.x, 95, and NT:

comp.os.ms-windows.apps.winsock.mail
> Winsock-based electronic mail applications and utilities

comp.os.ms-windows.apps.winsock.news
> Winsock-based Usenet news readers and servers

comp.os.ms-windows.apps.winsock.misc
> Winsock-based applications other than news and e-mail

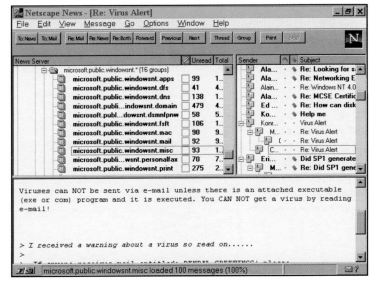

◀ Netscape Navigator's built-in newsgroup reader displaying a message in one of Microsoft's NT support newsgroups.

Microsoft support newsgroups for Windows NT:

The previous newsgroups are generally available on the Internet through your Internet Service Provider's news server. The ones below are available through Microsoft's news server, **msnews.microsoft.com**, which you will have to connect to separately. You can connect to the server without a password through your newsgroup reader.

microsoft.public.windowsnt.apps
> software for NT

microsoft.public.windowsnt.dfs
> DFS (Distributed File System) topics

microsoft.public.windowsnt.dns
> DNS (Domain Name Server) topics

microsoft.public.windowsnt.domain
> domain administration and related issues

microsoft.public.windowsnt.dsmnfpnw
> FPNW (File and Print Services for Netware) topics

microsoft.public.windowsnt.fsft
> NTFS (NT File System) issues

microsoft.public.windowsnt.mac
> networking Macintosh computers with NT

microsoft.public.windowsnt.mail
> electronic mail

microsoft.public.windowsnt.misc
> miscellaneous NT topics

microsoft.public.windowsnt.personalfax
> using fax programs under NT

microsoft.public.windowsnt.print
> printing issues

microsoft.public.windowsnt.protocol.ipx
> IPX networking protocol discussion

microsoft.public.windowsnt.protocol.misc
> miscellaneous networking protocol topics

microsoft.public.windowsnt.protocol.ras
> RAS (Remote Access Services) networking protocol issues

microsoft.public.windowsnt.protocol.tcpip
> TCP/IP networking protocol issues

microsoft.public.windowsnt.setup
> hardware and operating system setup

Appendix

The Glossary contains nontechnical definitions of some of the terms used in this book.

PART

I

PART

II

PART

III

PART

IV

PART

V

PART

VI

PART

VII

Glossary

Address Book   A file that contains a list of e-mail addresses.

Anonymous Login   Logging on to a network without using a user name or password.

Authentication   The process by which a computer or network determines a user's identity.

Autodial   An NT feature that automatically dials into a network when the connection to that network is needed.

Back Up   To make a copy of your data onto another hard drive, a tape, or a floppy drive. The Backup program in Windows NT 4.0 will back up only to a tape.

Bindings   NT's way of linking network protocols, adapter cards, and network services so that they will communicate and work together properly.

Bits (Binary digITs)   The smallest pieces of electronic data, either a zero or a 1.

Callback   A security measure by which a computer or network being connected to by phone hangs up the incoming call and then calls the caller back at a designated number.

Client   A computer that receives data or services from another computer, called a server.

Defrag   To undo the fragmentation of files on a disk.

Desktop   Refers to the screen you see after you boot up your computer. It can be viewed as the starting point from which you open various programs.

DHCP (Dynamic Host Configuration Protocol)   A network protocol that automatically assigns and configures IP addresses and related information for computers on the network.

DNS (Domain Name Server or Service)   A computer or program on a computer that translates Internet addresses from words to numbers and vice-versa.

Docking   The process of dragging the taskbar from the bottom of the screen to the top or one of the sides of the screen.

Double-click   To click the left mouse button twice in rapid succession while holding the mouse pointer on top of an object. The speed of the double-click can be modified in the Control Panel.

Drag   To place the mouse pointer on top of an object, press and hold the mouse button, and while holding the mouse button, move the mouse pointer. This will move, or drag, the object. As long as you continue to hold the mouse button, you can move the object. When you release the mouse button, the object will be placed at the spot where you released the mouse button.

Dual Boot   A computer set up with two operating systems, such as Windows NT 4.0 and Windows 3.11 for Workgroups. A user can select either system when booting up the computer.

Encryption   Turning information into a code to prevent its use by other persons.

Error Controls   Methods for preventing the corruption of transmitted data.

File Extension   Three letters at the end of a file name that identify the type of file. For example, in the filename glossary.doc, ".doc" identifies this file as a Microsoft Word document. In the filename resume.wpd, ".wpd" identifies the file as a Word Perfect document. In Windows NT, file extensions do not show unless you go into My Computer or Explorer and select the option to show file extensions.

Flow Controls   Methods modems use to signal each other when they are ready to send or receive data.

Folder   A place on your hard drive or floppy drive where you store information and programs. A folder in Windows NT 4.0 is analogous to a directory in Windows 3.1.

Fragmented Files   Files that have been split into more than one piece.

FTP (File Transfer Protocol)   A set of rules for moving files between two Internet sites.

Gopher   An Internet program that organizes information into text menus. By selecting an option on a Gopher menu, you go to either another menu of choices, or to a text file.

HTML (Hypertext Markup Language)   The code that is used to create Web pages, or files that are linked to other files.

Hyperlinks   Words, icons, or graphics in a Web page or file that, when selected, take you to another, related Web page or file.

Icon   A graphic symbol representing a file or an application. In many cases, the icon for an application or program looks like the product logo of the company selling the program.

Internet Address   The unique name or number for each machine on the Internet.

IP Address or Number   The unique name or number for each machine on a network.

Legacy Program   An application that was developed to run on an older version of the current operating system. For example, a program designed to run in Windows 3.1 would be called a legacy program if you are running it in Windows NT 4.0.

Links   *See* Hyperlinks.

LMHOSTS   An NT network file that translates numerical IP addresses into computer names and vice-versa.

Local Printer   A printer that is not shared. A local printer can be used only by the computer to which it is connected.

Log On   To enter your password and sign on to your computer.

Map a Network Drive   To assign a local drive letter on your machine to a drive located on another computer. For example, you might map another machine's C drive as the J drive on your machine. Thus, when you open the J drive on your machine, you are in fact opening the C drive on the mapped machine.

Marquee Screen Saver   Text that scrolls across your screen when you don't interact with your computer for a period of time. The message of the text can be customized using the Screen Saver tab in the Display Properties dialog box.

My Briefcase   A program that comes with Windows NT 4.0 that allows you to synchronize files that are used on more than one computer. My Briefcase will compare files and let you know if changes were made in the original version of the file or in the copy. You then have the option to update the older version with the new changes.

My Computer   An icon that sits on the desktop. Double-click on the My Computer icon to view local and network drives and the folders and files on the drives. You can perform file management functions, such as deleting, moving, and copying files in My Computer.

Network Drive   A network drive refers to a drive that is not on your computer but is located on another computer on the network.

Network Printer   A printer that is shared by more than one user on a network.

Network Protocols   Protocols, or sets of rules, used for transmitting data over networks.

Newsgroups   Electronic discussion groups.

ODBC (Open Database Connectivity)   A method that lets applications use SQL (Structured Query Language, a database programming language) to access data that is in another format.

Orphan   A file in My Briefcase that has been split from its original version on the hard drive. An orphan cannot be updated.

Paging File   *See* Virtual Memory.

Password   A unique combination of characters that identifies each user in an NT network. A password can be assigned by the network administrator or, if the network administrator agrees, can be selected by each user.

Path   A written description of the location of a file or program on your computer. A path statement includes the drive (e.g., C: drive), the folder (e.g., Winword), and the file name (e.g., test.doc) all separated by a back slash (\). Here's what a typical path statement looks like: c:\winword\my documents\test.doc.

Patterns   Graphic designs that can be applied to your desktop through the Display Properties dialog box. Patterns can use a lot of memory and slow performance.

Plus!   A tab in the Display Properties dialog box containing options that allow you to make specific changes in the appearance of your desktop and desktop icons.

Postoffice   A central set of folders and files for managing an electronic mail service.

Printer Driver   The software program that makes a printer work. Each manufacturer has its own printer driver that makes its printer work with your operating system.

Quick View   A way to preview a file in Windows NT Explorer or My Computer. Click on a file to highlight it and then click on Quick View in the File menu. If Quick View is grayed out on the File menu, it means that there is no viewer for that type of file.

Read Only   When a file is marked "read only," it cannot be edited. Changes must be saved under a new file name. This protects the contents of the original file. A file can be marked as Read Only from within the file or in the Properties dialog box for the file within Windows NT Explorer.

Recycle Bin   The metaphor that Windows NT 4.0 uses to describe a program that acts as a safety net when you are deleting files or folders. Instead of erasing the files when you click on delete, NT stores them in the Recycle Bin located on your desktop. You can restore files that were sent to the Recycle Bin.

Remote Access Service (RAS)   NT's programs that make dial-up communication with a network or workstation possible.

Restore   To copy files from a backup tape to a hard drive.

ScanDisk   A program in Windows NT 4.0 that scans (checks) a hard and/or floppy disk for errors and then repairs them.

Screen Saver   An image that appears on your screen when you have not interacted with your computer for a period of time. Screen savers were originally designed to prevent a static image from burning itself into your screen. Although they are no longer necessary with today's monitors, they remain popular for their entertainment value.

Script Files (for dial-up networking)   Files that contain information for automatically connecting to and logging on to remote networks or workstations.

Server   A computer that provides data or services to other computers, called clients.

Shortcut Icon   An icon you can create that will open a program when you double-click on the icon.

Shortcut Key   A sequence of three key strokes that opens a specific program (or toggles between open programs). The first two keystrokes are usually Ctrl and Alt. The third can be any letter or number. Shortcut keys are set up in the Properties dialog box associated with the shortcut icon for the program.

SSL (Secure Sockets Layer)   A method for safely sending data over a network or the Internet.

Subfolder   A folder that is contained inside another folder in Windows NT Explorer or My Computer.

Swap File   *See* Virtual Memory.

Systems Administrator   The systems administrator is the person assigned to control and manage a network in a large company. This person controls all access levels to the system. In a small company, there is usually no formal systems administrator but one or more of the owners may serve in this capacity.

Tape Device   A mechanical device that allows you to make a backup copy of data on your computer to a tape. Two popular brands of tape devices are made by Colorado Memory Systems and Conner.

Tape Driver   The software program that makes a tape device work. Each manufacturer has a tape driver that makes its tape device work with different operating systems.

Taskbar   In Windows NT 4.0, the bar at the bottom of the screen that contains the Start button and the buttons for minimized programs. The taskbar can be hidden or moved to another side of the screen.

TCP/IP (Transmission Control Protocol/Internet Protocol)   The standard for transmitting data over the Internet.

Telephony Dialing Properties   A dial-out access number, credit card number, or other special information that is associated with an entry in NT's Dial-Up Networking phonebook.

ToolTip   A balloon, or label, that appears describing the purpose of a button on the toolbar when you hold the mouse pointer on top of the button.

Usenet   A worldwide system of electronic discussion groups organized by subject into newsgroups.

User   In Windows NT, each person who uses a computer in the network.

User Profile   A description that contains the preferences and desktop settings of each person using the workstation. When a user logs on, the user profile is loaded and the preferences and settings are configured according to the user profile.

Virtual Memory   A file, called a swap file or paging file, on a computer's hard disk that is used to supplement RAM (random-access memory).

Wallpaper   A graphic design available on the Background tab of the Display Properties dialog box that can be applied to your desktop. Wallpaper designs can use a great deal of memory and slow performance.

Windows NT Explorer   A file management program that comes with Windows NT 4.0.

WINS (Windows Internet Name Server or Service)   A file on Windows network that translates Internet addresses from words to numbers and vice-versa.

Index

Check out Que® Books on the World Wide Web
http://www.quecorp.com

As the biggest software release in computer history, Windows 95 continues to redefine the computer industry. Click here for the latest info on our Windows 95 books

Make computing quick and easy with these products designed exclusively for new and casual users

Examine the latest releases in word processing, spreadsheets, operating systems, and suites

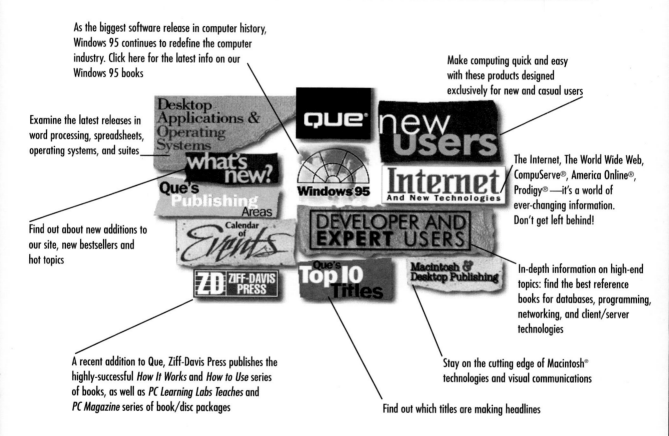

The Internet, The World Wide Web, CompuServe®, America Online®, Prodigy® —it's a world of ever-changing information. Don't get left behind!

Find out about new additions to our site, new bestsellers and hot topics

In-depth information on high-end topics: find the best reference books for databases, programming, networking, and client/server technologies

A recent addition to Que, Ziff-Davis Press publishes the highly-successful *How It Works* and *How to Use* series of books, as well as *PC Learning Labs Teaches* and *PC Magazine* series of book/disc packages

Stay on the cutting edge of Macintosh® technologies and visual communications

Find out which titles are making headlines

With 6 separate publishing groups, Que develops products for many specific market segments and areas of computer technology. Explore our Web Site and you'll find information on best-selling titles, newly published titles, upcoming products, authors, and much more.

- Stay informed on the latest industry trends and products available
- Visit our online bookstore for the latest information and editions
- Download software from Que's library of the best shareware and freeware

MACMILLAN COMPUTER PUBLISHING USA

A VIACOM COMPANY

Technical ---- Support:

If you need assistance with the information in this book or with a CD/Disk accompanying the book, please access the Knowledge Base on our Web site at **http://www.superlibrary.com/general/support**. Our most Frequently Asked Questions are answered there. If you do not find the answer to your questions on our Web site, you may contact Macmillan Technical Support **(317) 581-3833** or e-mail us at **support@mcp.com**.

Complete and Return this Card
for a *FREE* Computer Book Catalog

Thank you for purchasing this book! You have purchased a superior computer book written expressly for your needs. To continue to provide the kind of up-to-date, pertinent coverage you've come to expect from us, we need to hear from you. Please take a minute to complete and return this self-addressed, postage-paid form. In return, we'll send you a free catalog of all our computer books on topics ranging from word processing to programming and the internet.

Mr. ☐   Mrs. ☐   Ms. ☐   Dr. ☐

Name (first) ☐☐☐☐☐☐☐☐☐☐☐☐ (M.I.) ☐ (last) ☐☐☐☐☐☐☐☐☐☐☐☐☐☐☐

Address ☐☐☐☐☐☐☐☐☐☐☐☐☐☐☐☐☐☐☐☐☐☐☐☐☐☐☐☐☐

☐☐☐☐☐☐☐☐☐☐☐☐☐☐☐☐☐☐☐☐☐☐☐☐☐☐☐☐☐

City ☐☐☐☐☐☐☐☐☐☐☐☐☐☐ State ☐☐ Zip ☐☐☐☐☐ ☐☐☐☐

Phone ☐☐☐ ☐☐☐ ☐☐☐☐ Fax ☐☐☐ ☐☐☐ ☐☐☐☐

Company Name ☐☐☐☐☐☐☐☐☐☐☐☐☐☐☐☐☐☐☐☐☐☐☐☐☐☐☐

E-mail address ☐☐☐☐☐☐☐☐☐☐☐☐☐☐☐☐☐☐☐☐☐☐☐☐☐☐☐

1. Please check at least (3) influencing factors for purchasing this book.

Front or back cover information on book .... ☐
Special approach to the content .... ☐
Completeness of content .... ☐
Author's reputation .... ☐
Publisher's reputation .... ☐
Book cover design or layout .... ☐
Index or table of contents of book .... ☐
Price of book .... ☐
Special effects, graphics, illustrations .... ☐
Other (Please specify): _____ ☐

2. How did you first learn about this book?

Saw in Macmillan Computer Publishing catalog .... ☐
Recommended by store personnel .... ☐
Saw the book on bookshelf at store .... ☐
Recommended by a friend .... ☐
Received advertisement in the mail .... ☐
Saw an advertisement in: _____ ☐
Read book review in: _____ ☐
Other (Please specify): _____ ☐

3. How many computer books have you purchased in the last six months?

This book only .... ☐   3 to 5 books .... ☐
2 books .... ☐   More than 5 .... ☐

4. Where did you purchase this book?

Bookstore .... ☐
Computer Store .... ☐
Consumer Electronics Store .... ☐
Department Store .... ☐
Office Club .... ☐
Warehouse Club .... ☐
Mail Order .... ☐
Direct from Publisher .... ☐
Internet site .... ☐
Other (Please specify): _____ ☐

5. How long have you been using a computer?

☐ Less than 6 months   ☐ 6 months to a year
☐ 1 to 3 years   ☐ More than 3 years

6. What is your level of experience with personal computers and with the subject of this book?

	With PCs	With subject of book
New	☐	☐
Casual	☐	☐
Accomplished	☐	☐
Expert	☐	☐

Source Code ISBN: 0-7987-1106-0

7. Which of the following best describes your job title?

Administrative Assistant .... ☐
Coordinator .... ☐
Manager/Supervisor .... ☐
Director .... ☐
Vice President .... ☐
President/CEO/COO .... ☐
Lawyer/Doctor/Medical Professional .... ☐
Teacher/Educator/Trainer .... ☐
Engineer/Technician .... ☐
Consultant .... ☐
Not employed/Student/Retired .... ☐
Other (Please specify): _____ ☐

8. Which of the following best describes the area of the company your job title falls under?

Accounting .... ☐
Engineering .... ☐
Manufacturing .... ☐
Operations .... ☐
Marketing .... ☐
Sales .... ☐
Other (Please specify): _____ ☐

9. What is your age?

Under 20 .... ☐
21-29 .... ☐
30-39 .... ☐
40-49 .... ☐
50-59 .... ☐
60-over .... ☐

10. Are you:

Male .... ☐
Female .... ☐

11. Which computer publications do you read regularly? (Please list)

_____
_____
_____
_____
_____
_____
_____
_____
_____

Comments: _____

_____

Fold here and scotch-tape to mail.